The Art of Political Warfare

The Art of Political Warfare

JOHN J. PITNEY, JR.

UNIVERSITY OF OKLAHOMA PRESS
Norman

ALSO BY JOHN J. PITNEY, JR.

(with William F. Connelly, Jr.) *Congress' Permanent Minority? Republicans in the U.S. House* (Lanham, Md., 1994)

This book is published with the generous assistance of Edith Gaylord Harper.

LIBRARY OF CONGRESS CATALOGING-IN-PUBLICATION DATA

Pitney, John J. 1955–
   The art of political warfare / John J. Pitney, Jr.
      p. cm.
   Includes bibliographical references and index.
   ISBN 0-8061-3263-9 (cloth)
   ISBN 0-8061-3382-1 (paper)
      1. Politics, Practical. 2. Political participation. 3. Military art and science—Political aspects. I. Title

JF799. P57 2000
324.7—dc21   00-026710

The paper in this book meets the guidelines for permanence and durability of the Committee on Production Guidelines for Book Longevity of the Council on Library Resources, Inc. ∞

2 3 4 5 6 7 8 9 10

For Lisa

Contents

Acknowledgments   ix

1   Introduction   3

2   Strategy   21

3   Leadership   42

4   Coordination   61

5   Rallying the Troops   80

6   Demoralization, Deception, and Stealth   100

7   Intelligence   120

8   Geography and Logistics   138

9   Friction and Finality   158

10   Scholars and Metaphors   179

Notes   199

Index   237

Acknowledgments

I thank Kimberly Wiar at the University of Oklahoma Press for her encouragement at the beginning of this project, her patience at the end, and her advice and friendship throughout. Bill Rood and Alex Lamy provided me with substantive and stylistic help, offering their insights and saving me from many errors. Bob Faggen, Larry Arnn, Joe Rodota, and Chris Wiedey all pointed me toward valuable resources, contributing much more than they realized at the time. Bill Connelly and Jim Pinkerton have taught me much over the years: Many of the book's ideas took root while I was swapping thoughts with them during long-distance phone calls and email exchanges. Both generously took time from their busy schedules to offer comments that greatly improved the manuscript, as did several anonymous reviewers. And my wife, Lisa Minshew Pitney, helped me revise the first draft. This book would not have been possible without her intellectual guidance, emotional support, and loving forbearance.

This platoon of helpers went above and beyond the call of duty to improve *The Art of Political Warfare*. They bear no responsibility for any remaining errors. As Dwight Eisenhower was ready to say in case the D-Day invasion failed, "If any blame or fault attaches to the attempt, it is mine alone."

The Art of Political Warfare

1

Introduction

> We had to be battle ready just to be in the game—to break down the bureaucracy and replace campaigning by conference call with a single strategic center for attacks and counterattacks. Hillary got it immediately. "What you're describing is a war room," she said, giving us both a name and an attitude.
> —George Stephanopoulos
> *All Too Human: A Political Education*

This book develops a simple idea: politics resembles warfare, so military literature can teach us something about political action. This notion hardly means that politics is identical to war or that every activity in one field has a counterpart in the other. (There is no political equivalent to, say, rifle-cleaning.) Rather, it suggests rough similarities between the ways people organize to wage war and the ways they organize to win votes or to enact public policies. Thinking about the former can inspire insights about the latter.

We all assume this link whenever we use military metaphors. Lawmakers try to be good soldiers, except when Young Turks break ranks and overthrow the Old Guard.[1] Some standard-bearers let their lieutenants serve as their hatchet men, whereas others lead the charge. Candidates on the defensive may adopt a bunker mentality. Politicians gather ammunition, mobilize troops, mount attacks, launch blitzes, take hits, return fire, and beat retreats. Search for the word "battle" in an electronic card catalog and you find *The American Party Battle*, *The Battle for Democracy*, *Battle for Justice*, *The Battle for Municipal Reform*, *The Battle for Public Opinion*, and *Order of Battle: A Republican's Call to Reason*, among many others.

Yet none of these books has systematically applied military concepts to domestic American politics. This omission is striking. When a metaphor remains in common use for a long time, we can guess that it has a basis in experience, and so it is with military metaphors, whose frequency suggests many likenesses between politics and war. Consider a common emotion among politicians, namely, the feeling of "embattlement." In their classic work on metaphors, George Lakoff and Mark Johnson say that this sense comes from seeing yourself in a warlike situation in which you view other participants as adversaries and attack their position while defending your own: "Your perceptions and actions correspond in part to the perceptions and actions of a party engaged in war."[2]

While metaphors are expressing our thought, they are shaping it, too. When campaign volunteers hear their leaders talk about battling the enemy, they regard themselves as combatants, often unconsciously. In this sense, we live by military metaphors, for they structure many of the things we do.[3] Politics is like war, so people use military metaphors, which in turn make politics more warlike. Which has a stronger effect on the other: words or actions? Is it more a matter of military metaphors driving political behavior, or of politics naturally giving rise to military language? These are good questions—for another book. This one avoids such chicken-and-egg riddles. For now, it is enough to establish that political people speak in military terms and act in ways that military concepts can explain.

In what specific ways do the two realms correspond?

Both are organized struggles between opposing human wills: Most definitions of politics include the word "conflict," which connotes antagonism and combat.[4] People enlist in politics so they can work their will over others, an activity that they call "fighting," though it seldom involves violence. President Clinton once told residents of a Chicago housing project that their spirit inspired him to battle: "And I will take that back to Washington when we fight for the crime bill, when we fight to reform the welfare system, when we fight for the empowerment zones to get investment and jobs into these communities, when we fight to give you a chance."[5]

Both reach far and high: Politics and war recruit masses of people in an effort to settle vital issues.[6] After the 1860 election, Southerners saw Lincoln's victory as so ominous that they traded in their metaphorical armaments for real ones. Not all elections (or wars) are so decisive, but politicians portray the stakes as critical in order to keep up mass enthusiasm. Like generals, political leaders often cast their efforts as "crusades."[7] In 1948, Harry Truman told Democrats that "we are now engaged in one of the most important battles in our history. It is a crusade for the right, a crusade for the people against the special interests. I want you to join me in this crusade."[8]

Both arouse deep passions, especially hostility: It is not quite enough to invoke the Lord: one must also rally the troops against the Devil, whether in the shape of Saddam Hussein or of an opposing candidate. At the end of the novel *Primary Colors*, an insider story of presidential politics, the Clintonesque presidential contender tells the narrator: "Henry, you're a warrior, and we were at war—and you wanted to kill that pious [expletive deleted], just like I did."[9]

Both expose participants to peril and uncertainty: Despite the occasional assassination attempt, politicians seldom worry about violent death. They do, however, face the risk of a soiled reputation and humiliating defeat. According to Winston Churchill, "Politics are almost as exciting as war and quite as dangerous. In war, you can only be killed once, but in politics many times."[10] Clinton aide Leon Panetta described his own post "as a battlefield job, because you essentially set what you want to do in terms of how you'd like the battle to go, but you also wind up having land mines and mortars coming in and exploding around you."[11] (Panetta's title was Chief of Staff, a term from the U.S. Army.)

Both require elaborate strategies and tactics: Warriors and political activists seek intelligence about their opponents' strengths and aims, just as they try to thwart their foes' efforts to do the same. They also motivate their subordinates and outmaneuver the opposition. And they must adapt each battle plan to conditions at hand. In 1972, Gary Hart ran George McGovern's presidential campaign and had to take different approaches to the primaries and the fall election: "The nomination campaign for us was guerrilla warfare—scattered, ragtag troops, minutemen, roving bands of citizen volunteers, the people of Russia plaguing and harassing Napoleon's elite corps. The general election campaign was heavy artillery, panzer divisions, massive clanking movements of cumbersome weapons, mechanized, unwieldy warfare."[12]

PERENNIAL AND PERVASIVE

Military concepts are inescapable precisely because many basic political terms began their careers in uniform. "Strategy" comes from the Greek *strategia*, meaning "generalship." "Campaign," from the Latin *campus* ("field"), started as a military term for an organized struggle taking place over a distinct period and aiming at a definite result.[13] "Slogan" derives from the Scottish Gaelic *sluagh* ("army") and *ghairm* ("cry").

It is hard to think of any time when military ideas have not pervaded politics or to name any group of Americans who have not used them. In 1809, a North Carolina state legislator wrote about electioneering with his running mate: "Col. Bodinhamer & myself have been under a forced march since Sunday last—We have left none of the enemies [*sic*] ground in this quarter unexplored—and I think have succeeded in blowing up most of their strong places."[14] In 1840, young Abraham Lincoln looked ahead to the next presidential campaign: "We have the numbers, and if properly organized and exerted, with the gallant [William Henry] Harrison at our head, we shall meet our foes and conquer them in all parts of the Union."[15]

As the country grew, politics required an ever more rigorous approach. The Army supplied a handy model. After the Civil War, Union and Confederate veterans ran party organizations along military lines, complete with uniformed marching companies.[16] By the turn of the century, the uniforms and other martial trappings had faded from view, but military patterns still proved useful.[17] In 1896, when Mark Hanna took charge of the GOP presidential campaign, Republican elder statesman John Hay marveled: "He is a born general in politics, perfectly square, honest, and courageous, with a *coup d'oeil* for the battle-field and a knowledge of the enemy's weak points which is very remarkable."[18] Author Matthew Josephson later wrote: "Hanna set up a complete machinery for modern political warfare. The Republican National Committee, which he headed . . . became the general staff of the whole army."[19]

Franklin Roosevelt, who had served as assistant secretary of the Navy, embodied this military spirit. Like so many reformers, he saw warfare as a template for effective government power. World War I made a mark on many New Deal laws and agencies, such as the Civilian Conservation Corps, which mirrored the American Expeditionary Force.[20] FDR's "Hundred Days" program took its name from the period in 1815 between Napoleon's arrival in Paris and the restoration of King Louis XVIII after Waterloo. Before and after the Hundred Days, FDR spoke of war against the Depression. In his first Inaugural Address, he told Americans that they "must move as a trained and loyal army."[21] He later attacked conservative "Copperheads" for hindering his crusade: "It was the Copperheads who, in the days of the Civil War, the War between the States, tried their best to make President Lincoln and his Congress give up the fight in the middle of the fight, to let the Nation remain split in two and return to peace—yes, peace at any price."[22]

World War II and the Cold War fortified Americans' tendency to think of politics as a military exercise.[23] Just as FDR had called Americans to arms against the Depression, so politicians of later decades declared war on poverty, crime, cancer, drugs, and AIDS. This mindset lingered even after the Soviet Union's demise. The first post–Cold War president, Bill Clinton, named a former general to head the "drug war."

As a candidate, Clinton took political battle to new levels of expertise. In the spring of 1992, the Clinton campaign undertook "the Manhattan Project," an effort to address his vulnerabilities. In the fall, his aide James Carville set up a "war room" to issue attacks and counterattacks. As reporter Michael Kelly wrote, pacifists would have shuddered at its language: "Describing the campaign's reaction to an attack by President Bush on Mr. Clinton's health care proposals, Mr. Carville estimates the level of response in Pentagon jargon as 'Defcon-5,' or highest alert."[24] The Clinton crew remained on a war footing after the election. Room 433 of the Old Executive Office Building, where staff plotted strategy for ethics problems, acquired a telling nickname: "the Arsenal of Democracy."[25]

Betsey Wright, who fought off rumors about Clinton's character, was "the Secretary of Defense." Like Wright, more and more women are rising through the ranks—and they, too, speak of politics as war. In her memoir of the 1992 campaign, Bush aide Mary Matalin chose as her epigraph a Vietnamese battle cry: "Follow me if I advance. Kill me if I retreat. Avenge me if I die."[26] When Celia Morris wrote the story of the 1990 gubernatorial campaigns of Dianne Feinstein of California and Ann Richards of Texas, she called it *Storming the Statehouse*. EMILY's List, a committee for pro-choice Democratic women, offers such services as "targeting and candidate recruitment," "strategic research," and "ongoing tactical support." By following its advice, says its website, women "take command of the political environment" and "fight back against a negative attack."[27]

Military metaphors cross partisan and ideological boundaries. Pat Buchanan added a rare lively moment to the 1996 campaign when he told supporters: "Do not wait for orders from headquarters, mount up everybody and ride to the sound of the guns."[28] At the other end of the spectrum, German political sociologist Robert Michels observed in 1915: "There is hardly one expression of military tactics and strategy, hardly even a phrase of barracks slang, which does not recur again and again in the leading articles of the socialist press."[29]

The military model prevails even among those who oppose war. During the 1960s, no one thought it odd to talk about "anti-war militants." In 1972, George McGovern waged the most pacifist major-party presidential campaign in history. In a book dedicated to "the McGovern Army," campaign manager Gary Hart wrote that similar efforts had "relied heavily on the classic insurgency technique of rousing the countryside—the volunteers—to beat the entrenched powers. Like most political techniques, this one is based on military principles; it is New England citizens with pitchforks and muskets against George III's troops."[30]

READING ABOUT WAR

If Hart is right, then students of practical politics should learn about war. Scholars disagree about whether war sprang from natural aggressiveness, a genetic instinct for hunting, or a prehistoric need to defend against predators.[31] No matter which theory proves correct, the subject matter is ancient—and so is its literature. The *Iliad* described the archetype of combat deceptions, the Trojan Horse. Thucydides' *The Peloponnesian War* provided a panoramic view of a catastrophic conflict, and Xenophon's *The Education of Cyrus* analyzed military leadership. During the same period, several centuries before Christ, Sun Tzu wrote *The Art of War*, which remains in the curricula of the world's military schools.

Like Sun Tzu, Machiavelli wrote a book entitled *The Art of War*, and in his better-known works, *The Prince* and *The Discourses*, he interwove discussions of statesmanship with practical advice about combat. Carl von Clausewitz's *On War* took on scriptural status in European armies of the nineteenth and twentieth centuries, and in the post-Vietnam era it has influenced American military leaders, most notably Colin Powell.

Today's military publishes a huge amount of rigorous analysis, both in manuals and in periodicals such as *Parameters*. This literature covers a broad range of topics and draws upon many disciplines. Its breadth and depth should not surprise anyone, since the military stresses education: two-thirds of Army officers have advanced degrees, including many doctorates. "There is more interest in learning in the military than in most organizations I've seen," says business consultant Margaret Wheatley. "Generals take time to think."[32]

Believing that thousands of years of thought and battle must hold some lessons about human conflict, certain politicians and operatives have applied this body of literature to their own work. In a 1984 memo to the Walter Mondale presidential campaign, Democratic strategist Patrick Caddell quoted military writers from Sun Tzu to British theorist B. H. Liddell Hart. Caddell argued that the Mondale campaign would fail if it mounted a "frontal assault on Reagan" and followed the "trench tactics" that it favored: "What is needed is a strategy that reflects the doctrine of indirect approach. One that can exploit the numerous weak points of the Reagan position and finds the best grounds for forcing the position of the issue. [Mondale needs a strategy that] avoids and isolates Reagan's Maginot Line—his personality and leadership strengths."[33]

In planning for the first debate with Reagan, Mondale followed this advice while his aides mounted an elaborate "pantomime of deception" to mislead the press and the Reagan camp into expecting a frontal assault.[34] His indirect approach addled an already shaky Reagan, who botched the encounter. Although Reagan had daunting advantages, Mondale's debate victory narrowed the gap, at least for a while.

About the time that Caddell was writing his Mondale memo, a junior House Republican named Newt Gingrich was telling his staff to study Japanese samurai and World War II battle strategists, in hopes that they would learn about speed and maneuvering. Gingrich had a Ph.D. in contemporary European history and frequently lectured at the war colleges. Just before he became Speaker of the House in 1995, he explained: "Politics and war are remarkably similar systems."[35] A few months later he put it more boldly, paraphrasing Mao Zedong: "War is politics with blood; politics is war without blood."[36]

At Gingrich's direction, members of the House Republican leadership and their aides studied planning and training methods at U.S. Army Training and Doctrine Command (TRADOC) centers.

"Almost every major thing I have done for over a decade has been directly shaped by TRADOC," Gingrich said.[37] A lieutenant colonel on a fellowship helped the GOP leadership run "after-action reviews" to identify lessons from legislative battles.[38]

Gingrich's early successes made an impression on his opponents. Shortly after the new Speaker took the gavel, a Democratic political consultant wrote: "We need to follow the advice of jungle fighters, follow the example of the greatest light cavalry the world has ever seen (the Apaches), and read the teachings of Sun Tzu. When they expect retreat, attack; when they expect attack, retreat; when they rest, we move."[39]

Among recent American political figures, the most devoted student of Sun Tzu was Lee Atwater, who managed George Bush's 1988 presidential campaign and chaired the Republican National Committee until 1991, when he died of a brain tumor at the age of forty. The skill and intelligence with which Atwater used military principles are worthy of special attention.

ATWATER'S WAY

Mourners who attended Atwater's memorial service found something unusual in the program—passages from Sun Tzu: "The Way means inducing the people to have the same aim as the leadership, so that they will share death and share life, without fear of danger. Those skilled in defense hide in the deepest depths of the earth, those skilled in attack maneuver in the highest heights of the sky."

Atwater once explained his affinity for military ideas: "There's a whole set of prescriptions for success that includes such notions as concentration, tactical flexibility, the difference between strategy and tactics, and the idea of command focus."[40] Sun Tzu's *The Art of War* was his favorite book, which he claimed to have read at least twenty times. "Everything in it you can relate to my profession, you can relate to the campaign," he said. "Every time I read it, I am reminded of something very important."[41] (Atwater had a narrow attention span and a tendency to exaggerate, but in this case he was probably telling the truth. The book is short.)

Applying Sun Tzu's maxims on deception, Atwater confused opposing campaigns about his intentions—often by exploiting his own reputation for trickiness. The 1988 Bush campaign "would always announce our tactical and strategic decisions way out front because people would figure we were spinning them," he said. "The only way you could turn people off and keep them from following a strategy was to announce it first."[42]

"Know the enemy and know yourself" was another Sun Tzu dictum that Atwater took to heart.[43] "The only group that I was interested in having report to me," Atwater said, ". . . was opposition research."[44] Headed by Jim Pinkerton, the research team compiled a huge cache of material, first on Bush's GOP rivals, then on Democratic nominee Michael Dukakis. The "excellent nerds," as Atwater called them, were not just looking for hit-piece ammunition but for insight into the other candidates' personalities, working habits, ideologies, and bases of support. At the same time, they also searched Bush's own background for vulnerabilities. The idea was to anticipate the campaign's course, to know where the others could attack and how they would react to the Bush campaign's own moves.

In the nomination contest, Atwater and his lieutenants recognized that Bush's moderate public record had left him weak on his right flank. To head off conservative attacks, Atwater advised Bush to move rightward on key issues, especially taxes. Meanwhile, the Bush warriors also probed their opponents' soft spots.

Among other things, they learned much about Bob Dole's thin skin, which enabled them to follow Sun Tzu's counsel about harassing the opposition: "Anger his general and confuse him."[45]

The Bush campaign made numerous attacks, peeling off Dole's supporters and tapping into his bile. The payoff came with the New Hampshire primary, where Bush won an upset victory. When NBC reporter Tom Brokaw asked Dole if he had anything to say to the winner, Dole snapped: "Stop lying about my record." Those five words, which the networks repeated over and over, renewed doubts about Dole's temperament and helped scuttle his campaign.

Sun Tzu reminded Atwater of the importance of taking the initiative: "Generally, he who occupies the field of battle first and awaits his enemy is at ease; he who comes later to the scene and rushes into the fight is weary."[46] Atwater worked earlier than any of his counterparts to set up organizations in key primary states. Bush could thus recover from a loss in the Iowa caucuses, whereas the underprepared Dole had no way to regain momentum after New Hampshire.

In the fall campaign, the Bush camp defined the issue agenda before Dukakis could, stressing Republican strengths and Democratic weaknesses. Dukakis got stuck answering Bush attacks, usually too late. Bush's travels also caught Dukakis off guard. "Appear at places to which he [the opponent] must hasten," Sun Tzu taught; "move swiftly where he does not expect you."[47] Atwater read this passage literally, and he had Bush appear in Dukakis's home state to take a boat ride in polluted Boston Harbor and accept the endorsement of a Boston police union. These "sneak attacks" forced Dukakis to spend scarce resources to defend his home ground and highlighted issues that hurt him.

Atwater sought to divide the other side. The commentator Chang Yu elaborated on Sun Tzu's advice: "Sometimes drive a wedge between a sovereign and his ministers; on other occasions separate his allies from him. Make them mutually suspicious so that they drift apart. Then you can plot against them."[48] In the 1988 campaign, "wedge issues" such as Massachusetts's furlough program enabled the Bush campaign to split conservative Southerners and anti-crime Northerners off from the Democratic Party's base of liberals and minorities. Democrats later charged that the GOP's wedge issues deepened racial divisions, while Republicans answered that they were legitimate policy arguments.

After taking the helm of the Republican National Committee, Atwater stepped up his effort to split the Democratic Party, this time by encouraging its elected officials to switch to the GOP. He advised the administration to guard its "fortress" of low taxes so that it could advance an innovative domestic agenda: "As long as we hold the high ground, we can maneuver on this other stuff."[49] Bush, however, turned his administration into a target-rich environment by breaking the no-new-taxes promise and slighting domestic policy. In political terms, the administration neglected what Clausewitz called "moral elements," including what we now call "morale." By 1992, Republicans had read Bush's lips and lost their heart. His campaign proved indecisive, thus illustrating another observation from Clausewitz: "Given the same amount of intelligence, timidity will do a thousand times more damage in war than audacity."[50]

USES AND OBJECTIONS

Much of the political community has never heard of Sun Tzu or Carl von Clausewitz: mention such names at a local precinct meeting, and people will assume that you are recommending ethnic restaurants. Nevertheless, the Atwaters and Caddells are unusual only in the degree to which they explicitly cite military classics. As we have already seen, nearly everyone else in politics is implicitly thinking and acting along these lines.

Many observations from military literature should ring true to those who study and practice politics. This literature has much to offer on strategy and leadership—that is, laying out an overall plan for victory and getting people behind it. Followers require coordination, and military writings can help us understand how leaders achieve it. The idea of psychological warfare has clear political applications, in the sense of maintaining clear heads and stout hearts among one's friends while confusing and misleading one's enemies. Intelligence is a constant concern of political figures because they need an accurate picture of the opposition's strengths and weaknesses. In politics as in war, one must keep an eye on the mundane but essential matters of geography and logistics. No matter how carefully military or political leaders plan ahead, they will struggle with friction, the countless glitches that hinder effective action and spawn future conflicts.

This book analyzes these ideas. Note that its title is not "Twelve Easy Steps to Winning Political Wars." As columnist Maureen Dowd once wrote, the secrets-to-victory approach dissolves into the "intentionally Delphic and blindingly obvious advice for which modern political consultants get paid tons of money."[51] Chance, circumstance, and natural talent all shape the fate of warriors and politicians alike, so this book can no more guarantee political success than *The Art of War* can guarantee military victory. (Among Sun Tzu's most avid students was William Westmoreland, who led American troops in Vietnam.)

The goal here is more modest. By applying military ideas, we can better understand aspects of politics that would otherwise remain obscure. Politicians and bureaucrats already know many of these things in their bones: this book aims to put some of this knowledge on the printed page. Its approach may bother certain readers, so it is wise to address possible objections. Perhaps the most obvious is that a simpleminded application of military thought might make politics meaner than it already is, encouraging staffers and politicians to embark on take-no-prisoners jihads. In an address at the Air Force Academy, James F. Childress warned that "we will both trivialize real wars, and exaggerate other conflicts and problems our society faces, by our reckless and irresponsible use of the war metaphor."[52]

This warning deserves attention because we should avoid confusing analytic tools with literal descriptions. To say that politics resembles war in certain ways is not to imply that every political figure should always act like Patton. If anything, however, this form of analysis will make us more aware of the implications of our political language. It is better to be conscious of military images than to use them without reflecting on their origins and meaning. Seeing both their uses and limitations, we can put them to work for constructive purposes. That way, we become the masters of military metaphors rather than their servants.

Objecting to military metaphors can lead to ironies, since one can scarcely avoid them. When Gingrich became Speaker and tried to moderate his style, congressional Democrats remembered his earlier words and deeds. "In previous years he was following the Vietnam 'burn the village in order to save it' strategy, or calling in the artillery even if you took out some of your own people," one Democrat told reporter Elizabeth Drew. "The military metaphors come easily about him. There's something sociopathic."[53] Twenty pages later, she quoted another House Democrat on Gingrich: "Going after him is like trying to take out command and control."[54]

A second objection is that the precision and order of military operations cannot supply a model for the messy world of politics. True, politics is chaotic—but so is war. According to the official doctrine of the Marine Corps, "Disorder is an integral characteristic of war; we can never eliminate it. In the heat of battle, plans will go awry, instructions and information will be unclear and misinterpreted, communications will fail, and mistakes and unforeseen events will be commonplace."[55] A year after Desert Storm, General H. Norman Schwarzkopf mocked those who describe military operations as a form of precision dancing. "What I always say to those folks is, 'Yes, it's choreographed, and what happens is the orchestra starts playing and some son of a bitch climbs out of the orchestra pit with a bayonet and starts chasing you around the stage.' And the choreography goes right out the window."[56]

A third objection is that metaphor is just a gimmick, not a substantial means of serious political analysis. On the contrary, most political writing hinges on metaphors. Especially in academia, writers have relied heavily on the market metaphor, picturing the political world as a place where people dicker, barter, buy and sell. One reason this metaphor is so popular is that politics really does involve money. "I see the White House is like a subway," said one Clinton fundraiser. "You have to put in coins to open the gates."[57] Political scientists also like the market metaphor because it has enabled them to borrow concepts and methods from economics, a discipline that they envy for its rigor.[58]

Other metaphors have appeared in political writing. Using his imagination and drawing on anthropology, one writer described Congress as a set of tribes.[59] Another pictured politics as ritual, consisting of spectacles that elicit specific responses from their audiences.[60] And of course sports terms abound, though one scholar offered a memorable caveat to the common metaphor of football: "Politics is much more like the original primitive game of football in which everybody was free to join, a game in which the whole population of one town might play the entire population of another town moving freely back and forth across the countryside."[61]

A fourth objection naturally arises: if politics is like a marketplace, a ritual, or a football game, how can it also be like war? We can answer this question by remembering that all metaphors are like lenses that bring certain things into sharp focus while obscuring others. Putting different lenses on a camera allows us to see things in new and diverse ways. Likewise, different metaphorical lenses enable us to ask different kinds of questions and look for different kinds of evidence.[62]

Many scholars seem to think that we should look at politics through the market metaphor alone, which is a mistake. This metaphor does a fine job of clarifying aspects of politics that involve self-interested motives, large numbers, and easily measured elements. Alas, it tends to miss such hard-to-quantify phenomena such as duty, courage, and passion.[63] In the same vein, its emphasis on bargaining has merit but slights the importance of struggle and confrontation.[64] Thus, just as good photographers stock a variety of lenses, so we need a variety of metaphorical tools for analyzing politics. This book develops one such tool. It shows that military metaphors and concepts cast a clear light on things that the customary academic approach would leave in the blurry background. Chapter 10, which should be of particular interest to scholars, develops this discussion and also sketches alternative metaphors.

The military approach has limits. If war and politics were exactly the same thing, then great generals would automatically make great politicians. The troubled administration of Ulysses S. Grant and the stillborn presidential candidacy of Douglas MacArthur supply evidence to the contrary. Politics is not only about fighting, for it may also involve cooperation, compromise, and deliberation. Accordingly, military concepts work better in some situations than others. It is no accident that Newt Gingrich found his political home in the House of Representatives, where procedures foster tough, combative politics. Although there is conflict aplenty in the Senate, the warlike aspects of politics are more muted on that side of the Capitol. In a compact body in which every member has considerable power, there are practical limits on how intensely senators can fight their political adversaries.[65]

These objections and limitations aside, we can discover a great deal about politics by raiding the military's intellectual armory. This body of thought is not entirely uniform either in quality or in the substance of argument, but on many general points there is a broad consensus, and one that has faced the most rigorous test of all: life or death on the battlefield. Warriors have learned a lot because they have had to.

Finally, there is one more reason to explore the military analysis of politics: the topic is engrossing. As James Carville put it, "Anybody who's been on a battlefield, whether it's a real battlefield or a political battlefield, or a game, will know this: There's the smell, the odor, the feel that draws you back after it's done. They say in war it's the smell of cordite, of gunpowder. It stays in the air."[66]

2

Strategy

Strategy is the single most important factor in a
political campaign. This is the most important lesson
I have learned in 30 years. The right strategy can survive a mediocre campaign, but even a brilliant campaign is likely to fail if the strategy is wrong.
—Political consultant Joseph Napolitan
in Ron Faucheux, *The Road to Victory*

We often hear talk of legislative strategy, elec-
toral strategy, bureaucratic strategy, and legal strategy. Yet amid
all the discussion of "strategy," practitioners and scholars seldom say what they mean by the term. A military definition supplies a good starting point. "Strategy, broadly defined, is the
process of interrelating ends and means," explains a Marine
Corps handbook. "When we apply this process to a particular
set of ends and means, the product—that is, the strategy—is a
specific way of using specified means to achieve distinct ends.
Strategy is thus both a process and a product."[1] It answers three
related questions:

What goals do we want to achieve?

What resources can we use?

In light of goals and resources, what is our best course of action?[2]

These questions seem simple, but many a politician has fared badly by forgetting them. As this chapter shows, such questions lead to subtler and harder ones.

Throughout our discussion, it will be useful to make a rough distinction between strategy, which is a general plan or idea, and tactics, or the activities that carry out the strategy.[3] In practice, a very fine line can separate the two concepts, but we need not dwell on semantics for our purposes. We will also skip over differences between strategy and operations (the intermediate level of war), and among military strategy, grand strategy, and national strategy. Though such nuances are a proper concern for military theory, they are less relevant here.

In politics and war, writing out an explicit strategy can reduce confusion about ends and means. With his political high command, Dwight Eisenhower planned his 1952 presidential race with almost as much precision as an amphibious landing, tallying the campaign's goals and methods in unusual detail.[4] Many political activists and organizations follow this example only part way, drafting elaborate battle plans, then disregarding them as day-to-day pressures lead to haphazard decisions. Thus a strategy document does not equal an actual strategy. Conversely, the absence of such a document does not necessarily mean the absence of a strategy. When key decisionmakers share key assumptions and know one another's minds, they may follow an implicit strategy that observers can identify only after it has unfolded. (Although FDR never had an explicit long-term political strategy, reporter Frank Kent nicely summed up the spirit of the New Deal as "Tax and tax, spend and spend, elect and elect.")[5]

In practice, military and political strategies often involve both implicit and explicit elements.

OBJECTIVES

During World War I, French commander Marshal Foch used to ask, "De quoi s'agit-il?" (What's it all about?)[6] That is the first question of any strategy because the objective shapes every element of the conflict. Many discussions of political strategy take the question for granted, as if the answer were self-evident. It rarely is, either in politics or in war.

Survival is the minimum goal of any side in a conflict. During wartime, survival can mean different things, ranging from the well-being of the population to the protection of specific individuals or groups or the creation of a legacy that outlasts defeat.[7] The definition of political survival involves not individual life or death (at least in normal American politics) but the continuation of careers, policies, and organizations. A political strategist must ask: continuation in what form and under what conditions? Does an agency "continue" if budget cuts scuttle its mission? Does a minority party "survive" if it adopts the majority's views? Ideological factions often raise such questions when they think their party has moved too close to the center.

Your definition of death and survival determines how long and hard you fight. Pragmatists will yield much to maintain some form of existence, whereas zealots equate surrender with death. (In 73 c.e., a group of the original Zealots killed themselves at Masada rather than give in to the Romans.) When Gary Locke, the Democratic governor of Washington State, vetoed legislation banning gay marriage, many legislative Democrats voted to override, fearing voter backlash. A Democratic leader voiced the pragmatic view: "We need a new legislative majority. You live to fight another day." A state senator who fought the override said: "I was one of the ones who wanted to rally the troops, and I felt very much like Gen. Custer."[8]

Victory can be even harder to define than survival. If military victory means the unconditional surrender of the enemy and the overthrow of its political system, then it is rare. Of America's major conflicts, only the Civil War (from the Union's point of view) and World War II fully met this standard—and in both cases adoption of the goal took lengthy deliberation.[9] Other wars had more limited aims. In Vietnam, the U.S. government never did define what victory would be, or even whether it was seeking victory at all.[10]

Smart political strategists follow the example of the Eddie Mahe Company, a consulting firm that says it "assists in developing and clearly defining the ultimate goal which the client is hoping to achieve."[11] The key word here is "ultimate." Whether in public policymaking or electoral politics, people must ask themselves what end state they want. Their initial response typically describes a short-term goal, such as winning the next election or passing a particular bill. On reflection, however, short-term goals may turn out to be means to longer-range objectives. What seems puzzling at a one level may make sense in the broader scheme. In 1957, Majority Leader Lyndon Johnson (D-TX) pushed the Senate to pass the first civil rights bill since Reconstruction. From the standpoint of winning reelection in the segregated state of Texas, Johnson's position was costly. But the White House was his real goal, and from that perspective, support for civil rights was good politics. Richard Russell (D-GA), LBJ's mentor in the Senate, frankly assessed the strategic setting: "We can never make him President unless the Senate first disposes of civil rights."[12] The final compromise bill disappointed advocates of civil rights but did cleanse LBJ of the segregation stigma. Although he lost the 1960 nomination, his stand on civil rights enabled Kennedy to make him the vice presidential candidate—a decision that would put him in the White House when JFK died.

By pondering their long-term goals, decisionmakers often see that they must set higher short-term goals than the situation seems to demand. Campaign managers often say that strategy should aim for 50 percent of the vote plus one. That objective makes more sense for a cash-strapped challenger than for an incumbent who wants a long career, because a slender victory suggests weakness and attracts tougher opposition next time. "It's important for me to show strength to keep the young state representatives and city councilmen away," one House member told political scientist Richard Fenno. "If they have the feeling that I'm invincible, they won't try. That reputation is very intangible. [But] your vote margin is part of it."[13] In legislative struggles, a "minimum winning coalition" (i.e., the least number of votes needed to pass) is a logical approach if the goal is just to get one body to approve one measure one time. But if the goal is to change public policy, the proposal's sponsors must guide it through a long obstacle course—committees and subcommittees, upper and lower chambers, authorization and appropriation, executive signature or veto override—and large majorities make it easier for the proposal to clear all these hedgerows.[14]

Even after a bill becomes law, the battle goes on. Those who oppose the policy change will keep fighting in the courts and the bureaucracy. If supporters want to change the world, and not just some words in a lawbook, then their strategy must reach beyond the legislative process and include steps to ensure faithful implementation.[15]

When a strategy requires broad support, it helps to have a clear and understandable connection between means and ends. All other things being equal, the simpler the connection, the more readily a leader can rally supporters and coordinate their efforts. In 1981, President Reagan came to office promising to spur the economy with tax cuts. Although many economists criticized his plan, it proved politically popular. Simplicity "moves people," explained Representative Jack Kemp (R-NY), a key supporter of the measure: "It's what any real leader would do, any quarterback, Churchill at Dunkirk, MacArthur at Inchon, Philip of Macedonia or Alexander."[16]

In contrast, a complex link between means and ends will leave supporters without direction. As St. Paul asked, "For if the trumpet give an uncertain sound, who shall prepare himself to the battle?"[17] In 1993, President Clinton eloquently described a clear aim—universal medical coverage—but then proposed a health-care plan that few could understand. One analyst noted, "Rather than establishing a stepping stone toward eventual victory, a multiplicity of detail, complicated procedures and unfamiliar jargon separated groups who otherwise share common objectives and provided ammunition for hostile forces."[18]

As that observation suggests, political struggles often assume the character of coalition warfare, in which each side consists of disparate forces that bicker over strategies and objectives. Although many Americans wanted to finish the Gulf War by overthrowing the Iraqi government, Arab leaders saw the objective as restoring Kuwait's independence, not toppling Saddam Hussein. Because Arab participation was essential, President Bush stopped the war once the coalition had seized Kuwait. In this sense, a legislative party resembles the Desert Storm coalition. Although leaders may have grand policy goals, they cannot push farther than the rank and file want to go. Just as critics second-guessed Bush's decision not to march on Baghdad, so ideological partisans routinely attack legislative leaders for failing to press bold policy initiatives.

CRITICAL ASSUMPTIONS

Any strategy rests on critical assumptions about the following:

- **Leaders' qualities:** Are opposition leaders strong or weak, steadfast or faltering? How do they compare with our own?

- *Coordination of forces:* How does each side manage communication, command, and control?
- *Perceptions and intentions:* How do our opponents see the conflict? What courses of action are they likely to pursue?
- *Moral resources:* Is the other side's morale stronger or weaker than ours? Why? What keeps each side going—and what could cause it to quit?
- *Material resources:* What kinds of force can both sides bring to bear? Under what circumstances would each side have the material advantage?
- *The lay of the land:* At what points on the landscape would each side be strongest? What features of physical or human geography would help or hinder which side?

The answers to such questions are critical because serious trouble will result if they prove wrong. In 1950, General Douglas MacArthur assumed that the Chinese would stay out of the Korean War and that, in the unlikely event that they came in, the U.S. Air Force could crush them.[19] MacArthur pressed north toward the Yalu River, which separates North Korea from China. On November 25, he learned that his assumptions were wrong when Chinese troops stormed across the Yalu, forcing him into a humiliating retreat. Instead of ending by Christmas, as he had hoped, the Korean War dragged on until the summer of 1953.

Unless strategists are clairvoyant, they cannot eliminate the danger of false assumptions. All political and military conflicts involve both risk and uncertainty. No matter how much strategists know, they can never foresee outcomes with total confidence; they can only lay odds. That is risk. More often, strategists are missing information that could change their appraisal of the odds. That is uncertainty. (Intelligence, the means of reducing uncertainty, is the subject of chapter 7.)

In spite of these inevitable problems, a strategist can improve critical assumptions by making them explicit. The very process of writing them out requires thought and may spur healthy internal discussion.[20] One example is James Rowe's 1947 campaign memorandum for President Truman, which made acute observations about the politics of 1948:

- New York Governor Thomas Dewey would win the Republican nomination;
- Former Vice President Henry Wallace would run as the candidate of a left-wing third party;
- President Truman's base would lie in the South and West;
- U.S.–Soviet relations and foreign reconstruction would top the foreign-policy agenda; and
- The major domestic issues would be high prices and housing.[21]

The memo did err by assuming that the South would vote solidly Democratic. In fact, Truman's embrace of civil rights prompted Strom Thurmond, then the governor of South Carolina, to launch his breakaway "Dixiecrat" campaign, which took 39 electoral votes out of the Democratic column.

Much more accurate were the memo's comments on the "independent and progressive voter." Rowe not only foresaw the climate of 1948 but grasped a basic shift in American politics: "Better education, the rise of the mass pressure group, the economic depression of the 30's, the growth of government functions—all these have contributed to the downfall of 'the [party] organization.' They have been supplanted in large measure by the pressure groups." Rowe paid special attention to unions. "It is dangerous to assume that labor now has nowhere else to go in 1948," he wrote. "Labor can stay home. The rank and file of the workers are not yet politically minded; they will not, therefore, vote or work actively unless they are inspired to do so." During the campaign, Truman applied this advice by speaking to labor groups and flailing "anti-labor" legislation that the GOP Congress had passed over his veto.

By noting the death of political machines, the Rowe memo avoided a pitfall that has killed many strategies: assuming that the future will be merely an extension of the past. Although forecasts always rely on existing trends, strategists must watch for breaks in the pattern. In the years before the Civil War, rifles replaced smooth-bore muskets as the infantry's main weapon, making gunfire more accurate. But especially on the Confederate side, generals did not think through the implications of the new weapons and so committed their troops to needless bloodshed.[22] In a parallel fashion, congressional Republicans in 1995 still thought that they could win the perception battle against a "tax and spend" liberal. As Newt Gingrich later said, "The idea of a grand showdown over spending had long been a staple of conservative analysis."[23] The Republicans failed to grasp that "anti-government" sentiment had ebbed and that President Clinton had recast himself as a frugal "New Democrat." Clinton strategist Dick Morris recalled: "I had recently seen the movie *Gettysburg*, and told the president that it looked like Pickett's charge [where] the rebels marched suicidally into the lead of Union fire and fell in even rows."[24]

As the budget showdown suggests, any set of critical assumptions should frankly compare one's own strengths and weaknesses with those of the opposition. The Marine Corps advises combatants to avoid the enemy's strong points and instead to seek its critical vulnerabilities: "We may have to create vulnerability—to design a progressive sequence of actions to expose or isolate it, creating over time an opportunity to strike the decisive blow. . . . Just as we ruthlessly pursue our enemy's critical vulnerabilities, we should expect him to attack ours. We must take steps to protect or reduce our vulnerabilities over the course of the campaign."[25]

Murray Chotiner, a Nixon political advisor in the 1940s and 1950s, used similar language to describe an election campaign. Where an opponent is strong, he said, you "are not going to be able to tear down that strength. You can attack the weakness of the opposition and just keep hammering and hammering on those weak points until your opponent can no longer exist in the

election drive."[26] In the 1950 Senate race between Helen Gahagan
Douglas and Richard Nixon, Douglas ran as a supporter of FDR's
New Deal and Truman's Fair Deal. Nixon could not outbid her on
social welfare policies, so Chotiner advised him to keep talking
about communism, a critical Democratic vulnerability. Instead of
sticking to her own issues, Douglas figured that she could stun
Nixon by attacking him for weakness on communism. The move
failed. As Chotiner said, "She made the fatal mistake of attacking
our strength."[27]

A strategist has to know the difference between attacking the
opposition's strength and attacking a vulnerability that the opposition mistakenly regards as a strength. Despite MacArthur's
later mistake in pressing toward the Yalu River, he had earlier
executed a brilliant strategic move at Inchon. The North Koreans
reasoned that they did not need heavy defenses for this coastal
city because its 32-foot tidal range presented a huge obstacle to
landing craft. But MacArthur learned that tidal conditions did
sometimes allow landings. He exploited this latent vulnerability
with a surprise attack that routed the North Koreans, at least
until the Chinese came in.

A political Inchon occurred in North Carolina during the 1976
primary campaign between President Gerald Ford and Ronald
Reagan. Ford had already beaten Reagan in key primaries, and he
trusted polls showing him ahead in North Carolina. He did not
understand that many primary voters still liked Reagan's message, especially about Ford's "giveaway" of the Panama Canal.
Reagan won a surprise victory that revived his campaign, and
during the summer he came close to taking the nomination from
the incumbent.

CAPABILITIES

With objectives and critical assumptions in mind, strategists
must devise plans that make the most effective use of the means

at hand. In wartime, top military leaders decide on the appropriate roles for the Army, Air Force, Navy, and Marines, a choice that depends on terrain and relative strength, among other things. In the European theater of the Second World War, the Army played the leading role because most of the action took place on land. The Navy and Marines had a higher profile in the Pacific theater, where the fighting involved sea lanes and islands. In the 1999 Kosovo operation, NATO planners concluded that "smart bombs" could inflict decisive damage, so they dispensed with ground troops and relied on allied air forces.

In a nonmilitary context, strategists must also choose among different theaters, forces, and forms of action. For instance, those who want to improve race relations may forgo politics completely and turn instead to means such as church-based voluntarism. If they prefer political battlegrounds, their options include federal statutes, executive orders, departmental regulations, judicial rulings, constitutional amendments, state ballot propositions, or some mix of these. Each option entails a different set of activities and requires different resources, so this choice will frame the political strategy.[28]

Fighting for civil rights in the 1930s, the National Association for the Advancement of Colored People (NAACP) could not expect much from Congress because the seniority system gave disproportionate strength to long-serving Southern segregationists. Instead, the organization focused on the judicial system, where it could deploy its cadre of first-rate lawyers. This strategy resulted in legal victories, climaxing with *Brown v. Board of Education* in 1954. The strategic setting then changed. Civil rights advocates had gained strength on Capitol Hill, making legislative change more attainable. And by the late 1950s, the Southern Christian Leadership Conference (SCLC) was exploring nonviolent protest—a method that had become more practical with the advent of television news. Now demonstrators could reach beyond hostile locals and get their message to a sympathetic national audience.

Practicality is crucial. The Seabees' unofficial motto—"The difficult we do at once, the impossible takes a little longer"—may be good for morale but gives little guidance for strategy. An effort to do more than resources allow—a "strategy-capabilities mismatch," in military parlance—is bound to fail, by definition.[29] Weighing the available resources, a strategist should remember what Sun Tzu said: "He who knows when he can fight and when he cannot will be victorious."[30] Both parts of this saying are important because one should press ahead when strategic gain is possible and stay put when it is not.

Any strategist would say that it is easier to offer such advice than to apply it. Point well taken. In real-world conflicts, the golden mean is elusive. Even the most intelligent strategists may either aim too close and miss opportunities, or aim too far and court disaster. During the 1980s, Newt Gingrich justifiably chided Republican leaders for a failure to think big. After he assumed the speakership in 1995, his fondness for expansive goals ensured swift House passage of the Contract with America but led to defeat when congressional Republicans tried to pressure President Clinton on Medicare and other budgetary issues. The President responded by letting parts of the government shut down and blaming the Republicans, who were unready for the political cost. "The shutdown was a big mistake and a major strategic error," said Representative Tom Davis (R-VA); "You might say that our reach exceeded our grasp."[31] Leon Panetta, President Clinton's chief of staff, said that although Gingrich was "good at starting a war, I don't think he was able to strategize how in the end he was going to win the war or at least win some of the victories that would keep him in place." He likened Gingrich to Napoleon Bonaparte in Russia: "Bonaparte, you know, moved in quickly, but then bogged down, because he didn't look ahead at what he was going to face in terms of the winter and the troops that were there. And I think he [Gingrich] ran into the same problems on Capitol Hill."[32]

Once an imprudent strategy starts to falter, it will undermine morale instead of strengthening it. In lines that nicely describe how the shutdown hurt the GOP, B. H. Liddell Hart wrote: "Confidence is like the current in a battery: avoid exhausting it in vain effort—and remember that your own continued confidence will be of no avail if the cells of your battery, the men on whom you depend, have been run down."[33]

In such conflicts, tactical victories may backfire if they contribute to strategic defeats. About 281 B.C.E., Pyrrhus, a Greek king, led an effort to help a Greek colony that was fighting the Romans. He scored some gains, but the cost was so high that he had to withdraw. His famous remark, "Another such victory and I shall be ruined," gave birth to the term "pyrrhic victory." "While focusing on the contest at hand, don't lose sight of the big picture," advises Democratic consultant Victor Kamber, adding that "no one needs pyrrhic victories." Kamber cites the North American Free Trade Agreement (NAFTA). In winning congressional approval, the Clinton administration alienated allies and spent resources that it could have used for other priorities, such as health care. Kamber concludes: "What counts is that your public relations and political strategies be guided by your long-term goals; that your tactics are subservient to your strategies; and that you avoid getting sucked into the maelstrom of winning at all costs if you're not prepared to pay the price."[34]

The costs of a pyrrhic victory may not surface right away. Before the 1972 campaign, for example, the Nixon reelection committee decided to wage an extremely tough campaign against the Democrats while staying away from GOP candidates for other offices. (The Republicans lagged in voter support, so close identification with the GOP could have dragged Nixon down.) This strategy helped reelect Nixon in November 1972, but laid the groundwork for his ultimate defeat. Accusations about "dirty tricks" supplied Democrats with the motive and the means to bring him down. As Nixon himself said, "I gave them a sword."

Had Republicans controlled Congress, they might have down-played Watergate—but with no help from the White House in 1972, they did not come close to winning either chamber. And when the investigation closed in, many congressional Republicans abandoned Nixon.[35]

The opposite of a pyrrhic victory is a tactical defeat that contributes to strategic success. One might call it a "heraclitian defeat," after Heraclitus, the Greek philosopher who said that "Greater dooms win greater destinies."[36] Citing Heraclitus in their aptly titled book, *Losing to Win*, James Ceaser and Andrew Busch explain that the GOP's 1994 congressional victory and the Democrats' 1996 presidential victory both depended on each party's big loss in the previous election.[37] Consciously or unconsciously, voters have tended to support divided government, so a party wishing to hold Congress should plan to lose the presidency, and vice versa. The idea is far from whimsical. Before the 1992 campaign, some congressional Republicans privately (and, as it turned out, accurately) concluded that they would gain if George Bush lost reelection. Four years later, Republicans practically ditched Bob Dole, urging Americans not to give the presumably reelected Bill Clinton a "blank check."

Just as victory and defeat have a dynamic relationship, so do ends and means. Armchair analysts usually regard objectives as fixed, but real-life strategists often adjust them. Victories or unexpected increases in resources may prompt leaders to aim higher, whereas defeats or shortages may force them to trim their ambitions. According to Liddell Hart, "A plan, like a tree, must have branches—if it is to bear fruit. A plan with a single aim is apt to prove a barren pole."[38] Analyzing the 1995–96 budget battle, columnist Paul Gigot said that Gingrich "was so sure Mr. Clinton would sign a modified version of his budget that he lacked a fall-back strategy if the president refused. There was no Plan B—amazing for a man who reads Sun Tzu and Clausewitz."[39]

OFFENSE AND DEFENSE

A discussion of offense and defense might seem simple at first: the side with an offensive aim seeks more resources or relative power, while its opponent just wants to keep what it has. But the relationship is more complex. Although the term "defensive" connotes weakness, military analysts agree that defense is the inherently stronger form of combat. Carl von Clausewitz said that, all other things being equal, it is easier to hold ground than to take it. Why? "Time which is allowed to pass unused accumulates to the credit of the defender. He reaps where he did not sow. Any omission of attack—whether from bad judgment, fear or indolence—accrues to the defenders' benefit.... It is a benefit rooted in the concept and object of defense: it is in the nature of all defensive action."[40]

One political consultant explicitly made the connection: "It takes a whole company or four platoons on the offensive to overcome one platoon on the defensive. Now if you apply that to a political campaign, and you're the incumbent with a strong base, you can see that you don't need as many resources to hold your territory and win the election."[41] The electoral advantage of incumbency is the most obvious instance. When we speak of "entrenched" incumbents, we use a military term suggesting that they have dug themselves into fortified positions.

Another example is the durability of government organizations. Through persuasion and ingratiation, career bureaucrats routinely "capture" the political executives who are supposed to control them. To parry threats to their agencies, they also mobilize allies in Congress and the interest-group community. In the 1980 presidential campaign, Ronald Reagan promised to abolish the Legal Services Corporation, arguing that it was playing politics instead of supplying legal aid to the poor. When Reagan won, said one LSC attorney, "we then decided we had to get on doing what we had to do—either pack up our bags—or pick a place and stay and fight. And we have decided that we needed to fight."[42] LSC's "survival plan" got grassroots organizations to protest Reagan policies and even had grantees do opposition research on Reagan nominees to the LSC board.[43] The plan worked, and LSC lived on.

According to the Marine Corps, "while the defense is the stronger form of combat, the offense is the preferred form, for only through the offense can we truly pursue a positive aim."[44] Despite its difficulty, the offense provides the only way to achieve victory instead of mere survival. "The same passion for staying on the offensive marked the four greatest Civil War commanders, Grant, Jackson, Lee, and Sherman," says Gingrich. "All of them understood that wars are won by taking risks and that the side with the initiative always has a huge advantage."[45] In the 1997 Teamsters' strike against United Parcel Service (UPS), Gingrich notes, labor won though an aggressive strategy of interrupting a widely used service while mounting a public-relations blitz that cast management as the villain.

Offense and defense depend on each other because attackers must defend themselves and defenders must strike at the opposition. As Clausewitz said, defense "is not a simple shield but a shield made up of well-directed blows."[46] James Carville put it in an earthier way: "It's hard for someone to hit you when you have your fist in his face."[47] Though it is seldom possible to keep a fist in the enemy's face at all times, it is important to counterattack. In the fall of 1996, Democrats pounded Republican House members with campaign ads and at one point appeared ready to regain control of the chamber. Knowing that the attack would come, Republican National Committee chairman Haley Barbour had deliberately chosen to save party money for counterattack ads toward the very end of the campaign.

MASS AND MANEUVER

The simplest strategy rests on mass, or numerical superiority. For warriors, it is a matter of troops, weapons, ships, armor, and aircraft. For politicians, the relevant numbers involve such things as money and staff. In such a strategy, the main action consists of attrition as one side overwhelms or grinds down the other. According to the Marine Corps, "An attritionist sees the enemy as targets to be engaged and destroyed systematically. Thus, the focus is on efficiency, leading to a methodical, almost scientific, approach to war."[48] The approach is time-tested, for as Clausewitz said, "Superiority of numbers is the most common element in victory."[49]

A "mass" or "attrition" strategy would work for old-style political bosses, leaders of well-disciplined legislative caucuses, and for entrenched incumbents in reelection battles. One variation is the "firewall" strategy of building pockets of support that the opposition cannot overrun even if it wins some initial victories.[50] In preparing for the 1988 GOP primaries, Lee Atwater ensured that Bush would have insurmountable political support in Southern states. The strategy worked. Even though Dole won in Iowa, the Bush firewall kept him from recovering after his loss in New Hampshire. Eight years later, Dole used the same strategy to prevent early losses from breaking his hold on the nomination.

Rare is the military officer or political leader who can count on numerical superiority at all times. Each must also learn to maneuver around a problem and face it from a position of advantage. The Marines, who specialize in maneuver warfare, explain that their aim "is to render the enemy incapable of resisting by shattering his moral and physical cohesion—his ability to fight as an effective, coordinated whole—rather than to destroy him physically through incremental attrition."[51] This shattering of cohesion entails dislocation, in two senses:

Material or physical dislocation means causing the opposition to put its resources in the wrong places and use them at the wrong times.[52] Just before the ground phase of the Persian Gulf War, the United States and its allies deceived Saddam Hussein into thinking that they would attack from the south, so that the Iraqi troops massed on Kuwait's southern border. On the night before the attack, allied forces used cover of darkness to swing to the west, where the Iraqis were much weaker. The maneuver stunned the Iraqis, and the war ended within a hundred hours.

Psychological dislocation springs from what Liddell Hart called "the sense of being trapped."[53] This effect, which often follows and worsens physical dislocation, includes panic, confusion, and indecision. One can induce and maintain psychological dislocation by surprising the opposition and moving faster than it can react. "Speed is the essence of war," wrote Sun Tzu.[54]

Ever since the earliest wars, military leaders have understood speed as a "force multiplier" that allows one side to seize ground while the other is still getting ready. At the start of World War II, the German army used the latest technological developments to strike its enemies so quickly that they could not respond effectively. A journalist dubbed the strategy *blitzkrieg*, or "lightning war." (The term, often shortened to "blitz," instantly became a staple of military language.) In 1948, columnist Max Lerner helped import the term into American politics when he said that New York Governor Thomas Dewey's campaign for the GOP nomination "combined the age-old methods of power politics with the newest strategies of blitz warfare and the precision tools of American industry and administration."[55]

FDR's "Hundred Days" legislative campaign was an effective political blitz (though the term itself would not come into use for several years). Knowing that his opponents were still reeling from the Depression and the Democrats' 1932 landslide victory, Roosevelt pushed Congress to enact his New Deal program with unprecedented haste. In 1981, President Reagan used a similar logic for a different end: winning swift enactment of tax and budget cuts. Under Director David Stockman, the Office of Management and Budget produced analyses and proposals in a fraction of the usual time, leaving the opposition with little opportunity to marshal either arguments or constituents. When he wrote his memoir of the experience, Stockman entitled the relevant chapter "Blitzkrieg."[56]

Radical community organizer Saul D. Alinsky wrote: "Wherever possible go outside the experience of the enemy. Here you want to cause confusion, fear and retreat."[57] Alinsky cited Union General William Tecumseh Sherman, whose army lived off the land and dispensed with conventional supply lines: "The South, confronted with this new form of military invasion, reacted with confusion, panic, terror, and collapse."[58] A century later, Martin Luther King used civil disobedience to "go outside the experience" of segregationists. "Nonviolent resistance paralyzed and confused the power structures against which it was directed," King wrote. "The brutality with which officials could have quelled the black individual became impotent when it could not be pursued with stealth and remain unobserved."[59]

In warfare, guerrillas go outside the enemy's experience by avoiding the conventional combat that regular armies know well. Their strategy is to persist at irregular hit-and-run attacks, creating a climate of fear and uncertainty that eventually saps the enemy's will to resist. In politics, "guerrilla warfare" can take hard and soft forms. Alinsky perfected the hard form, in which activists take to the streets, physically confront the established powers, and sometimes invite arrest. The soft form shuns lawbreaking, opting instead for violation of etiquette and custom.[60]

In Congress, and especially the House, members of the minority party engage in guerrilla warfare by peppering the majority with procedural fights and ethics attacks. During the 1980s, Newt Gingrich and the Conservative Opportunity Society practiced this form of warfare against the Democrats. When the GOP took control, the Democrats copied this strategy. As one conservative lamented, the House Republicans went from "a wonderful sense of Agincourt, where conservatives thought they could win, to endless guerrilla warfare."[61]

WAR WITHOUT FIGHTING

Sun Tzu wrote, "To win one hundred victories in one hundred battles is not the acme of skill. To subdue the enemy without fighting is the acme of skill."[62] Military forces often win merely by threatening combat. In 1994, the prospect of an American invasion induced Haitian strongman Raul Cedras to flee his country, opening the way for a peaceful intervention. At other times, the implicit or explicit threat of force aims not at conquering the other side but at blocking offensive action. The familiar name for such a strategy is "deterrence." The United States relied on deterrence to keep the Soviet Union from launching its strategic nuclear weapons, and still counts on it to stave off smaller dangers from other countries.

The most straightforward way to carry out a deterrence strategy is to gain overwhelming firepower—hence the large military budgets of the Cold War period. For parallel reasons, lawmakers build up huge campaign warchests and cling to vote-getting official perquisites. When incumbents enjoy such advantages, strong potential challengers usually decline to run. Interest groups and other organizations follow this logic in building up their own resources. One analyst said that the Federal National

Mortgage Association ("Fannie Mae") "has the strongest mixture of political and economic power I have ever seen. They believe strongly they have to win, and win with overwhelming force, on every marginal issue because it builds their aura of invincibility."[63] Chapter 8 below, on logistics and geography, develops the discussion of physical and financial power.

Strategy also depends on intangibles. In chapter 3 we see how leaders must display willpower and determination in order to put their resources to effective use, and in subsequent chapters we look at how leaders sustain spirit in their own ranks while trying to intimidate the opposition. But as discussed in chapter 9 below, even the cleverest strategies are subject to chance and the thousand natural causes of failure. Philip A. Crowl, who headed the Naval War College's Department of Strategy, wrote the following advice: "After all your plans have been perfected, all avenues explored, all contingencies thought through, then ask yourself one final question: 'What have I overlooked?' Then say your prayers and go to sleep—with the certain knowledge that tomorrow too will bring its share of nasty surprises."[64]

3

Leadership

Perhaps because warfare has played a central role historically in the development of our conceptions of leadership and authority, it is not surprising that the ancient linguistic root of the word "to lead" means "to go forth, die."

— Ronald A. Heifetz, M.D.
Leadership Without Easy Answers

Notwithstanding Dr. Heifetz's observation, many people assume that leadership takes utterly different forms in politics and war. Political leaders have to deal with strict limits on their formal authority, so they spend most of their time changing minds instead of issuing commands. Military officers need not worry about persuasion, the common thinking goes, because they automatically enjoy the troops' complete obedience. In 1952, President Truman expressed this notion when he thought ahead to an Eisenhower White House: "He'll sit here, and he'll say 'Do this! Do that!' *And nothing will happen*. Poor Ike—it won't be a bit like the Army. He'll find it very frustrating."[1]

Eisenhower would have his share of frustrations, but Truman misread him. Only in recent years have scholars begun to grasp Ike's shrewdness. He knew perfectly well that he could not get his way just by barking orders, so he worked hard getting people to see his desires as in their own self-interest.[2] In part, his political savvy stemmed from his long career of staff jobs, in which he had worked with politicians and bureaucrats. As the Supreme Allied Commander in Europe, he had operated as both diplomat and warrior. But to a large extent, Eisenhower's understanding of leadership grew out of the same training and experience that all commanders undergo. Warriors have always known that they cannot automatically expect total compliance from their subordinates. Soldiers may mutiny—or worse. In Vietnam, American troops sometimes dispatched unpopular officers with fragmentation grenades, a process called "fragging."[3] More often, troops may follow orders, but with the least effort necessary to avoid punishment. Such low performance can hurt a military unit just as badly as a "work to rule" job action can ruin a private company.[4] To achieve greater effort, a leader must change attitudes as well as behavior. As Eisenhower said: "I would rather try to persuade a man to go along, because once I have persuaded him, he will stick. If I scare him, he will stay just as long as he is scared, and then he is gone."[5] Charles de Gaulle, whose career paralleled Eisenhower's in important ways, observed that a leader must inspire followers so that "they will look upon the task assigned to them as something of their own choosing."[6]

When it comes to persuasion and inspiration, the military has something to teach the political world, if only because it asks for greater sacrifices. It is challenging enough to champion unpopular positions, as politicians must sometimes do, but think about the task facing military officers: getting young people to risk death. Sometimes, as with the first landing at Omaha Beach on D-Day, that risk approaches certainty. In such settings, the threat of being court-martialed is not enough to secure obedience, for who would prefer a grave to a prison cell? Military leaders must convince troops that the risk is necessary for the sake of country, honor, or comrades. The world's armed forces have been pondering that task for thousands of years, so it is instructive to see what they have learned.

Obviously, political and military leadership are not alike in every way. Unlike military organizations, with their chains of command, political organizations spread power loosely among many hands. As Newt Gingrich said: "The need to devise a proper strategy is made even more daunting by the number of key players who must be in on it. Napoleon said that one mediocre general was better than three good generals who had to work together. Imagine what Napoleon would have thought of the House of Representatives!"[7] Even on this point, however, the distinction is scarcely airtight, because the modern military requires officers to work together and recommends that they involve subordinates in the planning process.[8]

Like any skill, leadership is partially a matter of talent: Some people just perform better than others. But field manuals stress that anyone can learn the basics, the specific things that a leader must be, know, and do. This chapter explains these basics and shows how they apply to politics.

TO BE: CHARACTER

On meeting a new commander, soldiers ask themselves whether that person deserves their wholehearted support. As an anonymous writer once put it in *The Infantry Journal*, "No man is a leader until his appointment is ratified in the minds and hearts of his men."[9] Accordingly, military leadership training emphasizes the need for strong character.

The concept of "character" consists in part of the mental habits that mold behavior. For leaders, though, private virtue does not go far enough, because they must also make others believe in them. In an official handbook on leadership, military analyst S. L. A. Marshall wrote that officers will falter if they have "not sufficiently regarded LOOKS, ACTIONS, WORDS" (emphasis in original).[10] That is the sense in which General George Washington dwelt on his own "character." Through his language and bearing, he consciously played the role of a leader who scorned wrongdoing.[11] Even though he yearned to command the Continental Army, Washington thought it would be unseemly to campaign for the job, so he made an elaborate show of reluctance.

Sociologist Erving Goffman analyzed face-to-face encounters as a form of theater in which people stage "performances" to sway the thoughts and actions of "audiences."[12] Significantly, Washington may have based his public persona on a play. He saw Joseph Addison's *Cato* many times, frequently quoting its dialogue and identifying himself with a character who puts the esteem of good men ahead of all else.[13] Washington's contemporary, Frederick the Great of Prussia, said that a general "should be constantly on the stage and should appear most tranquil when he is occupied, for the whole army speculates on his looks, his gestures, and his mood."[14] A century and a half later, de Gaulle added: "Whereas ordinary officers must be content with behaving correctly in front of their men, great leaders have always carefully stage-managed their effects."[15] Historian John Keegan extends this insight. The theatrical impulse, he says, drives politicians, athletes, ministers, and, most of all, generals. Anyone who would lead people into battle must reveal aspects of character that will inspire hard work and heroism while concealing traits that could undercut morale: "The leader of men in warfare can show himself to his followers only through a mask, a mask that he must make for himself, but a mask made in such form as will mark him to men of his time and place as the leader they want and need."[16]

Mystery enhances the effect. "In the designs, the demeanor, and the mental operations of a leader," said de Gaulle, "there must always be a 'something' which others cannot altogether fathom, which puzzles them, stirs them, and rivets their attention."[17] Officers may not fraternize with enlisted people, and the military reinforces the distinction with separate living quarters and dining areas. Though "of the people," strong political leaders also cultivate a subtle sense of distance. FDR camouflaged his disability at public events and withheld his innermost thoughts from aides and allies. And of that supposedly simple and easygoing president, Ronald Reagan, speechwriter Peggy Noonan observed: "He gleams; he is a mystery. He is for everyone there, for everyone who worked with him. None of them understand him. In private they admit it. You say to them, Who was that masked man?, and they shrug, and hypothesize."[18]

Warriors and political figures have donned a variety of masks, each reflecting its time and culture. In an era of divine myths, Alexander the Great's "Olympian" manner set him apart as a superior being. Thousands of years later, Ulysses S. Grant dressed and spoke plainly, remembering an early incident when civilians had mocked his fancy uniform.[19] In World War II, General George Patton worked on a tough, profane persona and would practice his "war face" in front of a mirror. When it came to choosing a president, however, voters much preferred Ike's smiling visage.

"The mask of command" is not mere fakery. In the long run, a leader can sustain an image only if it rests on some underlying reality. Conversely, the mask reshapes the face. As S. L. A. Marshall wrote, "It is good, also, to look the part, not only because of its effect on others, but because from out of the effort made to *look it*, one may in time come to *be it*."[20]

Amid all their differences, great military leaders share certain traits, especially courage. Distinct from the absence of fear, courage entails the ability to act effectively in spite of fear, to put a calm face atop jangling nerves and a racing heart. "Every man is frightened at first in battle," Patton told his soldiers. "If he says he isn't, he's a goddamn liar. Some men are cowards, yes! But they fight just the same, or get the hell shamed out of them watching men who do fight who are just as scared. The real hero is the man who fights even though he is scared."[21] Obviously, combat involves physical danger—especially for junior officers, whose bodies always litter battlefields. When a fight is under way, lieutenants must often dispense with complicated orders and instead utter the fateful words, "Follow me." Such exercises of courage set an example for the troops and cement their loyalty to the officer. "I knew if I flinched I was ruined," wrote a Union lieutenant at Bull Run. At the Western Front in 1915, Robert Graves found that "the only thing respected in young officers was personal courage."[22] Though contemporary generals rarely go into harm's way, the military prefers to give that rank to those who have undergone combat.

What does bravery have to do with politics? Politicians constantly talk about it, and the highest praise that one political figure can bestow upon another is the adjective "courageous." In his Senate memoirs, Warren Rudman (R-NH) wrote: "I came to respect those who proved themselves in political combat as much as I did heroes of the battlefield. A Bob Dole or a Howard Baker had to possess all the courage and resolve that a military commander needs."[23]

In one special way, politics does assume an aspect of actual combat. Nearly 10 percent of American presidents have died by gunfire, a higher casualty rate than American soldiers faced in Vietnam. Seeking and holding the office takes some physical courage, and Americans admire leaders who show such mettle. In 1981, while bleeding from a would-be assassin's bullet, President Reagan cracked jokes. Polls later showed that the incident raised his standing with the electorate.

Although lower-level politicians seldom face real peril to life and limb, they still confront serious risks. Political "killing" often takes the brutally clear form of electoral defeat. For a business owner, it may not be a disaster to go slightly into the red, but for a politician, a fraction of 1 percent of the gross vote can spell the difference between survival and ruin.[24] And "ruin" is the right word here, because a loss at the polls means a rejection not of one's work but of oneself. In effect, the politician's fellow citizens are saying, "We think your opponent is better than you."

People hate to be the objects of hatred. When green soldiers first come under fire, they react with bewilderment: "Why are they shooting at me? What did I ever do to them?"[25] Once the shock wears off, they can find small solace in remembering that war is anonymous. Politicians lack such consolations. In their world, attacks are inherently personal because opponents are deliberately trying to turn people against them. At best, they can look forward to charges of poor judgment. Often, they must fight smears about their public records and private lives. As politician and writer Stimson Bullitt put it, players in contact sports "need only keep in mind that their opponents feel no spite, while a politician must try not to remember, but to ignore, that his assailants often mean their blows to hurt; and therefore his defenses can be pierced."[26]

Government executives also have to watch out for attacks. When they run afoul of lawmakers, lobbies, or powerful superiors, they may find their careers in jeopardy. William Black, an attorney for the Office of Thrift Supervision, learned this lesson in 1987, when he uncovered congressional pressure to protect corrupt savings and loan institutions in Texas. House Speaker Jim Wright (D-TX) struck back by publicly denouncing Black as a Reagan puppet (even though he was a liberal Democrat) and privately seeking his dismissal. Black had cause for concern because Wright had earlier tried to discredit another regulator by spreading rumors about his sex life. In the end, though, the attacks backfired by deepening suspicions about Wright's ethics, and he had to quit Congress in 1989.[27]

When political analysts ponder why a qualified person forgoes public office, they often overlook the obvious reason: fear. Besides their opponents, people in public life must worry about investigative reporters. In a 1999 national survey, 80 percent of state legislative candidates said that press scrutiny of officials' private lives discourages good people from running for office.[28] It takes courage to overcome such concerns.

Boldness, another mark of a strong leader, consists of the imagination to see a new way of doing things and the backbone to follow through. Carl von Clausewitz said that this quality does "not consist in defying the natural order of things and in crudely offending the law of probability [but in] rapid, only partly conscious weighing of the possibilities."[29] By taking calculated risks in the tradition of Robert E. Lee, leaders can endow their followers with esprit de corps while demoralizing their opponents. A reputation for boldness can precede a leader to the battlefield, intimidating the other side before the fight begins. "I am heartily tired of hearing what Lee is going to do," Ulysses S. Grant told a panicky subordinate. "Some of you always seem to think he is suddenly going to turn a double somersault, and land on our rear and on both our flanks at the same time."[30] Bold political leaders, such as Lee Atwater and Bill Clinton, have the same effect on their foes.

Timidity, in contrast, may bring temporary safety at the cost of long-run success. In the Civil War, General George McClellan became the archetype of military timidity when he botched the Union's chance for early victory by refusing to strike boldly at the Confederacy. Despite his heroism in World War II and his decisive leadership in the Persian Gulf War, President George Bush proved fatally cautious in domestic policy. In his 1992 acceptance speech, Clinton said: "But right now I know how President Lincoln felt when George McClellan wouldn't attack in the Civil War. He asked him, 'If you're not going to use your army, may I borrow it?' And so I say, George Bush, if you won't use your power to help America, step aside, I will."[31]

Entering a battlefield or making a bold stroke is one thing, but it is another thing to stay on course after suffering a major blow. In such a situation, wrote Clausewitz, a general deals with conflicting and confusing pressures. "Perseverance in the chosen course is the essential counterweight, provided that no compelling reasons intervene to the contrary."[32] Grant showed this quality at the Battle of Shiloh. After the rebels had launched a stunning counterattack, some Union officers started to speak of retreat. "Well, Grant," said General William T. Sherman, "We've had the devil's own day, haven't we?" Grant agreed, but after drawing on his cigar, he added: "Lick 'em tomorrow, though."[33] And his troops did.

In war and politics, Eisenhower showed the same perseverance. Historian Stephen Ambrose uses a telling analogy in describing Ike's reaction to a 1952 flap over the ethics of running mate Richard Nixon: "In a way it was like the Battle of the Bulge—the opposition had launched a daring, surprise assault that threw most of those around Eisenhower into near panic; but Eisenhower felt instinctively that the Democrats, like the Germans in 1944, did not in fact have the resources to sustain the attack."[34]

Leaders must exude confidence as well as feel it. During World War II, Eisenhower said that "optimism and pessimism are infectious and they spread more rapidly from the head downward than in any other direction." Therefore, he added, "I firmly determined that my mannerisms and speech in public would always reflect the cheerful certainty of victory—that any pessimism or discouragement I might ever feel would be reserved for my pillow."[35] Nixon passed along Eisenhower's advice when he once told Republican candidates: "You as the candidate must keep your spirit up. Any time you show the audience in front of you that you're the least bit discouraged, any time you show that you have lost your zeal, it has a contagious effect and you are doomed to lose."[36]

A leader may have to withstand disappointment after disappointment. Grant repeatedly recovered from setbacks, prompting Lincoln to say, "It is the dogged pertinacity of Grant that wins."[37] Lincoln, like Churchill, suffered major defeats and endured a long time in the wilderness before returning to lead his country in wartime. Others have defied their own political obituaries. Richard Nixon was fond of St. Barton's Ode: "I am hurt but I am not slain! I will lie me down and bleed awhile—then I'll rise and fight again!"[38] Bill Clinton's "dogged pertinacity" sustained public support during scandals that would have finished anyone else.

A leader can be bold, confident, and physically brave yet still lack integrity. According to the Army, integrity consists of "utter sincerity, honesty, and candor . . . the avoidance of any kind of deceptive, shallow, or expedient behavior."[39] Because military and civilian organizations both depend on the integrity of their people, it would be reassuring to suggest a perfect correlation between integrity and individual success. Alas, history supplies too many exceptions. Integrity may keep good people from rising, as the Army itself acknowledged in its 1983 field manual on leadership: "There will be times when honestly stating your true beliefs to your seniors or the group may not be in your best interest—it may hurt your chances for promotion or even ruin your whole career. These times will test whether or not you have the moral courage to 'stand up and be counted.'"[40]

Integrity occupies a paradoxical place in politics. The virtue is popular, yet its real test is the willingness to do what is unpopular. Will citizens respect a leader who defies their views for the sake of principle? Only on occasion. As John F. Kennedy wrote of senators who stood against constituent opinion: "Some were ultimately vindicated by a return to popularity; many were not."[41]

TO KNOW: COMPETENCE

A leader must know many things, but the most important is human nature. In 1804, British military theorist Robert Jackson wrote that officers must study the human character, and that "the school is in the camp and the cottage rather than the city and the palace."[42] A century later, the Tammany Hall political leader George Washington Plunkitt used similar language: "There's only one way to hold a district: you must study human nature and act accordin'.... To learn real human nature you have to go among the people, see them and be seen."[43]

A good understanding of human nature helps leaders avoid the extremes of faintheartedness and rashness because it enables them to see their opponents as neither supermen nor oafs. It also helps them judge what to expect from their own followers. In politics and war, effective leaders know what their followers need— pride, self-respect, spiritual justification—and then appeal to these needs to get the desired result.[44] On a grand scale, this quality of understanding means a grasp of the motivations common to masses of people. On a more prosaic level, leaders need insight into the individual people with whom they work face to face. One battalion commander calls this aspect of leadership the ability "to know your soldiers by the backs of their heads."[45] That is how effective legislative leaders know their colleagues. As Senate majority leader in the 1950s, Lyndon Johnson studied each senator's personality, intellect, ideology, and home-state political situation. He knew exactly what he could get from each of them because he knew what they wanted, what they feared, and what they could do. Elsewhere in government and politics, leaders gain a similar understanding of their staffs and key line personnel.

With such knowledge, leaders can pick the right people for the right tasks. General George C. Marshall had a particular genius for identifying and promoting talented officers, such as Matthew

Ridgway and Dwight Eisenhower. Among American political figures, Nelson Rockefeller and Robert F. Kennedy showed a similar
knack for spotting talent. The example of Barry Goldwater, in
contrast, shows what happens when a leader lacks this ability.
Despite some gifted outside advisers, Goldwater failed to choose
staffers who could provide him with a steady stream of material
and act as a check on his own tactlessness. "Barry Goldwater
could not or would not perceive shortcomings in his entourage,"
wrote two of his consultants. "He elected to do battle at the head
of a cordon of political tyros rather than an action-hardened professional army."[46]

Military officers must grasp their own strengths and weaknesses so that they will know when to do things themselves,
when to delegate, and when to defer to higher authority. Because
leadership involves image, says General Aubrey "Red" Newman,
officers "should look into the mirrors of their minds with the
power of imaginative introspection and empathy to visualize
how they look to others—and try to improve what they see."[47]
Political leaders need similar self-knowledge. In 1998, California
Republican gubernatorial candidate Dan Lungren figured that he
could win on personality but failed to see that voters did not like
him. Had he recognized his limitations, he might not have suffered a landslide defeat.

To get "reality checks" on their performance, leaders need can-
did advice. When General Marshall had completed his first week
as Army chief of staff during World War II, he told his aides: "I am
disappointed in all of you." When they asked why, he answered:
"You haven't disagreed with a single thing I have done all week."[48]
Like Marshall, effective political leaders know that internal
debate can help them identify and avoid problems.

Though knowledge of self and others is paramount, leaders
need technical and historical knowledge as well. In 1949, historian Douglas Southall Freeman told students at the Naval War

College: "First, know your stuff. Know your stuff, just that. If you are an aviator, know it. And know something else besides. . . . Know—know your own branch, know the related arms of the service; you can't know too much if you are going to be a successful leader. And know the yesterdays."[49] To help officers gain such knowledge, the U.S. armed forces maintain a system of special postgraduate schools, including the Army War College and the Naval War College. The military also encourages independent reading. According to the Marine Corps, "Self-study in the art and science of war is at least equal in importance—and should receive at least equal time—to maintaining physical conditioning. This is particularly true among officers; after all, an officer's principal weapon is his mind."[50]

Obviously, a certain level of technical knowledge is essential for job performance: artillery officers have to know one end of a cannon from the other. It is also essential for winning the esteem of superiors and subordinates. Soldiers respect officers who have mastered their jobs and quickly look down on those who have not.

Throughout the world of government and politics, people acknowledge the importance of "knowing your stuff." Though political executives sometimes come into office with only a dim comprehension of what their organizations do, they have to learn fast. Such an executive must master the details of administration, said former Reagan official Donald Devine, "because if he does not, the political leader will lose control of policy, which is his first responsibility. . . . He will become a figurehead, and turn policy over to those below him who do not have the legal or moral authority to set policy for the public."[51] In every legislative body, members can tell which colleagues know what they are talking about and which ones rely too much on staff. All other things being equal, the former gain influence more readily than the latter.[52] Similarly, lobbyists can have impact only if policymakers can trust them to supply reliable information about their issues.

In all these positions, political figures—like military officers—must keep learning about their field through both self-study and formal training. (Chapter 4 discusses training in greater detail.)

Anyone with good study habits can gain a working knowledge of details. Political and military leaders of the top rank need something rarer: *coup d'oeil*, or "intuition," loosely translated. The idea, wrote Clausewitz, "refers to the quick recognition of a truth that the mind would ordinarily miss or would perceive only after long study and reflection."[53] Willie Brown, Speaker of the California Assembly from 1980 to 1995, used this gift to dazzle allies and flummox opponents. Even his initial election as Speaker was a masterstroke. When fellow Democrats split badly over the choice, he saw that he could win by breaking with normal practice and reaching out to the other party. Thinking that they would have the upper hand, Assembly Republicans gave him enough votes to win the speakership. Although Brown honored the specific commitments he had made to the Republicans, he consolidated his power and emerged as the scourge of the GOP.

TO DO: CONDUCT

As chapter 2 explained, leaders need strategies that link ends and means. Leaders must also explain those ends and means to their troops, so they must express ideas effectively. General George Meade's chief of staff once explained that Ulysses S. Grant was a splendid communicator: "There is one striking feature of Grant's orders; no matter how hurriedly he may write them on the field, no one ever has the slightest doubt as to their meaning, or even has to read them over a second time to understand them."[54]

With such examples in mind, the armed forces devote a great deal of time and money to improving officers' skills in writing and speaking. Colin Powell recalls how the Army trained him to serve as an Infantry School instructor. The course taught officers how to move, gesture, and speak with authority, and how to transmit information with clarity. "If I had to put my finger on *the* pivotal learning experience of my life, it could well be the instructors course, where I graduated first in my class. Years later, when I appeared before millions of Americans on television to describe our actions in the Gulf War, I was doing nothing more than using communicating techniques I had learned a quarter of a century before in the instructors course at Infantry Hall."[55]

Americans expect their leaders to be articulate, which is one reason we revere Lincoln and both Roosevelts—and why those Gulf War television briefings made Powell a potential presidential contender. It is telling that Powell's communications training came in a school for instructors. In war and politics, leadership is teachership. Admiral James B. Stockdale said: "Every great leader I've known has been a great teacher, able to give those around him a sense of perspective and to set the moral, social and particularly the motivational climate among them."[56] In this sense, teaching goes beyond the transmission of facts to the transformation of people. As teachers, leaders can change their followers by causing them to think in new ways and to adopt new values. During boot camp, Marine drill instructors indoctrinate recruits in the corps' language, lore, discipline, and habits of mind. By the time their young charges come out, they have forsaken their civilian ways and are thinking like Marines—sometimes to the point of harboring contempt for the world they left behind.[57] In less intense and dramatic ways, military leaders at all levels work to mold and remold those who serve under them. The Corps advises all commanders to "foster a personal teacher-student relationship with their subordinates."[58]

Many political scientists see leaders as mere brokers of material interests who have to deal with their followers' preferences as given. From the perspective of teachership, however, we see that leaders can change those preferences. On the highest level, Abraham Lincoln and Martin Luther King led people to national reconciliation. On less lofty planes, other political leaders have remade their followers' minds. Newt Gingrich came to power by persuading House Republicans to unlearn their "minority party mentality" and to study ways of winning the majority. "My strategy is essentially teaching," he explained.[59]

According to Gingrich, General Marshall embodied the leader as teacher. "From his years as an infantry officer," Gingrich wrote, "Marshall knew that Americans were very poor at *taking* orders but would fight better than anyone if they *understood* why they were fighting."[60] Such an assertion assumes that the leader is giving voice to aims that deserve extraordinary effort. As a mid-level officer in 1932, de Gaulle said that a leader's plans must "respond to the cravings felt by men who, imperfect themselves, seek perfection in the end they are called upon to serve."[61] In his first Inaugural Address, FDR did not merely say that he would shorten bread lines and stop bank failures but that he would lead a disciplined citizenry toward greatness, "pledging that the larger purposes will bind upon us all as a sacred obligation with a unity of duty hitherto evoked only in time of armed strife. With this pledge taken, I assume unhesitatingly the leadership of this great army of our people dedicated to a disciplined attack upon our common problems."[62]

While exhorting the troops to pursue the larger good, a leader also has to take care of their needs. Douglas Southall Freeman put it this way: "Look after your men and your men will look after you. I don't believe there has ever been an exception to that dictum."[63] Freeman cited the case of Robert E. Lee, who cemented the loyalty of his men by seeing to such mundane matters as hot food and clean uniforms.

Political leaders rarely supply food and clothing to each of the citizens they represent. In important ways, however, they too must look after their followers. Through such devices as committee assignments and schedule adjustments, legislative leaders tend to the political needs of their members. These lawmakers, in turn, track down lost benefit payments and provide other services to their constituencies. And whether elected or unelected, all leaders have to care for their aides and other subordinates. General Omar Bradley said that "it is well to remember that loyalty goes down as well as up. The sincere leader will go to bat for his subordinates when such action is indicated."[64] William Niskanen, a member of President Reagan's Council of Economic Advisers, echoed the general's advice: "Share credit with your staff. Be prepared to accept blame for innocent mistakes by your staff, at least in any public role. Recognize that loyalty down is an essential condition of loyalty up."[65]

The military teaches leaders to think about personal touches, such as remembering names, listening to problems, and offering recognition for good work. Julius Caesar and Napoleon were famous for their ability to identify individual soldiers in their armies. Patton also spoke of the bond between leaders and followers: "Always talk with the troops! They know more about the war than anybody. Make them tell you all of their gripes. Make sure they know we are doing everything we can to help them. The soldiers will have to win the war. We cannot do it. Talk with them. They will not trust you if you do not trust them."[66]

Smart political leaders tend to their troops by knowing names, observing birthdays, offering tokens of appreciation, and lending a sympathetic ear when necessary. A well-timed thank-you note or a few moments of "face time" with the leader can help motivate a staffer or volunteer to extend an already lengthy workday. Conversely, a perceived slight can prompt a resignation or an act of outright disloyalty. Whereas soldiers in Vietnam did their "fragging" with hand grenades, bureaucrats and political aides can do it with leaks to the press.

OBSERVATIONS

The criteria for good leadership in war and politics are diverse and demanding. By this point, the reader should have gathered that no human being could possibly excel in all of them, and that every leader has flaws. Douglas MacArthur's strategic brilliance enabled American forces to work wonders in the Pacific theater; but at the same time, he also suffered from vanity and pomposity, which often made him an object of soldiers' discontent. Ronald Reagan was a great communicator and political teacher of the first rank, but in key areas of policy and management he simply did not "know his stuff." His neglect of detail gave free rein to ambitious subordinates, leading to such botches as the Iran-Contra affair.

Often, leaders' vices are caricatures of their virtues. Through oratory, for instance, leaders should be able to inspire their followers, but after a certain point eloquence balloons into verbosity and a leader's orations may undercut confidence instead of bolstering it. "The man who is moved by desire or fear is naturally led to seek relief in words," explained de Gaulle. "Men instinctively distrust an officer who is prodigal of speech."[67] House Speaker Newt Gingrich and Senator Joseph Biden (D-DE) both got into serious political trouble by talking too much. Their loose tongues irritated their colleagues, supplied ammunition to their opponents, and distracted attention from their genuine strengths.

Where does a leader find the right balance? Where are the bright lines that distinguish wordsmith from windbag, enthusiast from zealot, bold risk-taker from reckless gambler? Such lines can be hard to see during political or military combat; and historians may still not find them years later. Scholars of the late twenty-first century will debate the Clinton impeachment just as they still debate the Battle of Gettysburg today. Some will see the House Republicans as heedless fanatics jeopardizing their party and their government, whereas others will see them as courageous statesmen willing to brave partisan abuse for the sake of principle.

The obvious (but difficult) remedy is for leaders to recognize their own limitations and compensate for them through procedure or personnel. William Gavin, a longtime aide to the House GOP leadership, once compared political leadership to jazz. Soloists can achieve greatness through improvisation and musical risk-taking, he explained, but they need a reliable accompaniment that sets a formal structure within which creativity can take place. In politics, a leader needs both the soaring riffs of the idea-driven revolutionary and the steady back-beat of the Main Street establishment figure. "Combine both," said Gavin, "and you have the great synergism called art."[68]

General Gordon Sullivan, Army chief of staff in the early 1990s, used jazz to describe military leadership: "Our military plans have the complexity of orchestral scores, but the certainty of that sheet music does not parallel the changing conditions under which the military leader performs his tasks. Versatility—the improvisation of the jazzman—has been a hallmark of great leaders in our past and is in even greater demand today."[69]

In jazz, war, and politics, improvisation consists of building on a theme, of working from the known to the unknown. Teamwork is what keeps it from turning into chaos. And teamwork, in turn, depends on people who have solid training in their work (be it musical, military, or political), who share an understanding of what they are trying to accomplish, and who can readily communicate with one another. And so it is to these concepts—training, doctrine, and communication—that we now turn.

4

Coordination

The greatest discovery ever made in the art of war
was when men began to perceive that organization
and discipline count for more than numbers. . . . By
degrees, for even in America great truths do not burst
full-grown upon the world, it was perceived that the
victories of the ballot-box, no less than of the sword,
must be won by the cohesion and disciplined docility
of the troops, and that these merits can only be
secured by skillful organization and long-continued
training.

—James Bryce
The American Commonwealth

Generals and admirals have to move their forces
across long distances, making sure that they all do the right things
at the right place at the right time. Politics also involves the coordination of large numbers, often over vast areas. In a caucus, campaign, or bureaucracy, leaders have to get people working by the
same plans and striving toward the same goals. If the legislative
whip decides that Monday is the day to push the crime issue, the

effort will fizzle if lower-ranking figures pick that day to empha-
size playground construction. In his classic study of the Forest
Service, Herbert Kaufman listed obstacles to coordination that
could break the Service "into an aggregate of separate entities,
destroying it as an integrated, functioning organization."[1]

In the military, the stakes are higher. When everything works
right, the forces act as one large body, with each limb supporting
the others. When coordination fails, troops come under fire without support, artillery shells land on empty ground, supplies go to
the wrong units, and airplanes bomb their own soldiers. During
the close-quarter fights of the seventeenth century, armies found
that sparks from their primitive muskets could trigger a chain of
accidental discharges. The solution consisted of a drill in which
everyone loaded and fired in unison.[2] Hence the origin of a phrase
that has come to denote unity of action—"knowing the drill."

The modern military uses a variety of tools to promote coordination:

1. *Doctrine—fundamental statements of how a military
   organization runs its operations.* Doctrine fosters a
   shared professional culture, helping troops understand one
   another's language and assumptions.
2. *Recruitment—enlisting people with a talent for certain
   tasks and a willingness to adopt the organization's culture.* The Roman warrior Vegetius wrote: "An army raised
   without proper regard to the choice of its recruits was never
   yet made good by length of time."[3]
3. *Training—the teaching of skills, habits, procedures,
   and doctrine.* Training includes the initial orientation of
   recruits (in basic training, or boot camp), but it also involves
   ongoing educational efforts by which the military turns
   good troops into better ones.
4. *Communication.* Obviously, action depends on the internal flow of information, but that is not enough. People at

both ends have to understand what the signals mean and what they must do as a result. When soldiers misread these signals, they will do the wrong things—hence the need for doctrine.[4]

Politics has its own forms of doctrine, recruitment, training, and communication. Although these versions tend to be less formal than their khaki counterparts, the military model still helps us see how political figures achieve coordination.

DOCTRINE

Whereas strategy is a plan that links ends to means in a particular conflict, doctrine is a basic, standing approach to combat and other activities. Doctrine sets a mode of thinking and fighting, providing guidance on military methods. It does not dictate a response to every situation, but it does tell officers how to make decisions.[5] Doctrine enables officers to communicate via mutually understood shorthand, and even to anticipate one another's thoughts.[6]

Field manuals are guides to military doctrine. In its major doctrinal publication, *Warfighting*, the Marine Corps lays out the assumption that it will be "the first to fight" in any military conflict, landing ahead of the Army and often facing numerically stronger foes. The Marine warfighting doctrine, says the manual, depends on "rapid, flexible and opportunistic maneuver." Unlike military forces that work by attrition, the Corps "seeks to shatter the enemy's cohesion through a series of rapid, violent, and unexpected actions which create a turbulent and rapidly deteriorating situation with which he cannot cope."[7] Steeped in this doctrine, Marine officers know that they should fight fast and hard—and that fellow Marines will do likewise. As *Warfighting* puts it, "We seek unity, not through imposed control, but through *harmonious* initiative and lateral coordination. . . . While a situation may change, making the task obsolete, the intent is more permanent and continues to guide our actions."[8]

Civilian agencies have their own doctrines.[9] Bureaucracies try to foresee events and conditions in the field, and then suggest how to choose a course of action—often in field manuals that resemble those of the military. Once officials figure out the category into which a particular circumstance falls, they know how to respond.[10] As in the military, however, these responses need not grow out of point-by-point rules; instead, they may result from a commitment to the agency's overarching philosophy. Consider the Social Security Administration in its youth. Its publications reflected the belief that the organization supplied "social insurance," not welfare; that it sent checks to "clients," not recipients; and that its long-range goal was to expand the program, not curb expenditures. This doctrine encouraged employees to take good care of recipients and to help lawmakers who wanted to enlarge the program.[11]

In the world of electoral politics, doctrine is usually implicit, although we can still trace its outlines and track its influence. When thinking about national party committees, for example, Republicans focus on technical and organizational concerns, or the "nuts and bolts" of raising money and winning elections. Democrats focus on procedural issues involving which groups have a voice in party decisions. In response to presidential-election defeats, Republicans restructure their forces whereas Democrats reform their nomination procedures.[12]

Doctrine shapes election campaigns. In advising President Clinton on his 1996 reelection, consultant Dick Morris analyzed GOP campaign doctrine in a search for weaknesses that the Clinton camp could exploit. Although no party official had ever explained this doctrine in a public document, Morris teased out its major elements by drawing on his experiences as a sometime

GOP advisor. First, he said, was a bias against early advertising, a belief that commercials can shift votes only in a campaign's last weeks. Second was a reluctance to answer attacks, on the grounds that rebuttals merely let the other side drive the agenda. Third was the assumption that challengers can beat incumbents only by raising their "negatives," that is, their unfavorable perceptions among the voters.[13] As Morris convinced the President and his staff, each part of GOP doctrine was flawed. The Clinton campaign leadership correctly concluded that it could make effective use of early ads and tough rebuttals, and that the Dole campaign would not. It also defused Dole attacks by making GOP "negativity" an issue in itself.

The politician who did the most to make doctrine explicit—and to base it on military models—was House Speaker Newt Gingrich. He had long studied Army doctrine, and once in power, he sent Republican members and staff to seminars of the Training and Doctrine Command (TRADOC). A spokesman for TRADOC said that the GOP visitors wanted to learn "how we develop doctrine, how we achieve consensus in the Army. . . . We want people to understand it [doctrine] and sign up to it, not just have it dictated to them." An Army officer who worked with the GOP on "after-action reviews" explained how these ideas applied to the House: "Newt knows that twisting arms is not sustainable. He wants them to internalize what the plan is."[14]

In 1994, at Gingrich's urging, House Republican members and candidates adopted the Contract with America, a policy agenda that they promised to bring to a quick vote if they won a majority. The Contract was a doctrinal document, aiming to break House Republicans' old "minority mentality" and get them thinking as a governing team. In May 1995, Gingrich called the Contract a "training implementation document masquerading as a public relations device." It guaranteed that the House GOP "would have to behave in a deviant manner from what it would normally be expected to do. The theory being that if you could get them through the first 100 days being deviant, then the deviancy would become normal."[15]

Two years later, House GOP leaders worked with military officers on a doctrinal handbook. "A Framework for House Republicans" spoke of "a foundation for mutual understanding [that] explains how Members and staff think about the way we work."[16] It defined such terms as "strategy" and spelled out procedures for military-style "after-action reviews," in which members would study legislative successes and failures, then derive the appropriate lessons.

After another two years, however, Gingrich had to quit. GOP factional fights and legislative failures had enabled the Democrats to make unprecedented midterm gains. What had happened? During the Republicans' long years in the wilderness, their implicit doctrine had depicted House politics as a constant struggle for power and publicity. "As the minority party," wrote Gingrich, "we were in the position of having to fight every day just to get some media attention. We tended to say and do things that were far more strident and dramatic than are prudent to do and say as the leaders of the majority."[17] Just as military forces must revise doctrine in light of historic events (e.g., the end of the Cold War) or technological advances (e.g., the development of aircraft), so parties must change theirs when they face new situations, such as majority status. Doctrinal shifts can roil the military, as the Army showed in 1925 when it court-martialed General Billy Mitchell for his aggressive advocacy of air power. Similarly, the Republicans had difficulty adjusting to majority status. Despite Gingrich's efforts to craft a new "governing" doctrine, many of his colleagues were still operating according to the old minority-party doctrine.

Gingrich could not impose his changes because of an important difference between an army and a legislative body. Soldiers must answer to a well-defined hierarchy, so they have a strong motive to heed doctrine from above. In the tangled legislative chain of command, however, lawmakers respond not only to party leaders but to committee chairs, constituent groups, Washington lobbies, and executive officials. A leader can maintain coordination through constant persuasion, but Gingrich's own political problems made him less and less persuasive over time.

RECRUITMENT

In the seventeenth century, the term "recruit" entered the English language as a term meaning "to replenish or 'recrew' a body of troops."[18] For most of American history, the military has relied on volunteers. It does not want just anyone: criminals, psychopaths, and racists would all disrupt order, so the military tries to keep them out. To encourage enlistments by good people with valuable aptitudes, the services offer educational and financial incentives. At the same time, they want to prevent these rewards from becoming the sole attraction. "Soldiers motivated by the lure of a college education or technical training for future civilian application may not be ideal choices for our future Army," writes Major Brian R. Reinwald. "Above all, our recruits must be disciplined and prepared to sacrifice their lives for their country in the performance of their duties."[19] Recruits acting on patriotism and personal challenge are more likely to accept discipline and doctrine because they put military goals ahead of their material interests.

In general, it is easier to sustain unity of effort by recruiting like-minded people than by changing the values of people who already belong to an organization.[20] When the Social Security Administration was starting up, it hired people from the social sciences or social services because they presumably had more sympathy for program goals than people from the insurance industry.[21] In the 1950s, recruiters for the Forest Service stressed that its mix of tough work and modest pay was not for everyone, just those with a passion for the outdoors. Through this approach, the Service hoped to screen out potential troublemakers, taking only those who would adopt the organization's ways.[22]

When politicians recruit policymakers or staff aides, they also seek people who are already "with the program." According to political aide Lyn Nofziger, the test for Reagan Administration job candidates was: "Are you a Republican, and if you are, are you the best Republican for the job—or is there a Reagan Republican out there?"[23] The idea was not simply to reward partisans but to fill the government with loyal soldiers of the Reagan agenda.

Acceptance of discipline and doctrine hardly means mindlessness. One may back an organization's beliefs and still disagree with its actions. As chapter 3 suggested, wise leaders should seek subordinates who will engage them in internal debate and provide a "reality check" against error. But good leadership requires good followership, so once a decision is final, subordinates should salute and comply. The political world uses military metaphors to describe such loyalty:

- On learning in 1996 that the White House did not want him to attack Independent Counsel Ken Starr, James Carville responded: "Well, if that's the decision, . . . I'll be a good soldier."[24] (The White House later changed its mind, and the good soldier went back on the attack.)

- "I pleaded internally with people to let me take a different position," said Clinton aide Lanny Davis of his efforts to defend the President against charges of scandal. "But I was a good soldier, thinking I'm a lawyer and I'll do the best I can for my client with a bad set of facts."[25]

- Journalist Gloria Borger said of Clinton's defenders: "Such situational ethics, as they were called in the 1960s, require loyal troops. Leaders who live more bureaucratic, rule-managed existences require less personal devotion; this White House demands total fidelity to its crusade for the greater good."[26]

Political organizations try to enlist good candidates to run for office. For an advocacy group, the definition of "good" usually includes agreement with its positions. EMILY's List, for instance, seeks Democratic women who support legal abortion. Of course, parties do most of the recruiting. In a 1996 article entitled "Replenishing the Troops for a Revolution," the *Washington Post* said that the House GOP's campaign chief was "winning the recruiting war" and quoted him as saying, "We play offense, offense, offense, never defense. Our priority is finding candidates."[27] When recruiting, parties differ from advocacy groups by downplaying issues in favor of "electability." Ideological soulmates may be nice, but parties prefer candidates who have money, organization, and a victory record. If armies recruited this way—looking only at certain attributes without regard for the recruits' willingness to heed doctrine—they would suffer serious lapses of discipline. As we shall see, American legislative parties confront this very problem.

Political parties depart from the military model in another way. Party organizations can encourage a candidate, but the selection usually belongs to primary voters, who can pick somebody else. Thus the organization may not only fail to get its favorite candidate but also end up with the worst possible one. The 1990s brought the recurring nightmare of David Duke, a racist who won Republican nominations in Louisiana, thereby giving Democrats a chance to paint the GOP as the party of brown shirts and white sheets. The military can pick its own people, so it has an easier time excluding Nazis and Klansmen.

In another way, political parties do resemble the all-volunteer military. After all their recruitment efforts, both rely on the individual's decision to sign up. Neither can enlist a true cross-section of the American public because certain kinds of people are more likely than others to choose careers in politics or the armed services. Military leaders must accept physical danger and separation from loved ones, while political figures risk personal attack, public humiliation, and loss of privacy. Most people shun these sacrifices, so by definition, those who answer the call are different from everybody else. Even if they look like the rest of society in many ways, they still have a distinct outlook—specifically, a willingness to put their work ahead of family. Dwight Eisenhower's blunt words to his wife apply equally to politics and the military: "Mamie, there's one thing you must understand. My country comes first and always will. You come second."[28]

Some observers fear that the all-volunteer military is becoming a caste apart from the larger society, even turning hostile to the world outside.[29] Critics have long raised similar concerns about the permanent bureaucracy. More recently, there have been signs of a "a new governing class" of office-seekers and staffers for organizations in the political world. Whereas politics was once a part-time avocation or brief detour from a nonpolitical job path, it now draws many people who see it as a career. Political life has taken on many of the airs of professionalism, meaning degree programs, vocational journals, and special ways of thinking and speaking.

Even though political figures try to be "responsive" to the public, they often see themselves as a class apart, which is why they refer to nonpolitical people as "civilians." One former Senate aide displayed this mindset when he explained why President Clinton would sometimes sacrifice personal friends to political necessity: "If you give me a political context, I'll just tell you that you're not going to find what you out there in the world, civilians, think is friendship."[30]

TRAINING

Los Angeles Times reporter Jennifer Warren once described a training program for California lawmakers: "Soldiers have basic training. Pilots have flight school. Now comes boot camp for politicians, an intensive, exhaustive crash course on how to be a legislator."[31] Writers use such metaphors when describing training in politics and other realms of civilian life. Military training— which includes everything from boot camp to the service academies to the postgraduate war colleges—offers a vivid model because it can transform attitudes, behavior, and personality.

Although the military tries to recruit people who are highly motivated, it still takes work to turn them into warriors. Beyond learning such basics as the proper use of firearms, they have to shed their civilian habits and acquire a military frame of mind. Especially at the entry level, training is what the Marines call "a socialization process," which changes people so they can do things they would not have thought of doing otherwise.[32] When the process works well, recruits quickly come to identify with their service, seeing themselves as servants of a larger purpose. They absorb military values and doctrine—hence the term "indoctrination." S. L. A. Marshall said that the process fosters coordination: "Instruction is the generator of unified action. It is the transmission belt by which the lessons of experience are passed to untrained men."[33]

So it is in politics. Though nothing in civilian life matches the intensity of Parris Island, nearly all political and governmental organizations do have some form of basic training. Such programs can be quite elaborate. Take the Green Corps, a Philadelphia-based environmental group that prepares college graduates for careers in political advocacy. An article in *Earth Journal* said that the Corps "might be likened to a boot camp for young activists," describing its "intensive one-year training program" as a "no-frills curriculum that teaches everything from how to organize effective postcard drives to how to study a gas station's compliance with the federal Clean Air Act."[34]

Just as boot camps deliberately isolate newcomers from the civilian world, so orientation or training sessions often take place in out-of-the-way locales where trainers can get the recruits' full attention and temporarily shield them from anything that would interfere with the effort to reshape their values.[35] As part of its Latino Academy leadership program, the Southwest Voter Registration Education project holds "boot camp" at a Christian meditation center 20 miles from Santa Fe, New Mexico. With no television or outside transportation, participants focus on learning the group's approach to electoral politics and community organizing.[36] One of Social Security's founders recalled that its training program aimed to teach the program's philosophy and its commitment to the program's beneficiaries: "We kept clerks here, as well as the high-ups for months before they went out and set up local offices. So they just had religion. They had it complete."[37]

The process goes on after orientation. Like their military counterparts, civilian bureaucracies supply members with continuing education programs that hone their skills and bolster their adherence to doctrine. In partisan politics, such activities are less structured but no less important. In the early 1980s, the Reagan administration put a great deal of effort into indoctrinating executive branch officials, both in cabinet meetings with the President and in larger subcabinet sessions with other senior officials.[38] A few years later, Newt Gingrich worked to turn GOPAC into the party's "mechanism for distributing ideas and doctrine through training."[39] He made innovative use of videotapes and audiotapes that instructed Republican politicians in policy, rhetoric, and campaign technique. "It was like subscribing to a motivational course," write journalists Dan Balz and Ron Brownstein, "with Gingrich a cross between Norman Vincent Peale and a Marine drill sergeant."[40]

In the political and military worlds, training always involves the teaching of new language. Every organization or activity has its own technical terms, which recruits must learn simply to know what is going on. A new Army officer should learn that

ADA stands for Air Defense Artillery, whereas a partisan campaign activist should recognize the initials as representing the liberal group Americans for Democratic Action and a domestic policy analyst should read them as the abbreviation for the Americans with Disabilities Act. Groups also cultivate their own argot to deepen a sense of identity and to separate insiders from outsiders. Marine drill sergeants teach recruits that they must refer to floors as "decks," doors as "hatches," pens as "inksticks," and sneakers as "go-fasters."[41] One can find parallels at all levels of government and politics. Newcomers to Los Angeles city government learn that a "skin patch" is a layer of asphalt used to repair a pothole, and a "LULU" is a "locally unwanted land use." According to the president of a homeowners' association, "The jargon is intimidating. The uninitiated go to a public hearing and they don't know what's going on, but a lawmaker or a lobbyist knows what is going on."[42]

Some organizations even try to change their recruits' personalities. Many political activists believe that cultural norms keep women out of politics by discouraging assertiveness. "You've got to throw that stuff out the window," one veteran politician told prospective candidates at a Buffalo training forum. "I didn't run for office until I was 35, because I was uncomfortable saying good things about myself."[43] Pacifists, not surprisingly, need help with developing aggressiveness. Training for Change, a Philadelphia-based organization that helps people "stand up more effectively for justice, peace, and environmental harmony," offers a schedule of "powerful, transformational workshops which affirm the spiritual roots of change while challenging people to increase their effectiveness by giving up limiting habits and beliefs."[44] One of its workshops is "The Nonviolent Warrior: Confrontation and Long-Range Strategy."

Political training typically includes role-playing simulations that the trainers call "war games."[45] One newspaper account of a

1996 Democratic training session supplies a good illustration: "Last week's training session here for hundreds of eager volunteers from around the country featured a war-games approach. The Henry VIII hotel in Bridgeton [Missouri] was transformed into a political battlefield known as the State of Flux. There, activists experienced firsthand the glory and defeat of modern campaigns while surviving the accompanying bloody attacks and counterattacks."[46]

In these exercises, participants try to learn how the other side thinks and how to anticipate what it will do. Such tasks are easier for those who can identify with aspects of their opponents' training or experience. During the Civil War, many leaders of both armies were graduates of West Point who had drawn first blood during the Mexican War. Similarly, many of today's Republican and Democratic operatives are graduates of the same schools of public policy or political management.[47] And although Republicans and Democrats seldom work for the same politicians, primary campaigns often pit former office-mates against each other. An instruction sheet for Birch Bayh's 1976 volunteers said that "the techniques we are using are also being used by other campaigns as well. This is natural, as many of us had the same training ground—the McGovern campaign."[48]

Whether in war or politics, each side's training programs crib from the other side's writings. During the 1980s, Marine General Al Gray required officers to read Mao Zedong's *On Guerrilla Warfare* and North Vietnamese General Vo Nguyen Giap's *How We Won the War*.[49] Ralph Reed, director of the Christian Coalition in the 1990s, followed a similar practice by studying the works of Saul Alinsky and Tom Hayden.[50] In a turnabout, the Gay and Lesbian Victory Fund then lifted some of Reed's training methods. "We use the Christian Coalition training manual," said a leader of the group. "We just changed it around a little. I'll send Pat Robertson a thank-you note."[51]

COMMUNICATION

Political leaders often speak of "mobilizing" their supporters. Needless to say by now, the term has military connotations. The *Oxford English Dictionary* quotes this line from a book on the Franco-Prussian War: "It only requires a simple telegraphic order to mobilise . . . to set in perfectly harmonious movement the colossal machinery spread over the whole country."[52] Even the best-trained forces do not spring into action of their own accord. A leader must send them commands and then learn how well they are carrying out their tasks. This information may point to unexpected problems or opportunities, prompting the leader to issue new orders, which in turn require monitoring, and so on. This process (oversimplified here) is what the military calls "communication, command, and control."

Until the nineteenth century, commanders faced daunting constraints in this area. Enemy forces could kill or capture couriers, while bad weather or darkness could foil visual communication methods such as smoke signals. Because military leaders could not count on rapid long-distance transmission of information, they had to run things by word of mouth, and key moves could take place only in their immediate presence.[53] These limitations curbed the size of armies and battlefields.

By the mid-1800s, however, technology enabled the military to operate on a wider scale than ever before. Because of railroads, troops could now cross hundreds of miles a day. Because of the telegraph, leaders could now communicate instantly over enormous distances. Though the telegraph initially had only limited use in field command, it proved crucial for mobilization, deployment, and communication between armies and their headquarters.[54] Abraham Lincoln spent much of the Civil War in the War Department telegraph office, using the new device to supervise military operations from Maryland to Texas.[55]

These same technological innovations also changed politics. Railroads expanded the scope of electoral campaigns just as they had enlarged military ones: in their 1858 Senate contest, Abraham Lincoln and Stephen Douglas covered a combined total of almost ten thousand miles, mostly on trains, which they could not have done just a few years before.[56] And together, the ability to send information by wire, and to ship masses of printed material by rail, fostered the growth of mass-circulation newspapers. During this era, the papers were party organs that coordinated the activists. Historian Richard Jensen says: "The troops waited for the morning paper to learn how the enemy was to be ruined today, his arguments torn apart, his silly programs ridiculed. If the weekly *New York Tribune* did not arrive on time, a Republican farmer in upstate New York would be speechless around the hot stove in the village store."[57]

During the twentieth century, science changed the scope and speed of military operations. Radio opened the way for instantaneous two-way communication between mobile forces, thereby making *blitzkrieg* possible.[58] In the decades after World War II, the military helped develop computers, communications satellites, and the Internet. By the 1990s, military commanders could use this array of equipment for instant oversight of activity just about anywhere on the globe—and all from a single war room.

Knowing the importance of communication, and instinctively reaching for military models, political figures began to use the term "war room" for the center of any intense electoral or legislative campaign. As the epigraph to the introduction mentions, Hillary Clinton christened the "war room" of the 1992 Clinton campaign. The following year, at a senior staff meeting on the President's economic program, she voiced frustration at the breakdown of communication between the political and economic policy experts. "First, we need a War Room to coordinate this," she said. Having already established such a center for her health-care proposal, she volunteered it for the economic plan: "Take the War Room and do something with it."[59]

In any political war room, leaders can now coordinate troops via a network of faxes, Internet, talk radio, and cellular phones. In 1994, a congressional conference committee added a provision to a lobbying bill that would have imposed reporting requirements on grassroots organizations. "We were able to energize the nation in two hours," said Tom DeLay (R-TX). "We met with our Wednesday lunch group, informed the outside groups about the bill, and within two hours people were tying up the phone lines from all across the country. It killed the bill." Jonathan Adler of the Competitive Enterprise Institute, said of the improvement in communications: "That has totally changed the battlefield."[60]

In 1998, public-health advocates set up a war room to fight for anti-tobacco legislation. "It's a war. An absolute war," said a spokeswoman for the American Cancer Society. "The tobacco companies are so powerful you don't see them. They can push buttons from their offices and send a thousand letters to a senator."[61]

The rapid development of information technology has contributed to what defense experts call "the revolution in military affairs," a radical increase in effectiveness of military units that changes warfare and its strategic setting. Microchips now endow commanders with unprecedented power to watch and shape events all over the world, yet each leader can only focus on a few events at any given time. Meanwhile, technology gives the lower ranks access to vast amounts of real-time information and enables them to communicate up, down, and across the chain of command. Therefore, one emerging element of the revolution in military affairs may be a decentralization of authority. "'The strategic corporal,' we call him," said General Charles Krulak, commandant of the Marine Corps, speaking of the typical American in uniform. "He's going to do amazing things."[62] It still remains a matter of speculation as to what those amazing things might be.

The same is true of government and politics. Though many organizations post information online, the systematic use of the Internet is still in its embryonic stages. The first major election campaign in which the Internet played a central role was Jesse Ventura's third-party bid for the governorship of Minnesota. Though short on money, Ventura had the advantage of running in a state with a high level of computer usage. "It's tailor-made for my campaign," Ventura said. "It's reaching a huge amount of people at a very low price."[63] Just as Republican farmers relied on the *New York Tribune* more than a century earlier, so Ventura's troops used his website to learn what they should tell their friends and neighbors. Web bulletins and email messages also enabled the campaign to coordinate volunteers, ensuring that they would show up for rallies at the right place and the right time. The campaign webmaster said: "The Internet for us served as the nervous system for the campaign. The Web site was not the difference; it was the mobilization."[64]

As in the military, the Internet can have both centralizing and decentralizing effects. On the one hand, it can enable leaders to coordinate their followers and supply them with instant access to doctrine. On the other hand, it may also create the political equivalent of "the strategic corporal," providing even the lowest-ranking activist with high-level research and communication capabilities. Marine General Krulak could have been speaking for the political world when he said,"We're experimenting. We're 'riding the dragon' of change. Chinese proverb. I've got the Chinese character for 'chaos' from the *I Ching* on my wall in my office. Below, it says, 'Chaos—where brilliant dreams are born.'"[65]

Because this chapter has focused on coordination, it has mainly discussed internal communication—that is, how people within an organization transmit information to one another. Chapter 5 includes a discussion of external communication, the use of the mass media to spread propaganda. Subsequent chapters analyze the closely related topics of intelligence and deception. At this point, we should think ahead to the topic of chapter 9: friction. As we shall see, even the most sophisticated means of communication are subject to simple human error, a point that became painfully clear during a tense moment in the Cuban Missile Crisis. Although the United States sought to avoid escalating the conflict, a U-2 spy plane briefly strayed into Soviet airspace. President Kennedy commented, "There is always some son of a bitch who doesn't get the word."[66]

5

Rallying the Troops

Politics is battle, and the best way to fire up your troops is to rally them against a visible opponent on the other side of the field. If a loyal supporter will fight hard for you, he will fight twice as hard against your enemies.

—Richard M. Nixon
In the Arena: A Memoir of Victory, Defeat and Renewal

Political and military operations require machines, vehicles, and other physical resources. But even the best-equipped outfit can achieve nothing without the will to use these assets. In any conflict, each side fights for hearts and minds, gaining new allies and strengthening the resolve of its own troops. The importance of such efforts is among the oldest themes in military literature. "In war," said Napoleon, "the moral is to the material as three to one."[1] Carl von Clausewitz said that moral elements "constitute the spirit that permeates war as a whole, and at an early stage they establish a close affinity with the will that moves and leads the whole mass of force, practically merging with it, since the will is itself a moral quality."[2]

For millennia, necessity has forced wartime leaders to pioneer techniques of persuasion. The Assyrians used public inscriptions to bolster military confidence and warn malcontents about the bloody consequences of rebellion. The Greeks developed oratorical weapons: the speech texts in Thucydides' *History of the Peloponnesian War* reveal that they knew how to exploit appeals to family and national pride. By the Thirty Years' War (1618–1648), advances in printing technology enabled the combatants to produce illustrated books, posters, and leaflets. In World War I, telephone and telegraph lines shot propaganda across continents. With the formal study of psychology gaining respectability, leaders used its findings to encourage enlistments, strengthen home-front morale, and engender hatred for the enemy. This effort became a template for business and politics. The father of public relations, Edward L. Bernays, once reflected on his work in the American "public information" effort during World War I: "It was, of course, the astounding success of propaganda during the war that opened the eyes of the intelligent few in all departments of life to the possibilities of regimenting the public mind."[3]

NECESSARY ENEMIES

If military writers are unanimous on the importance of motivation, they are equally emphatic on enmity. Combat, said Clausewitz, "is essentially an expression of *hostile feelings*."[4] Sun Tzu said, "The reason troops slay the enemy is because they are enraged,"[5] and Machiavelli wrote, "As for the means of animating your men and inflaming them with a desire to fight, it would be good first to enrage them against the enemy; to tell them they are despised."[6] Many political figures have voiced similar thoughts. In 1953, GOP strategist Robert Humphreys wrote: "As in all forms of conflict, attack is the strongest political weapon. It is axiomatic in politics that you must have an enemy."[7] In 1979, liberal direct-mail consultant Robert Smith gave this advice to campaign managers: "Find your candidate a nasty enemy. Tell people they're threatened in some way. . . . It's a cheap trick, but the simplest."[8]

As noted in chapter 1, some political settings suppress open hostility. In the United States Senate, where a single member can cause serious delays in legislative business, comity usually makes more sense than confrontation. But politics ultimately involves conflict. In elections, challengers try to deprive incumbents of their livelihoods and good names. In legislative and bureaucratic life, political figures routinely thwart one another's dreams. After all, both the creation and the abolition of programs impose real costs on real people.

Political and military leaders do not simply rely on conflict itself to produce ill will toward opponents. They stoke it. Such effort is necessary because most people curb their own aggressiveness and avoid hurting others. Some scholars attribute these tendencies to social conditioning, whereas others speculate that an innate "moral sense" may also be at work.[9] Whatever the case may be, "killer instinct" seldom shows itself without coaxing. In a study of combat in World War II, S. L. A. Marshall found that many frontline soldiers never fired their weapons, and asserted that not more than one-quarter of them would ever strike a real blow unless overpowering circumstances compelled them to do so.[10] He added that "if resistance to the idea of firing can be overcome for a period, it can be defeated permanently. Once the plunge is made, the water seems less forbidding."[11] Responding to Marshall's findings, the Army revised its training regimen to quash such resistance. By the time of the Vietnam War, training had raised the firing rate to 90–95 percent.[12]

The key is to depict the enemy not as a fully rounded human being but as an evil force who deserves attack, or at least as a mere target whose fate is unimportant. Political figures rarely go that far in "dehumanizing" opponents, and they should not, lest they provoke actual violence. But on a different level, they, too, must paint the enemy in dark hues. In the case of candidates, the process begins with their own attitudes toward opponents. In everyday life, many of us try to think the best of other people and to withhold harsh personal criticism, and expect others to do the same. For candidates, such a mindset will create two problems. First, it will cause them to withhold attacks, thereby forgoing political advantage and depriving the voters of potentially important information about the other side's record. Second, it will leave them demoralized when opponents attack them. Coming under fire for the first time, people new to battle often react with bewilderment, wondering, "What do they have against me?"[13] Such feelings persist until one comes to view the enemy as unworthy of moral concern. Similarly, political assaults hurt less when they come from a despised opponent than from a respected colleague. "Psyching" oneself up against a political competitor is just as essential to defense as it is to offense.

A good cause can make a powerful weapon, as we shall see shortly, but it is not enough. Anger and hatred reach deep inside, and in a very real way. Such emotions cause a physical response, often a tightening of the midsection, which is why we speak of "gut feelings" or "visceral reactions." Negative information packs more psychological firepower than positive information, because people remember it better and are more likely to change their behavior as a result.[14] As everyday experience reminds us, dark emotions are more reliable over the long run: love fades while hatred lingers. From Belfast to Baghdad to Belgrade, current conflicts stem from animosities that have been raging for centuries. Have any friendships or alliances lasted so long?

Wartime propaganda always relies on negative appeals. The target audience consists not only of troops but of civilians on the home front who support the effort with hard work and financial sacrifice. In World War I, the American government issued posters showing evil Germans and bearing the caption: "Beat Back the Hun with Liberty Bonds."[15] Political fundraising letters apply the same technique by telling addressees that their checks can help sustain the fight against a dastardly foe. Every political group has a "Hun." In the mid-1990s, Republicans raised millions by getting contributors angry at Bill Clinton, just as Democrats did with Newt Gingrich. For years, the Christian Coalition and the American Civil Liberties Union (ACLU) have played the Hun to each other, to their mutual benefit.

THEM AND US

When you view another person as similar or close to you in important ways, you find it harder to define that person as an enemy. Physical or emotional distance makes enmity easier,[16] so when firing up the troops against an opponent, political figures often pick individuals or groups who come from far away—and better yet, who have no representation within the constituency. Until World War II, England was a bogeyman, particularly in Irish constituencies. When the King of England visited the United States, Chicago Mayor William Hale Thompson threatened to punch him in the nose. During the Cold War, hawkish politicians ran against the Soviet Union, and in the 1980s, the apartheid regime of South Africa was a favorite target of liberals. (At the end of the 1989 movie *Lethal Weapon 2*, a Los Angeles detective executes an unarmed South African diplomat. No major American political figure uttered a word of protest.) The enemy need not be foreign, since "nonlocal interests" will do just fine, especially if they excite regional hostilities. In upstate New York, politicians run against New York City. In the South, they run against the North. And in the West, they run against the East. During his 1958 reelection campaign, Arizona Senator Barry Goldwater cast himself as David against the Goliath of Eastern labor leaders.[17] In 1982, Montana's Democratic senator John Melcher ran a famous television ad in which talking cows mocked the "city slickers" who were running an independent campaign against him.

The gap between "them" and "us" can be social or cultural as well as geographical. Nixon championed the "silent majority" against hippies, leftists, and what Spiro Agnew called "an effete corps of impudent snobs who characterize themselves as intellectuals."[18] Speechwriter William Safire later explained: "'They' could be useful to 'us,' as the villain, the object against which all of our supporters, as well as those who might become our supporters, could be rallied."[19] Nixon tried to link all of "them" with their most extreme elements. Following a bombing at the University of Wisconsin, he approvingly quoted an editorial: "It isn't just the radicals that set the bomb in the lighted, occupied building who were guilty. The blood is on the hands of anyone who encouraged them, anyone who talked recklessly of revolution, anyone who has chided with mild disparagement the violence of extremism, while hinting that the cause was right all the time."[20] A quarter of a century later, the Clinton political team followed this example. According to consultant Dick Morris, the 1995 bombing of a federal building in Oklahoma City provided a political opportunity "by demonstrating so vividly the danger of right-wing extremists." In a memo to the President, Morris and other consultants said that a common element of the Nixon and Clinton eras was "a common national enemy from one side of the ideological divide"—the extreme left in the former case, the extreme right in the latter. By responding with anti-violence measures that Republicans opposed, says Morris, Clinton forced the GOP to "link itself to the extremists."[21]

Conflict with an enemy can be a force for unity.[22] During wartime, people "rally around the flag" and lay aside their internal conflicts so that they can beat the foe. In 1945, President Truman referred to the Nazis as "the common enemy in Europe."[23] The next year, he called on Americans "to close ranks in the face of a common enemy—the enemy which after the last war turned our military victory into economic defeat"—namely, inflation.[24] In 1948, he said: "Now it is time for us to get together and beat the common enemy. And that is up to you."[25] In this case, his audience was the Democratic National Convention, and the "common enemy" was the Republican Party. Facing a walkout by Southern segregationists and possible defections to a leftist third party, Truman figured that he could unify his party by attacking Republicans for a variety of sins, such as passage of an "anti-Semitic, anti-Catholic" displaced-persons bill. To a large extent, the tactic worked. The third-party challenges waned as Truman rallied Democrats against the GOP.

A similar approach succeeded half a century later. In 1998, when charges arose that President Clinton had lied under oath in a sexual harassment case, many observers thought that his own party might yield to possible Republican moves for impeachment. Congressional Democrats distrusted him, in part because he had undercut them on issues ranging from international trade to welfare reform. But Clinton and his allies shrewdly framed the conflict as a battle with Republican "extremists." Democratic voters and politicians thus thought that they should lay aside their misgivings about the President and join arms against the common enemy. "If there is one thing that unifies Democrats, it is Gingrich," said a White House official. Using a phrase from the post–Civil War era, a GOP strategist observed: "Evoking Newt Gingrich's name is the equivalent of waving the bloody shirt for the libs."[26] When Gingrich's resignation deprived them of a convenient enemy, the President's defenders redirected their fire to other targets, including majority whip Tom DeLay (R-TX). Right after the House narrowly approved articles of impeachment, House Democrats joined Clinton in a boisterous rally on the South Lawn of the White House.

CUNNING AND DANGEROUS

Chapters 6 and 7 discuss deception, stealth, and intelligence-gathering. Although these practices are commonplace in war and politics, people see them as despicable when they take place across enemy lines. (Our side is crafty whereas theirs is underhanded. We surveil whereas they spy. We are foxes, and they are snakes.) Propaganda often plays up the other side's cunning, in part to encourage alertness. The famous World War II slogan "Loose lips sink ships" was a response to the real danger that Axis agents could gain intelligence from the casual chatter of American defense workers. Depicting the enemy as a dangerous serpent also serves to deepen hostility, since fear and loathing are kindred feelings.

In military propaganda, the enemy often runs a conspiracy that reaches across national borders and employs a "fifth column" of subversives. Comparable themes have long pervaded politics. Historian Richard Hofstader told of a "paranoid style" in American politics whose exponents "regard a 'vast' or 'gigantic' conspiracy as *the motive force* in historical events." The enemy is "a perfect model of malice, a kind of amoral superman."[27] The first important third-party movement in the United States was the Anti-Masonic Party, which held that the Freemasons governed the country through stealth and violence. The Lincoln-Douglas Senate campaign of 1858, which reformers constantly cite as a model of lofty political exchange, involved dueling accusations of conspiracy. Stephen Douglas charged Abraham Lincoln with plotting to turn both parties toward abolitionism, while Lincoln accused Douglas of secretly scheming with President James Buchanan and Chief Justice Roger Taney to spread slavery throughout the land.[28]

Conspiracy theory has thrived throughout the twentieth century. In the 1928 presidential campaign, foes of New York Governor Al Smith, the Democratic presidential nominee, charged that he was conniving with the Pope to make Catholicism the national religion. Some of the anti-Smith propaganda included a photo of construction on the Holland Tunnel, identifying it as a passageway to the Vatican.[29] FDR was not above using conspiracy accusations. In the 1940 campaign, some of his partisans suggested that GOP nominee Wendell Willkie was pro-German.[30] Just before the election, FDR warned that his GOP opponents were forming an "ominous" combination of "the extreme reactionary and the extreme radical elements of this country." These groups had nothing in common, said FDR, except "their common will to power, and their impatience with the normal democratic processes to produce overnight the inconsistent dictatorial ends that they, each of them, seek." He concluded the attack with an allusion to Nazism: "Something evil is happening in this country when vast quantities of Republican campaign literature are distributed by organizations that make no secret of their admiration for the dictatorship form of government."[31]

During the 1950s, Senator Joseph McCarthy became the embodiment of conspiracy politics when he tried to link the Democrats to international communism. "How can we account for our present situation unless we believe that men high in this government are concerting to deliver us to disaster?" he said in 1951, referring to communist advances in Eastern Europe and Asia. "This must be the product of a great conspiracy, a conspiracy on a scale so immense as to dwarf any previous such effort in the history of man."[32] McCarthy and his cohorts went far outside the loose norms of political attack. They not only went after major public figures—who could defend themselves by returning fire— but also smeared lesser-known people whose careers suffered irreparably.

Conspiracy rhetoric resounded in the 1990s. Some of President Clinton's opponents tried to link him to a plot involving drug-running and the assassination of material witnesses. Few believed these charges. In 1998, when more credible accusations threatened his presidency, First Lady Hillary Clinton moved into what one aide called her "battle mode."[33] *Today Show* host Matt Lauer asked her about her purported comment "that this is the last great battle and that one side or the other is going down here." She did not recall the remark, she said, "But I do believe that this is a battle." She then attacked "this vast right-wing conspiracy that has been conspiring against my husband since the day he announced for president."[34]

Appeals to fear are risky. By making the enemy out to be vast and superhuman, you may render your own side too frightened to fight. One solution is to play up the consequences of defeat, thereby making people more afraid of potential enemy victory than of present enemy behavior. "Look at your houses, your parents, your wives, and your children," a Federalist newspaper wrote in 1800, summing up the case against Thomas Jefferson. "Are you prepared to see your dwellings in flames, hoary hairs bathed in blood, female chastity violated, or children writhing on the pike and halbert?"[35]

In the Civil War, Confederate propaganda said that the Union wanted to enslave the South. If the North won, wrote one soldier to his wife, "our property would all be confuscated [*sic*] . . . & our people reduced to the most abject bondage and utter degradation."[36] More than 120 years later, Newt Gingrich applied similar terms to partisan conflict. Liberals, he said, understood "in a way that Grant understood at Shiloh that this is a civil war," that only one side could win. "This war has to be fought with the scale and duration and savagery that is only true of civil wars. While we are lucky in this country that our civil wars are fought at the ballot box, not on the battlefield, nonetheless, it is a true civil war. . . . The hard Left will systematically root us out and destroy us if they can."[37]

CAUSES AND CRUSADES

People fight better when they have a cause, which is why Oliver Cromwell wanted "a plain russet-coated captain that knows what he fights for, and loves what he knows."[38] The U.S. Army has long believed in this principle. During World War II, General George C. Marshall had director Frank Capra (*Mr. Smith Goes to Washington*) create the *Why We Fight* documentary series. Similarly, political activists issue their own versions of *Why We Fight* in the form of broadcast advertisements, website postings, pamphlets, and speeches. In 1988, AIDS activist Vito Russo gave a speech entitled "Why We Fight," in which he passionately called for more government funding for treatment and education. To convey the depth of his emotion, he reached for military metaphors: "Living with AIDS in this country is like living through a war that's happening only for those people in the trenches. Every time a shell explodes you look around to discover that you've lost more of your friends."[39]

In both arenas, leaders often describe their efforts as crusades, a term with deep connotations. The word "crusade," which comes from the Latin *crux* ("cross"), refers to the central symbol of Christianity. In the original Crusades, between the eleventh and the fourteenth centuries, European Christians fought Muslims for territory around Jerusalem. Although many Crusaders joined the fray for land and loot, the original impulse was a papal call to make the Holy Land safe for Christians.

Military and political "crusades" often march under God's banner. Appeals to piety breed enthusiasm, a term that derives from the Greek *enthousiasmos*, meaning "possession by a god." The more people believe in a crusade, the less heed they give to earthly costs or obstacles, for no price is too high for the infinite benefit of doing God's will. Even when a conflict involves secular interests, leaders highlight or inject religious elements. Barbara Ehrenreich calls this process "the sacralization of war."[40]

This "sacralization" is especially evident when the foe has a radically different faith (e.g., the Crusades) or overtly professes atheism (e.g., the Cold War). It may also appear when coreligionists fight each other. In the Civil War, both Northerners and Southerners saw themselves as upholding a holy cause and believed that God would see them through. The rebels sang "The Star-Spangled Cross and the Pure Field of White" (a reference to the Confederate flag), which had a chorus that ended with the lines, "Our trust is in God, who can help us in fight,/ And defend those who ask Him in prayer." The federals sang "The Battle Hymn of the Republic."

In the years after the Civil War, Republicans adopted "The Battle Hymn" as an unofficial anthem, mingling all war, politics, and religion into one. Other political figures have invoked God's terrible swift sword. During his 1912 "Bull Moose" campaign, Theodore Roosevelt fought for direct democracy and expanded federal power, thundering: "We fight in honorable fashion for the good of mankind; fearless of the future; unheeding of our individual fates; with unflinching hearts and undimmed eyes; we stand at Armageddon, and we battle for the Lord."[41] His distant cousin Franklin D. Roosevelt accepted the 1932 Democratic nomination in a similar spirit. Though his policy details were sketchy, he proclaimed his cause to be equality in the name of the public good.

He acknowledged that many Americans had "made obeisance to Mammon" (a New Testament personification of materialism) and called on them to "abandon the false prophets." Near the end, FDR uttered his famous line, "I pledge you, I pledge myself, to a new deal for the American people." He then resumed the language of holy war: "Let us all here assembled constitute ourselves prophets of a new order of competence and of courage. This is more than a political campaign; it is a call to arms. Give me your help, not to win votes alone, but to win in this crusade to restore America to its own people."[42]

Leaders of crusades always speak of lofty ends. In human conflict, however, leaders can hardly define what they are fighting for without describing what they are fighting against. To take the Holy Land, the original Crusaders had to smite "infidels." To establish the Four Freedoms, the United States had to destroy the Nazis. In Capra's *Why We Fight* documentaries, the world needed the "lighthouses" of the Allied nations because the Axis powers were trying to put out "the lights of freedom and equality."[43] Ironically, then, a crusade's high-mindedness depends on hostility, because the more fiendish the foe, the nobler the cause.[44]

Wartime propaganda has often pictured the enemy leader as the devil himself. In domestic politics, such heavy-handedness can backfire. During the 1986 campaign, Representative Mark Siljander (R-MI), facing a tough primary challenge, sent an audiotape to local ministers asking for their support as a way to "break the back of Satan." Voters ousted him, resenting the implication that his mild-mannered opponent had horns. "That was it, no question," Siljander acknowledged afterward. "There's no question the major bomb was the tape."[45] Other leaders have found subtler ways of suggesting that their foes are, at the very least, not on God's good side. In his 1933 Inaugural Address, in which he urged Americans to "move as a trained and loyal army," FDR attacked the financial interests that had opposed him: "The money changers have fled from their high seats in the temple of our civilization."[46] The line alluded to the money changers whom Jesus drove from the temple in Jerusalem (Matthew 21:12–13). In 1992, Jesse Jackson equated the Virgin Mary in Bethlehem to a homeless person, referring to King Herod as "the Quayle of his day."[47] According to the Gospel of Matthew (2:1–18), Herod murdered all the infants in Bethlehem while trying to kill the Christ child.

In military and political crusades, the cause need not be overtly religious nor the enemy explicitly satanic. What is essential is that the opponents represent something bad, so that fighting them is praiseworthy. In a 1936 campaign speech, Franklin Roosevelt recalled those who had fought with him in 1932: "We still lead that army in 1936. They stood with us then because in 1932 they believed. They stand with us today because in 1936 they know. And with them stand millions of new recruits who have come to know." He declared their cause to be peace—for the individual, the community, the nation, and the world. The "old enemies of peace"—greedy financial interests—stood in the way: "We know now that Government by organized money is just as dangerous as Government by organized mob. Never before in all our history have these forces been so united against one candidate as they stand today. They are unanimous in their hate for me—and I welcome their hatred."[48]

Through these words, FDR recast antagonism as altruism: to fight his enemies was to fight greed, hatred, and warfare. By deploying similar rhetorical weapons, leaders can make their followers see virtue in rancor.

Warring nations routinely accuse each other's forces of rape, pillage, torture, and murder. The accusations are often true. Atrocity stories provide the most direct means of equating the enemy with evil, and they perform a similar function in domestic politics. Environmental activists try to turn the public against corporate polluters by pointing to such incidents as the toxic gas leak in Bhopal, India, which left thousands dead. During the early 1960s, civil rights leaders not only drew attention to past atrocities but deliberately exposed themselves to new ones. When they marched in hostile Southern cities, they fully expected local authorities to react with brutality, revealing the evils of segregation to a national audience. One activist said of Birmingham Public Safety Commissioner Bull Connor: "He was the perfect adversary.... He believed that he would be the state's most popular politician if he treated the black violently, bloodily, and sternly. We knew that the psyche of the white redneck was such that he would inevitably do something to help our cause."[49]

CONFIDENCE

"The enemy may be dangerous, obstructive, and satanic," wrote political scientist Harold Lasswell in a landmark 1927 study of propaganda, "but if he is sure to win, the moral[e] of many elements of the nation will begin to waver and crumble.... The will to win is ultimately related to a chance to win."[50] As we saw in chapter 3, General Eisenhower flashed his famous grin because American troops expect confidence from their leaders. A good morale campaign includes the home front, too. Paul Fussell wrote of World War II: "For years, nothing was apparently fit to appear without *Victory* attached to it. A vegetable garden was not a wartime garden but a victory garden. *Victory* taxicab companies sprang up everywhere. Film theaters were renamed *Victory*. The bad cigarettes issued British troops were called *Victory* cigarettes."[51]

Faith in victory is just as important to political organizations and social movements, which is why the civil rights marchers sang "We Shall Overcome." Like good military officers, political leaders reassure their troops that, despite setbacks and disappointments, their cause will prevail in the end. Media consultants coach public figures on how to exude confidence through body language and tone of voice. In the rhetoric of electoral or legislative campaigns, talk of "victory" is as pervasive as it was during World War II. When signs point to defeat, speakers invariably remind listeners that Truman beat Dewey and David slew Goliath. Such efforts go on behind the scenes as well. When he served as President Ford's chief of staff during the 1976 campaign, Dick Cheney knew that reporters and fellow staffers saw much more of him than of the President: "I felt an enormous responsibility at that point just to send out positive signals to everybody, regardless of the polls, just to keep the organization going, so you have a chance to maybe pull it out."[52]

People find it hard to see how a noble cause can lose a fair fight, so the beaten side will often claim that the victor won only through trickery or treachery. Democrats charged that Reagan fooled the voters in 1980 with Hollywood gimmickry and that Bush divided the nation in 1988 with "wedge issues" such as the Massachusetts furlough program. Many Republicans blamed their 1992 and 1996 defeats on Clinton's alleged deceptions and coverups. Losers may also claim that the winners had unfair material advantages, or "overwhelming numbers and resources," as General Robert E. Lee told his Confederate army at Appomattox. Defeated political figures often complain of their opponents' lavish finances or incumbency perquisites, thus sounding much like the Virginian who said, "If we had had anything like a fair chance, or less disparity of numbers, we should have won our cause."[53] Numbers and resources do count for a great deal, but they often give vanquished fighters a way to rationalize their own errors.

Defeat is easier to handle in politics than in war. When a country loses a military conflict, it may forfeit its wealth and perhaps its very existence. Political losses seldom have such grave consequences because the individual or the cause may live to fight another day. Consequently, defeated political figures typically speak of "losing the battle but not the war." Even when Nixon resigned in disgrace after Watergate, he said that "we think that when we lose an election, we think when we suffer a defeat that all is ended. . . . Not true. It is only a beginning, always."[54] Shortly thereafter, Nixon launched a two-decade campaign to rehabilitate his place in history.

SYMBOLS AND RITUALS

On boarding the presidential helicopter for the last time, Nixon gave the crowd the V-for-victory salute. The gesture has military origins. During World War II, Churchill popularized it as a sign of defiance, but an older form derived from the Hundred Years' War. When French soldiers captured an English archer, they would cut off the two fingers he used for drawing the bowstring. Thus, just before a battle, the English would taunt the French by waving their index and middle fingers, as if to say: "I've still got mine, so watch out!"[55] (In Britain, the palms-in version of the gesture has rude connotations.)

It is natural that war and politics feature so many gestures and rituals because these forms of communication provide ways of arousing the troops' passions. From the dawn of combat, fighters have used battle cries to intimidate the enemy. During the Civil War, few Union soldiers could forget the Confederates' "rebel yell," which their great-grandsons would revive during World War II. Soldiers have also used shouts to express hostility, celebrate victory, or release tension—as have political figures. *New York Times* reporter Francis X. Clines got the point across in his account of Newt Gingrich's hard-fought reelection as speaker in 1997: "The roar that finally goes up from the victor's side after a bare-knuckled fight for career and leadership in the House of Representatives must be heard in person for the full sense of power to register. It both rings with jubilation and booms with dominance as if echoing all the way from the tribal conflicts of prehistory with the true meaning of partisan zeal."[56]

Whereas battle cries are more or less spontaneous, most military symbolism is methodical. The armed forces mount elaborate ceremonies to mark such events as graduation from basic training or return from a successful campaign.[57] These rituals bond the individual to the group by dramatizing a sense of continuity and high purpose. The formalities surrounding legislative bodies play a similar role,[58] as do political conventions and rallies, which heighten the interest of activists, bolster their self-esteem, and strengthen their willingness to work for candidates. Lord Bryce likened an American convention to "a medieval pilgrimage, or the mustering of a great army."[59] Political scientist Robert Dahl has written, "The ceremonies are in this respect not unlike the traditional tribal rites prescribed for warriors before battle."[60] At such events, participants honor their heroes and ritually abuse their enemies, all with the appropriate applause or catcalls. Often, musical bands will stir the audience by playing cavalry charges. Anyone who loses an internal power struggle is supposed to make gestures of unity, such as holding the winner's arm aloft.

Prayers are part of the routine, and major speakers often heighten the sense of gravity by calling for divine help. At the 1980 Republican National Convention, Ronald Reagan ended his acceptance speech this way: "I will confess that I have been a little afraid to suggest what I am going to suggest. I am more afraid not to. Can we begin our crusade joined in a moment of silent prayer? [Pause.] God bless America."[61]

In wartime, people develop their own rituals, even superstitions, as a way of restoring order amid chaos. Soldiers come to believe that if they hold onto a talisman or rigorously perform a certain practice, then they will survive. For centuries, Catholic warriors have worn St. Christopher medals. Even the supremely rational Dwight Eisenhower had a set of lucky coins that he rubbed before major events. Frequently, the superstition involves an article of clothing that a warrior will always wear even if she or he has to forgo washing it.[62] The same is often true in politics. Throughout a 1988 New Jersey Senate race, campaign manager James Carville wore a pair of garden gloves, taking them off only to sleep. Three years later, in a Pennsylvania special election, he wore the same underwear for the last ten days of the campaign (though he did wash it).[63]

METHODS

In winning the hearts of their troops, warriors cannot forget their minds: messages have to be believable, though not necessarily true.[64] Propagandists who blatantly contradict self- evident facts are not likely to change feelings the way they want to. When soldiers are retreating in the face of enemy fire, for instance, they will scorn rosy official assessments of the situation—and they will also doubt future pronouncements from the same source. As the Dole campaign learned in 1996, it is hard to convince people that the economy is doing poorly when it is in the middle of history's longest peacetime expansion.

Predispositions are crucial. To create support for their cause, or to turn people against their enemies, propagandists must understand their target group's values: what they like, dislike, revere, or despise. In particular, they must pick the right enemy. During the 1996 campaign, Dole ran against teacher unions, forgetting that most people—even conservative Republicans—actually approved of these groups because they linked them with education instead of union power. Clinton, in contrast, ran against tobacco companies, knowing that even people in tobacco states had little affection for the executives of these corporations. "If voters view the parties by their opponents," said one Republican operative in 1996, "it's pretty clear who has the better enemies this cycle."[65]

It helps to define the struggle as personal. During the Vietnam War, the American government failed to demonize Ho Chi Minh's successors; indeed, few Americans knew who was leading enemy forces. When America entered the Gulf War, Saddam Hussein became "public enemy number one." In domestic politics, Saul Alinsky understood this principle. He pointed to CIO labor organization of the 1930s, which "never attacked General Motors, they always attacked its president, Alfred 'Icewater-In-His-Veins' Sloan; they never attacked the Republic Steel Corporation but always its president, 'Bloodied Hands' Tom Girdler."[66]

Messages must be clear and consistent. It would have been strange for American depictions of Saddam Hussein to note good things that he had done for Iraq. Alinsky recalled a grassroots fight against a segregationist: "Many liberals, during our attack on the then-school superintendent, were pointing out that after all he wasn't a 100 per cent devil. . . . Can you imagine in the arena of conflict charging that so-and-so is a racist bastard and then diluting the impact of the attack with qualifying remarks such as 'He is a good churchgoing man, generous to charity, and a good husband?' This becomes political idiocy."[67]

Here we must observe a caveat. Beyond a certain point, attacks may backfire because ordinary voters do not like them to be too blatant or harsh. It is one thing to "demonize" opponents in a metaphorical sense, but it is quite another to suggest that they really are in league with Satan. As noted earlier, Representative Mark Siljander learned this lesson a bit too late.

Up to this point, we have discussed the opposition's own attitudes and behavior as a given. But a large part of any political or military conflict consists of trying to affect the opposition, to dim its mind and render its behavior less effective. We now turn to this subject.

6

Demoralization, Deception, and Stealth

I'll play the orator as well as Nestor,
Deceive more slily than Ulysses could,
And, like a Sinon, take another Troy.
I can add colours to the chameleon,
Change shapes with Proteus for advantages,
And set the murderous Machiavel to school.

—Gloucester
in William Shakespeare, *King Henry VI, Part 3,* Act 3

Defeating the enemy depends not just on conquest of physical forces, said Carl von Clausewitz, for "one also has to weigh the loss of order, courage, confidence, cohesion, and plan."[1] In any conflict, each side tries to inflict such losses on the other. The idea is to get adversaries to forgo opportunities, fall into traps, and do other things that will hasten their own defeat.

One may reach for this goal by sapping the opposition's will to carry on or by keeping it from thinking clearly. That is, one may attack its heart or its mind. The first process—demoralization—represents the obverse of the activities discussed in chapter 5. Just as leaders seek to make their followers heroic and hopeful, so they want to render the other side's forces timid and unsure. In the Vietnam War, the North used this psychological approach to overcome American material advantages. The 1968 Tet Offensive, though a military defeat for the communists, became a political victory by convincing American voters that their government's policy offered only endless warfare. "You know you never defeated us on the battlefield," Colonel Harry Summers said to a North Vietnamese counterpart after the war. "That may be so," the North Vietnamese officer replied, "but it is also irrelevant."[2]

One may attack the opposition's mind by falsifying one's capabilities and intentions; as Stonewall Jackson put it, "Always mystify, mislead, and surprise the enemy, if possible."[3] Attacks on heart and mind work together, for panic clouds the brain while confusion wounds the spirit. Both forms of attack pervade political life. The logic resembles that of warfare because one can vastly economize on tangible resources by manipulating the other side's feelings and thoughts.

VEXATION AND DECAPITATION

Chapter 5 explained that strong passions can motivate rank-and-file troops. For leaders, however, rational decisions require cool heads. Sun Tzu thus pinpointed one line of attack against the enemy: "Anger his general and confuse him."[4] In politics, an assault on the opponent's composure can be especially effective during campaign debates or legislative sessions. In preparing Walter Mondale for his first debate against Ronald Reagan in the 1984 presidential campaign, Pat Caddell offered the advice that many strategists give their candidates: "The critical element to making the debate an overwhelming success is SURPRISE. Surprise Reagan and throw him off stride."[5] It worked. Mondale flustered him with deft jabs, especially when he turned Reagan's famous "There you go again" back on him.

In the wake of Mondale's success, Caddell amplified his advice for the second debate: "The overriding objective of this debate must be to 'break' Reagan—hurt him on age, his lack of knowledge, on his grasp of issues. Mondale must not simply beat Reagan, he must take him apart. From the very first moment he must engage, disorient, pick Reagan apart, and put him on the defensive."[6] Reagan was ready this time, however, so the tactic fell short.

There are other ways to fray nerves. During the Gulf War, President Bush kept pronouncing the name of the Iraqi leader as "SAD-am," which loosely means "shoeshine boy."[7] On Capitol Hill, the ritual mispronunciation of a member's name is a time-tested way to rattle opponents or haze newcomers. Lyndon Johnson was a master of the practice. When Johnson was Senate majority leader, writes J. McIver Weatherford, he applied it with junior members who voted the wrong way: "While slapping the young chap on the back and telling him he understood, Johnson would break his name into shreds as a metaphorical statement of what would happen if the disloyalty persisted."[8]

House Speaker Tip O'Neill used a similar trick with Republicans, referring to Newt Gingrich and Vin Weber as "Jin-rich" and "Wee-ber." The GOP also knew how to rankle a foe. In 1980, the party ran generic television ads featuring an O'Neill lookalike, an affront that stung him for years. In 1984, Gingrich confronted O'Neill in a floor debate, goading him into remarks so intemperate that the chair had to rule him out of order. The leader-baiting intensified when Jim Wright became Speaker: Republicans attacked his ethics, forcing him to resign in 1989.

In military parlance, the GOP achieved "decapitation," the act of disrupting opponents by striking down their chief. Sometimes, the mere attempt will have psychological impact by itself. In 1986, President Reagan sent F-111 fighter-bombers to attack the Tripoli headquarters of Libyan strongman Muammar Qaddafi. Nodding to an executive order against assassination, Reagan denied that the bombers aimed to kill Qaddafi, while administration officials hinted to reporters that he was indeed a target. After the raid, Qaddafi scaled back his terrorism.

Similarly, political organizations often target opposition leaders. National Democrats repeatedly backed efforts to defeat Newt Gingrich in his home district. If they could not beat him outright, they reasoned, they could at least throw a scare into him. As campaign chairman Vic Fazio (D-CA) put it: "You always want to play the game of decapitation."[9]

THREATS

Military threats, whether explicit or implicit, are more common than uses of military force. Nations employ the prospect of combat to deter aggression or to bend other nations to their will. To make their threats effective, they must convince other nations that they have both the means and the will to fight. The best method is simply to maintain actual military strength and establish a record of using it. Paul Seabury and Angelo Codevilla offer a vivid example: "Mongols developed such a reputation for torturing to death anyone who put up the slightest resistance to them that the appearance of a single Mongol horseman in a Russian village would provoke the inhabitants to line up, docilely offering their necks to be decapitated."[10]

Politics is full of "Mongols." In 1981, presidential aide Ed Rollins explained that the White House got Senator Roger Jepsen (R-IA) to switch on a key vote by threatening to withhold political favors: "We just beat his brains in." Jepsen erupted when the remark got into the papers, but Rollins quieted him by threatening to back a challenger in the next GOP Senate primary: "I'll bomb your ass back to the Stone Age."[11] Mongols are especially plentiful in the U.S. Senate, where the rules allow a skillful lawmaker to bog down proceedings on the floor. Howard Metzenbaum (D-OH) built a hard-won reputation for using delaying tactics, so other senators would often offer him concessions at the mere hint of a filibuster. Sometimes, he would not have to say anything: even before submitting legislation, colleagues would ponder whether it would pass "the Metzenbaum test."[12] Although not all senators are as adept at procedural combat, the possibility of all-out warfare encourages mutual respect. As one senator said, "You have to think of the Senate as if it were 100 different nations and each one had the atomic bomb and at any moment any one of you could blow up the place."[13]

Congress and the White House routinely threaten each other. For the presidency, Alexander Hamilton wrote, the veto power is among the strongest "constitutional arms for its own defense."[14] A president can force lawmakers to change legislation by brandishing the veto pen, an act that reporters call "saber rattling." Conversely, Congress uses the appropriations process as its own saber, threatening spending cuts as a way of winning concessions from the President. James Madison called the power of the purse "the most compleat and effectual weapon with which any constitution can arm the immediate representatives of the people."[15]

If opponents lack mettle, the mere shadow of combat can scare them away from the field. In 1937, a Texas congressman suddenly died of a heart attack. Young Lyndon Johnson started planning to run in the special election to succeed him, then learned that the man's widow was thinking of entering the race. Knowing that widows usually win such contests, Johnson was distraught until his father reminded him of the power of deterrence: "She's an old woman. She's too old for a fight. If she knows she's going to have a fight, she won't run. Announce now—before she announces. If you do, she won't run."[16] LBJ announced. The old lady did not run.

Non-establishment figures use threats, too. In the middle of the twentieth century, radical community organizer Saul Alinsky and his followers became notorious for their ferocity. Alinsky later told the story of a boycott against "Tycoon's Department Store." After the company had hired goons to stop the boycott, the organizers saw an opportunity. "Here was the psychological moment to attack," one organizer recalled, "both to win the war without a war, and yet to provide a satisfactory outlet for the high-running passions and aggressions of our people." The demonstrators would "prepare an attack of such devastating proportions and so utterly diabolical in character that in some respects it would even shock the morals of such people as the Tycoon officials."[17] The plan was simple. The boycott organizers leaked word that they would seek an injunction restraining the company from murdering Protestant ministers and Catholic priests. Although a court probably would not have granted the injunction, the publicity would have devastated the company, which caved in before the organizers had to go any farther.

On another occasion, the city government of Chicago seemed ready to break its commitments to a ghetto organization. According to Alinsky, the group responded by planning to occupy all the toilets at O'Hare Airport. It was a simple way to cause great discomfort to many people in a place that would catch the world's attention. When the city administration learned of the threat, it immediately surrendered.[18]

Sometimes nations try to make their point just by showing military power. The Soviet leaders, who were normally sensitive about maintaining secrecy, liked to hold parades that allowed Westerners to view their latest armaments. Politicians have their own May Day parades. At fundraisers and receptions, party leaders and other VIPs serve the same function as the missiles in Red Square: their quantity and quality say that no one should trifle with the host. *Washington Post* reporter Dan Balz described an early event of the 2000 presidential race: "Texas Gov. George W. Bush launched his presidential exploratory committee here today with a show of political muscle designed to intimidate his rivals."[19] By announcing that major GOP figures had joined his exploratory committee, Bush was trying to convince other candidates that the contest was ending before it even began.

RESISTANCE IS FUTILE

Harold Lasswell identified the keynote message of most demoralization efforts: "Your cause is hopeless. Your blood is spilled in vain."[20] In the nineteenth century, French military theorist Ardant du Picq wrote, "Make the enemy believe that support is lacking; isolate; cut off, flank, turn, in a thousand ways make his men believe themselves isolated."[21] During the Gulf War, the United States and its allies air-dropped pamphlets telling Iraqi soldiers that they had no chance and giving them instructions on how to surrender safely. Because the Iraqis were already witnessing an awesome display of American military power, they found the message persuasive, and many did surrender.

Politicians sometimes use the "inevitability" tack to cow their opponents into quitting. "You know, New York could do it; it could do it," said Bob Dole before the 1996 New York GOP primary. "It could demoralize every other candidate in this race. They wouldn't even be able to write checks anymore, they would be so nervous and so shaky about the election. You can do it right here."[22] Soon after New York, Dole did clear the field. Politicians have to take care in copying this approach, however, because high expectations can backfire. The promise of an overwhelming victory can make a merely respectable one look like a defeat.

According to a British expert in PsyOps (psychological operations), "Causing the enemy to defect is a crucial part of the PsyOps battle."[23] Such an effort causes turmoil in several ways. First, the side that loses defectors has to wonder what secrets they carried off with them. Second, each defection raises the possibility of others, thereby undermining the mutual confidence that fighting forces need. Third, defectors often become propagandists for their new friends. During the Cold War, the United States made very effective use both of Soviet emigrés and of domestic communists who broke with their cause.

Defectors play a key role in the politics of issues and interest groups. In the wake of the health industry's "Harry and Louise" ads against President Clinton's health-care proposal, an operative for the Democratic National Committee tried to get the actress who played Louise to endorse the Clinton plan. (The effort failed when the operative resorted to bullying tactics.)[24] In the 1990s, some tobacco company scientists and employees turned against the industry, supplying damning information to the press and the government. CBS reporter Leslie Stahl introduced a profile of FDA Commissioner David Kessler this way: "The war in this story is the one he fought against the tobacco companies. Allied with defectors from the enemy camp, Kessler fought much of the war behind enemy lines."[25]

Political parties dread defections. Before the 1994 election, House Republicans suggested that if they won or approached a majority, they could persuade some Democrats to switch. One Democratic leadership aide saw an element of bluster, saying, "They're engaging in psychological warfare."[26] After the Republicans took control, they made good on their suggestion, with five Democrats crossing over. When Nathan Deal of Georgia made his announcement, an aide to House Speaker Newt Gingrich said that Deal's switch would be "psychologically demoralizing" to the Democrats.[27]

DEMOBILIZATION

Propaganda efforts try to show the enemy that its cause is not just futile but unworthy, that its aims are flawed, its leaders corrupt, and its allies undependable. America's Gulf War propaganda told Iraqi soldiers that Saddam Hussein was stealing, lying, murdering, and violating Islamic law. In politics, a rough equivalent consists of messages that depress the opponent's support: borrowing a military term, scholars refer to this process as "demobilization."[28] In 1964, Lyndon Johnson's campaign ran a spot that quoted criticisms of Barry Goldwater by his rivals for the GOP nomination. According to analyst David Beiler, "This spot masterfully plays on feelings of violation by depicting the physical carnage one might find in the wake of a riotous political battle: skimmers, streamers, confetti, and the downtrodden banners of the defeated."[29]

To make their messages more credible, warriors often use "gray propaganda." By influencing media outlets in a target country, a government can launder the origins of its messages and make them appear to come from neutral sources.[30] Political figures use gray propaganda all the time, especially when they go on the attack. Suppose a campaign unearths damaging material about an opponent but worries that a direct assault will look too mean. No problem: with adequate documentation, it can hand the source material over to reporters, who then print the information without revealing who did the original research. "Far from being detached observers, reporters constantly call oppo staffs looking for tidbits and sometimes trading information," wrote three *U.S. News* reporters in 1992. "Because they often have more money, more staff and more time than news organizations, the campaigns are almost always ahead of the reporters—and they're usually happy to help."[31]

Rumors are an effective way to spread morale-busting information because they are hard to trace and gain credibility through repetition. During World War II, the Office of Strategic Services set guidelines for spreading rumors: tell the story casually, and if especially hot, confidentially. Never speak the rumor more than once in the same place, and never disclose a source that a skeptic could easily discredit.[32] Obviously, no written handbooks exist for political rumors, but operatives have their own rules of thumb. Before he became White House press secretary, Mike McCurry said that standard procedure consists of "getting a dozen people aggressively asking 'Have you heard the one about...' until enough chatter develops so that the press starts to think it's true."[33] In a 1940 conversation that the White House taping system accidentally recorded, Franklin Roosevelt told an aide how to use rumor in the fall presidential campaign: "[We can] spread it as a word-of-mouth thing, or by some people way, way down the line. We can't have any of our principal speakers refer to it, but the people down the line can get it out."[34] (Because of a garbled patch on the tape, it is not certain which rumor FDR wanted to use, but he and the aide did go on to discuss the extramarital affair of his GOP rival, Wendell Willkie.)

Recent campaigns have used a technique called "push polling" in which the caller pretends to be gathering survey data but is actually spreading negative messages. Because this method aims to suppress the opponent's turnout, experts call it "suppression phoning."[35]

"DIVIDE AND RULE"

The Latin maxim *divide et impera*, meaning "divide in order to rule," refers to a tactic in which one side physically splits the opposition's forces, blocking unified action. In military and political circles alike, it also means creating emotional rifts. FDR forged alliances with certain GOP office-holders such as New York Mayor Fiorello LaGuardia, making it difficult for Republicans to build a broad base of opposition. He used subtle language to divide Republican leaders from their voters. "So never attack the Republicans or the Republican party—only the Republican *leaders*," he said. "Then any Republican who hears it will say to himself: 'Well, he doesn't mean me.'"[36] In the first Nixon term, a White House aide wrote a blunt memo, entitled "Dividing the Democrats in 1972," that laid out a plan for isolating liberal Democrats from moderates. Republican leaders should congratulate top Democrats who attack left-wing extremism, the memo advised: "Give thought to secret funding of certain candidacies we know will divide the Dems. Make sure [segregationist governor George] Wallace gets on the Dem ballot in Florida, North Carolina and Tennessee primaries—this should cause vast division. . . . If a fourth party comes about on the left of the Dem party—we should give it assistance any way we can."[37]

In 1999, both sides in the House's partisan war tried to split the other. "The Democratic caucus is riven with internal conflict," said Republican majority leader Dick Armey of Texas, trying to drive a wedge between the Democratic leadership and pro-tax-cut moderates. Democratic Caucus chair Martin Frost, also of Texas, responded in kind: "I think the Republicans are being driven by their right wing. . . . They obviously have problems in their own ranks."[38]

DECEPTION

Sun Tzu's most famous observation is: "All warfare is based on deception."[39] Although we often use the terms "deception" and "lying" interchangeably, they do not mean the same thing. Lying is simply the intentional making of false statements. Deception includes not only lying but also many other means of creating false impressions, such as statements that are technically true but misleading.[40] During the Clinton impeachment case, the President's defense depended on distinguishing such deceptive statements from outright lies. One may also deceive through disguise, camouflage, or silence.[41] At the climax of the Gulf War, for instance, allied forces massed at the border between Saudi Arabia and Kuwait, making it appear that they would head directly north. Instead, the main force used cover of darkness to swing west and hit through Iraq, achieving strategic surprise.

Deception is commonplace in politics. Investigative journalists often use "stings" to expose crooked politicians. Government agencies have also used deceptive tactics to infiltrate criminal operations—and, occasionally, legitimate groups of political dissidents. Seldom does academic political science pay much attention to practical deception, but military writers have given it a good deal of thought. Among their most important findings, says the Center for Army Lessons Learned, is the following: "It is generally easier to induce a target to maintain a preexisting belief than to deceive him for the purpose of changing his belief. The Germans did this to us in their operation 'Wacht am Rhein.' Even the code name for their winter offensive in the Ardennes in 1944 connoted a defensive operation, which is what we believed would occur."[42]

One often wants to sustain an illusion of weakness where strength exists. When you can get your opponents to underestimate your power, they will fail to prepare, making themselves easier to attack. A number of American politicians have enjoyed this talent. Bill Clinton displayed it as early as his law school years, when he would often enter a debate with the demeanor of a yokel. Classmate Nancy Bekavac would say to herself of whomever Clinton was debating, "Oh, you poor bastard, you are about to be rolled over."[43] In the same vein, Senator Alfonse D'Amato (R-NY) deliberately kept up his image as a simple-minded lout. The artifice cropped up briefly in an interview with a *New York Times* reporter:

> "People underestimated you," I said.
> "Of course," he said. "There's an expression in Italian, '*Faccia contenta*,' which means 'Keep a happy face, a face of contentment.'

Sometimes you allow people, because it doesn't make any sense to argue a point, to believe what they want to believe because you're not going to change it, and my mother and father have both drummed that into me. Leave it alone, even if someone else is there, even if they're talking nonsense." He turned to his father. "How do you say that, Dad, *faccia contenta*?"

"It's an idiomatic expression," his father said. "It's play the fool, rather than be wise."

The Senator said, "Yeah, make a happy—let them just talk."

"You may come out losing but in the end you're a winner," his father said. "Very complex."[44]

People may catch on eventually because it is hard to keep playing the fool after years in power. In 1998, Representative Charles Schumer defeated D'Amato with a tough campaign whose slogan was "Too many lies for too long."

At times, leaders use the opposite deception—namely, creating an illusion of strength that conceals weakness. In the 1990s, the Christian Coalition reportedly overstated its base by keeping thousands of dead people and duplicate names on its list of supporters. Former staffers revealed that when journalists toured the group's headquarters, a roving band of staffers would leapfrog ahead to fill empty offices and work idle telephones.[45]

An illusion of strength is important for politicians who suffer from health problems that their opponents could exploit. Throughout his presidency, Franklin Roosevelt went to great lengths to hide the extent of his paralysis and to give the impression that he could walk, after a fashion. Political elites knew of this disability but did not fully grasp the extent of his physical and mental decline in his final years. To convey a facade of health toward the end of his 1944 campaign, he made a grueling four-hour parade in a cold New York rain. At various points, the Secret Service had commandeered garages where the car could slip in and agents could dry Roosevelt off, change his clothes, and give him a bracing rubdown and shot of brandy.[46] The illusion got FDR through the election but could not prevent his death several months later.

Deceptive information or signals should come from sources that the enemy will believe. "Gray propaganda" is useful here. Before the release of President Clinton's videotaped grand jury testimony in the Lewinsky case, many newspapers reported that he had lost his temper and stormed out. When the broadcast revealed a cool performance, public opinion swung in his favor. The original story apparently had elements of a deception to it. At least one of its sources was a Hill Democrat, and although White House aides knew it was false, they did nothing to discourage it.[47]

Small details enhance deceptions. Robert Moses, a powerful unelected figure in New York government, plotted in 1936 to surprise Mayor Fiorello LaGuardia with a radio speech. The announced topic was housing policy, but the speech was actually planned to rally voters behind a massive urban-renewal plan that the mayor opposed. Unbeknownst to Moses, however, LaGuardia had gotten wind of his plan. Moses confidently strode to the microphone and saw technicians twisting dials and going through all the motions of making a broadcast. When they made a thumbs-up gesture, he started. Toward the end of his speech, someone handed him a note saying that the radio station had been off the air all the time. Apparently, LaGuardia had given the order to block the program and have the technicians trick Moses into thinking all was going smoothly.[48]

DISTRACTION

Through distraction, a military force can keep its adversaries from focusing their efforts on the right places. Distraction takes two basic forms: decoys and dazzles.[49] The first of these can draw adversaries to places where they will either waste their firepower or expose themselves to ambush. Before D-Day, the Allies invented a decoy army to trick the Germans into thinking that they would land at the Pas de Calais. Complete with fake radio traffic and the presence of General George Patton, the "First U.S.

Army Group" decoyed enough Germans away from Normandy so that the Allies could gain a beachhead. In 1988, Republicans staged highly visible rallies in Michael Dukakis's home state of Massachusetts. "A lot of this is aimed at getting into their minds," said a Bush aide. "The more we can distract them from what they should be thinking of—California, for example—the better off we are. . . . I make them think. I make them spend resources."[50]

Four years later, the Bush forces put out word that the President would attack Clinton's draft record at a National Guard convention. Clinton hastily rearranged his schedule to defend himself at the event. Bush then gave a statesmanlike speech that forced Clinton to rewrite his own remarks at the last minute. Mary Matalin recalls: "We disrupted Clinton's schedule, we wasted their time and got the entire campaign off message for four days solid. It was the coolest strategic fake-out we did in the entire election. . . . A little psychological warfare goes a long way. We got them, we'd sucked them in."[51]

Dazzling, the second major form of distraction, means presenting the opposition with more signals or options than it can handle. "The enemy must not know where I intend to give battle," wrote Sun Tzu, "for if he does not know where I intend to give battle, he must prepare in a great many places. . . . And when he prepares everywhere he will be weak everywhere."[52] Toward the end of the 1992 campaign, rising poll numbers enabled Clinton to turn the tables on Bush. His campaign announced a late swing through states that Republicans had expected to carry, forcing the GOP to shift resources from marginal states back to their base. "These are all states where we feel we have a reasonable chance of winning," said Clinton spokesman Bruce Lindsay. "But if it spooks the Bush-Quayle people a bit, so much the better."[53]

The Clinton impeachment was also dazzling, but not in the good sense. According to Clinton supporters, the President's foes were deliberately throwing a huge array of charges at him, in hopes that he could not simultaneously defend himself against all of them. House Judiciary Committee counsel David Schippers threw the accusations back at them, comparing the President's case to air chaff during World War II: "The planes would carry packages of lead based tinfoil strips. When the planes flew into the perimeter of the enemy's radar coverage, the crews would release that tinfoil. It was intended to confuse and distract the radar operators from the real target. Now, the treatment that Monica Lewinsky received from the Independent Counsel, the legality of Linda Tripp's taping, the motives of some of the witnesses, and those who helped finance the Paula Jones lawsuit—that's tinfoil."[54]

For lawmakers and bureaucrats, the dazzling chaff may sometimes consist of paper, which may misdirect attention through its sheer volume. In 1924, Robert Moses drafted a lengthy bill for the New York State Legislature providing for parks and roads on Long Island. Deep within the act, hidden beneath page after page of tedious prose, were provisions allowing him to seize land, hire police officers, and take other extraordinary powers. The distraction worked, and the bill passed unanimously.[55]

SECRECY AND STEALTH

"Military metaphors come easily whenever secrecy is at issue," writes Sissela Bok; "they are perhaps more common than all others."[56] No wonder: military activity has always depended on secrecy. "If you have the finest plans in the world but divulge them," wrote Frederick the Great, "your enemy will learn about them, and then it will be very easy for him to parry them."[57] Commanders hold their plans as close as possible and try to restrict access to data about deployments and weapons. Secrecy scarcely stops at the Pentagon's outer ring. Though the mechanisms are especially rigorous in the national security establishment, nearly all government organizations seek to control knowledge. Despite the Freedom of Information Act (FOIA), researchers may find it difficult to dislodge papers from government agencies. Even public information is subject to distortion. Reporter Scott Armstrong says: "Given the government's propensity to conquer, control, and manipulate information, individuals, journalists, scholars, and concerned citizens must fight an ongoing low-intensity guerrilla war for government information."[58]

One weapon in that war is "deniability." Lower-ranking intelligence officials may withhold details from superiors so that the latter can plausibly deny knowledge, leaving the former to take the blame if something goes wrong. Testifying about the Iran-Contra affair, Admiral John Poindexter defined deniability as "the ability of the President to deny knowing anything about it and be very truthful in that process."[59] Loyal staffers, bureaucrats, and campaign aides routinely engage in the practice. In the 1858 Illinois Senate contest, Stephen A. Douglas accused Abraham Lincoln of making deals with a faction of state Democrats. Lincoln denied any contact. But William Herndon, his law partner and political handyman, did keep in touch with the faction. "They make 'no bones' in telling me what they are going to do," Herndon said. "Lincoln . . . does not know the details of how we get along. I do, but he does not."[60]

In all parts of the political world, smart operators know the value of stealth. In a confidential circular telling fellow Whigs how to "overthrow the trained bands that are opposed to us" in the 1840 campaign, a young Lincoln closed with a note of caution: "Our plan of operations will of course be concealed from every one except our good friends who of right ought to know of them."[61] Such instructions could have come from Lyndon Johnson. When he was a minor congressional aide, he closed innocuous personal letters with the words "Burn this." As an undergraduate, he learned that certain pages of the college yearbook contained information about him that he did not like, so he arranged for someone to slice those pages from hundreds of copies.[62] And as a politician, he carefully concealed his campaign finances so that no one could easily identify his contributors or reckon the size of his warchest.[63]

Johnson's experience raises a larger point: in war and politics, money means stealth. During World War II, the Roosevelt administration used accounting tricks to hide expenditures for the Manhattan Project, eventually enlisting key lawmakers to assist in the concealment. Until recently, the overall budget for U.S. intelligence operations was a secret; and even now, detailed breakdowns of that budget are unavailable, so that potential adversaries cannot find clues to operations and capabilities.

In some ways, political finance is similar. Although the law now forbids the cash transactions that fueled LBJ's races, politicians and interest groups have developed many lawful and semi-lawful smokescreens. Knowing that candidates can catch flak for taking "cancer money," tobacco companies make contributions through party committees or have the funds come from the political action committees (PACs) of subsidiaries. Since data on expenditures can tip off opponents about strategy and tactics, politicians and issue groups can cover their tracks with nonprofit organizations and "shadow" political committees that nominally engage in general political education, not candidate support.[64]

There are other ways to "fly under the radar." In 1999, Representative Jerry Lewis of California, chair of the House sucommittee in charge of defense spending, deftly maneuvered to cut funds for a controversial fighter plane. The *Los Angeles Times* explained how Lewis's "tactical acumen" did the deed: "To blunt an anticipated counterattack from the F-22's congressional supporters, Lewis and his subcommittee allies gave no advance warning—even to their staffs—that they planned to excise the

$1.8 billion in procurement money."[65] For the time being, at least, Lewis had outmaneuvered the professional warriors.

In the 1950s, GOP activist Stephen Shadegg explicitly followed Mao Zedong's "cell group" model. Just as Mao's cells would lay the basis for guerrilla warfare, so Shadegg's cells would quietly build support for his candidates apart from formal political organizations. "The individuals we enlisted became a secret weapon possessing strength, mobility and real impact," Shadegg wrote. "They were able to infiltrate centers of opposition support, keep us informed of opposition tactics, disseminate information, enlist other supporters and to do all these things completely unnoticed by the opposition."[66] In the early 1990s, local affiliates of the Christian Coalition sometimes backed "stealth candidates" for local office who would downplay their affiliations in order to attract broader support. Ralph Reed, longtime director of the Christian Coalition, once summed up the value of the quiet approach: "It's like guerrilla warfare. If you reveal your location, all it does is allow your opponent to improve his artillery bearings. It's better to move quietly, with stealth, under cover of night. . . . It comes down to whether you want to be the British army in the Revolutionary War or the Viet Cong. History tells us which tactic was more effective."[67]

KNOWING THE OTHER SIDE

Knowledge of the opposition is essential to all the activities discussed in this chapter. To wage psychological warfare, one needs to know the adversary's sensitivities and vulnerabilities. A lawmaker can gain maximum advantage by learning about other members' schedules and legislative priorities. That way, the legislator can threaten dilatory tactics at exactly the moment when delay would hurt the most. A candidate trying to bait an opponent has to understand what throws the opponent off guard. In a

1992 debate, Clinton deftly exploited Bush's reverence for his father, Senator Prescott Bush (R-CT). "Your father was right to stand up to Joe McCarthy," he said. "You were wrong to attack my patriotism."[68] Bush did not know how to respond.

Deception and stealth also require knowledge of the opposition. To hoodwink adversaries, one must know what they will believe. An ignorant or careless enemy is easy to fool; even a smart one may fall prey to manipulation of assumptions and prejudices. (The Trojan Horse worked because the Greeks played on the Trojans' hubris: though good warriors, they were too ready to believe that they had won.) Either way, one can maintain appearances only by monitoring whether or not the other side suspects the truth.

"If your assessment of the enemy is good," wrote General H. Norman Schwarzkopf in 1988, "then you probably have anticipated his actions or reactions and will be able to quickly develop or adjust your plan accordingly. If your assessment is bad, . . . then you will probably get surprised, react slowly, lose the initiative, and cause your unit to be defeated."[69] Intelligence, the process of reaching these assessments, is our next topic.

7

Intelligence

> Therefore I say: "Know the enemy and know yourself;
> in a hundred battles you will never be in peril."
>
> —Sun Tzu
> *The Art of War*

According to one military coursebook, intelligence is "the product resulting from the collection, evaluation, analysis, integration and interpretation of all available information."[1] This definition reaches too far because it includes matter that has little bearing on the battlefield. For our purposes, intelligence consists of usable knowledge about current or potential conflicts. Note that the definition employs the word "knowledge" rather than "information": raw facts gain value only when someone makes sense of them through analysis and interpretation.[2] To be usable, this knowledge must help leaders devise and weigh their alternatives; it must also arrive in time for them to do so. It does not involve all conceivable questions, but only those that could come into play during a fight. When we gather intelligence, we try to learn:

- Who will join which side? What are their intentions?
- What are the other side's strengths and weaknesses? How do they compare with ours?
- How would our adversaries fare against us in a variety of circumstances?
- Are they asking these questions of themselves? What answers do they get?[3]

These questions cover a great deal of ground. The roster of possible combatants is broad and shifting, because changes of leadership and clashes of interest can turn friends and neutrals into enemies, and vice versa. The history of the twentieth century successively made Russia our ally, our adversary, and our uncomfortable partner. Strengths and weaknesses may be psychological or material, permanent or temporary, generic to the opposition's culture or specific to individual leaders. They also depend on the situation and the relative status of the opposing sides. Naval power is critical in a war between two island nations, but it matters much less if one of the warring parties is landlocked Afghanistan.

All political leaders and organizations collect intelligence, although many shy away from the term because it conjures up images of secret agents digging up smear material. Political intelligence, however, also encompasses more benign activities, such as monitoring media stories and public statements. Intelligence-gatherers often worry less about preparing attacks than anticipating what adversaries might do. In preparing for debates, political figures need intelligence on what their opponents are likely to say so that they can prepare accordingly. Despite technological innovations that we shall discuss shortly, the basic process is nothing new. In 1858, Abraham Lincoln sent his law partner William Herndon to the Illinois State Library to collect what Herndon called "all the ammunition Mr. Lincoln saw fit to gather in preparation for his battle with Stephen A. Douglas."[4]

WHO WATCHES WHOM

The formal United States intelligence community consists of thirteen government agencies, both civilian and military. These organizations gather all sorts of data from nearly every part of the planet, but their main focus is on threats from conventional armed action, guerrilla warfare, terrorism, and the development of weapons of mass destruction.

Outside the world of national security, the intelligence function has more flexible boundaries. Every government agency and political organization has people who act as its "eyes and ears."[5] This category embraces "facts and figures" specialists in bureaucracies and opposition researchers in campaigns. The "eyes and ears" also include "contact" people, such as lobbyists and press secretaries, who not only write and speak for the organization but also pick up information from their contacts by talking shop and hearing gossip.

Outside each organization's membership list or personnel roster lie the informal agents who make up the "grapevine" or "old-boy/old-girl network."[6] These loose sets of acquaintances consist largely of organization alumni who have moved to other positions but stay in touch with their old workplaces. (In Washington, D.C., with high levels of both professionalism and turnover, such networks are as numerous as they are invisible.) Grapevines serve as distant early warning systems. On learning of developments that could hurt the organization, members of the grapevine will call or email with a "heads up" message. (This slang term for an alert dates back to World War II.) Lawmakers, lobbyists, and bureaucrats usually benefit when an able employee takes another job, because they are not losing an aide so much as gaining an intelligence source. During the 1990s, political Washington envied Senate Majority Leader Trent Lott (R-MS) and informal Clinton adviser Vernon Jordan for their networks of protégés.

With information coming from diverse sources in diverse forms, organizations must assemble these fragments into a realistic picture of current events.[7] In the national intelligence community, this job belongs to the aptly named Central Intelligence Agency. The CIA is supposed to coordinate intelligence from other agencies, though bureaucratic rivalries get in the way. (Soviet spy Aldrich Ames escaped detection for years because the FBI and CIA failed to tell each other about him.) Political organizations vary widely in their collating mechanisms. Some require their departments to report intelligence to a director of communications, whereas others rely on staff meetings where everyone supposedly shares information. The latter method works poorly. Just as spies in the field often have a distant relationship with analysts at headquarters, so the "contact" people and the "facts and figures" people may disdain each other.[8] In 1992, candidate Bill Clinton's contact people referred to his researchers as "propeller heads."[9]

Coordination is less of a problem when political leaders themselves play an active part in the intelligence effort. When he was Senate majority leader, Lyndon Johnson cultivated an extensive intelligence system with sources all over Washington. At one point in the 1950s, Johnson complained to a reporter that he was focusing on internal Democratic problems while failing to cover divisions in the Senate GOP. To make his point, he pulled out a memorandum on a recent private meeting at which the reporter and several of his colleagues had gotten a briefing on GOP factionalism from Senator Thruston Morton (R-KY). Rowland Evans and Robert Novak recalled: "The Intelligence System was a marvel of efficiency. It was also rather frightening."[10]

Even in the White House, Johnson believed in firsthand political intelligence. According to his aide Harry McPherson, "I guess he called a lot of people, but I could usually count on it in the late afternoon, as he woke up from his nap, that I would get a call which would usually say, 'What do you know?'" McPherson would then pass along the latest news that he had picked up from reporters and political figures. Johnson did not stop there. "Then he would start reading the afternoon papers, and then he would want to, of course, see the evening news."[11]

LOOKING INWARD

The more an organization depends on the loyalty of its own people, the more closely it will keep track of them.[12] In the armed forces, officers and noncommissioned officers watch for insubordination or personal problems that could undermine unit performance. Throughout the national security community, experts in counterintelligence and internal security look out for espionage or reckless behavior. For political jobs in the executive branch, the question is not just national allegiance but loyalty to president and party. The Office of Presidential Personnel checks the political backgrounds of potential appointees, keeping supporters in and opponents out. When they go to the agencies, some of these appointees have the task of monitoring career civil servants who might otherwise thwart policy or leak information to political enemies. Within the White House, certain aides keep an eye on their colleagues. During the Bush administration, Chief of Staff John Sununu had a deputy annotate negative articles about him; the aide would guess the identity of the leaker, who would then get a tongue-lashing from Sununu.[13]

Internal intelligence works differently when its objects are not employees but peers, colleagues, or volunteers. In legislatures, the task falls mainly to party whips. Besides counting votes, whips serve a broader intelligence function by maintaining constant contact with their members, alert to hints of discontent that could spell trouble for the party leadership. While whips gather human information from face-to-face contact, their staffs maintain databases that track members' voting records and constituency characteristics.

Candidate and political organizations also have whips at events such as party conventions. At the 1960 Democratic convention, John Kennedy seemed ready for a first-ballot nomination but feared slippage. "We therefore set up an elaborate intelligence system so that we would know what was happening in each state delegation at all times," said Kennedy aide Lawrence O'Brien. "One of our trusted people was assigned to each delegation as a permanent liaison. He was to eat with the delegates, live with them, and know exactly where each delegate stood at all times."[14] Thanks to the intelligence system, the Kennedy forces remained calm during a passionate demonstration for Adlai Stevenson: the elder statesman may have enjoyed the applause, but Kennedy still had the votes.

COVERT OPS

As mentioned above, many people equate political intelligence with spying. And political espionage does take place—sometimes with the national security apparatus as a participant. The Watergate break-in involved veterans of the FBI (G. Gordon Liddy), the CIA (E. Howard Hunt and James McCord), and CIA-sponsored anti-Castro operations (Bernard Barker). Some of the Watergate figures, in turn, had taken part in domestic intelligence activities, such as the break-in at the office of psychiatrist Daniel Ellsberg, the defense analyst who leaked the Pentagon Papers to the press. Nixon's defenders claimed that previous presidents had condoned similar activities. Whatever its merits as a legal or ethical defense, this argument had a basis in history.

In 1964, Lyndon Johnson persuaded the FBI to send a thirty-agent team to the Democratic National Convention in Atlantic

City. Its nominal purpose was to help the Secret Service avert assassination and violent protests, but Johnson's request also reflected his desire to keep tabs on his hated rival, Attorney General Robert Kennedy, and to monitor civil rights activists who were making controversial demands.[15] During the same campaign, Johnson put GOP nominee Barry Goldwater under surveillance, which included electronic eavesdropping.[16]

Such cases are exceptional, for most political spying is the ad hoc work of amateurs. A California assemblyman once said, "In every campaign I have someone in the opponent's camp spying for me."[17] People became his spies, he said, because they liked him, hated his opponent, sought some payoff, or just wanted to express "sheer cussedness." Politicians seldom acknowledge specific cases of covert intelligence, but one example became public in 1983. Three years earlier, before the lone major-party presidential debate in the fall of 1980, Reagan campaign chief William Casey got a stolen copy of President Carter's briefing book. The foreknowledge enabled Reagan to anticipate Carter's lines and prepare his responses accordingly.

Despite the popular culture's fascination with espionage, covert sources have severe limits, both in the national security community and in politics. One drawback is the potential cost of exposure. When the Soviet Union shot down an American U-2 spy plane in 1960, the Eisenhower administration responded that the aircraft was doing "weather research." The Soviets then revealed that the pilot had survived and confessed, making it clear that the United States government had lied. U.S.–Soviet relations soured, and American prestige plunged. Similarly, any benefit that the Nixon team reaped from its spying was trivial compared to the long-term damage that Watergate caused the GOP. Accordingly, experienced political operatives are leery of black-bag jobs. In 1976, when an aide to Jimmy Carter devised a plan to listen in on all wireless communication at the Democratic convention, Carter's television advisor stopped it immediately, shouting: "You must be crazy. Didn't you ever hear of Watergate? If somebody finds out, it'll destroy Carter."[18] Even in the briefing-book affair, in which the Reagan camp merely received a document from a disgruntled Democrat, the publicity hurt the GOP, and a subsequent congressional investigation cost Republican aides thousands of dollars in legal fees.

Both in national security and in domestic politics, clandestine intelligence has debatable value because turncoats and leakers are inherently untrustworthy—and may be working as double agents. Similarly, political organizations get little return from planting their own people as moles in the enemy camp. As one political consultant told Larry J. Sabato and Glenn R. Simpson, "All a ringer volunteer finds out is that the coffee machine broke and that a hundred voters were called and twenty-eight are coming to the picnic."[19]

OPEN-SOURCE INTELLIGENCE

In 1989, a young aide for the Republican National Committee (RNC) went to Democratic National Headquarters. Posing as a student, he asked for a copy of a speech that New York Mayor David Dinkins had delivered at the 1988 Democratic convention. A suspicious Democratic staffer gave him an unreadable photo-copy and then had someone tail him right back to the Republican headquarters. Gleeful Democrats then embarrassed their GOP counterparts by telling the press about the "slimy covert operation."[20] The skullduggery was needless. All along, the official published record of the convention—complete with the Dinkins text—was sitting in the RNC's basement library.

This incident illustrates the importance of "open-source intelligence," which comes not from espionage but from libraries, government document depositories, newsstands, broadcasts, and electronic databases. Around the world, military and civilian intelligence agencies have always gathered these data, which are abundant in free societies. During the 1960s, Soviet defectors said that their military attachés in the United States could get most of their material through lawful channels—including toy stores. Admiral Hyman Rickover testified that a toymaker had produced such an detailed model of the Polaris nuclear submarine that a good ship designer could study it for an hour and get millions of dollars of free information.[21]

Open sources can supply better information than secret ones. On May 8, 1999, during their strike against Serbia, NATO forces accidentally bombed the Chinese embassy in Belgrade. Drawing on classified sources, NATO intelligence officers believed that this address was a military target and that the Chinese embassy lay elsewhere. When news of the fatal mistake became public, computer enthusiasts found the embassy's street address on the Internet.

One cannot always spot bombing targets on electronic maps, but it is indisputable that open sources are becoming more vital to the intelligence process. In 1996, the National Security Agency reported that "in the past ten years the amount of detailed, accurate, and timely information available to the public and U.S. adversaries has expanded dramatically."[22]

Technology is propelling this trend, in politics as well as military intelligence. "The computer was the first breakthrough. Going online is the second," said one opposition research expert in 1996. "Remember, the biggest domestic spy agency is the newspaper industry."[23] Thanks to the growth of the Internet (a product of the Defense Advanced Research Projects Agency) and the proliferation of online databases, a world of intelligence is available to everyone, from analysts in the Russian army to opposition researchers in an Arkansas legislative campaign.

The Clinton impeachment was the first domestic political war in which cyberspace was a major theater of operations. News of Clinton's liaison with White House intern Monica Lewinsky first broke on the *Drudge Report*, an online newsletter. Throughout the yearlong conflict, Republicans logged onto the Drudge site for ammunition, while Democrats checked it for early warning of new accusations. The pro-Clinton electronic newsletter *Salon* worked in the opposite direction by, among other things, reporting that the GOP chair of the House Judiciary Committee had himself engaged in an extramarital affair. When Independent Counsel Kenneth Starr released his lengthy report on Clinton, Internet availability enabled political operatives to do quick word searches and analyses. On both sides of the fight, researchers constantly searched Nexis and the Internet for evidence that their foes were inconsistent and hypocritical.

Television technology has also contributed to intelligence. Cable and satellite systems enable more people to get more broadcast information than ever before. The Iraqi regime, like many governments, uses CNN as a prime source of real-time political and military information.[24] In the United States, political organizations also monitor news channels, and those with a special interest in Congress keep a close eye on C-SPAN. Clinton's 1992 war room used a satellite dish to pull in broadcasts, including intercepts of yet-unaired GOP advertisements on their way to local affiliates.[25] Consulting firms provide monitoring services, for a price. POLARIS, or the "political advertising reporting and intelligence system," allows real-time tracking of political advertising in numerous markets, enabling operatives to gather research quickly so that they can launch immediate responses. "This is going to intensify combat," said a partner in the sponsoring firm. "This is intelligence that helps you deploy your troops on the frontline."[26]

Sometimes, the technology is as commonplace as a VCR or handheld video camera. Senator Joseph Biden (D-DE) dropped out of the 1988 Democratic presidential race because of videotapes showing him plagiarizing a speech and making inflated claims about his education. Ten years later, Al Checchi, running in California's Democratic gubernatorial primary, sent operatives to videotape his rivals' campaign appearances. One of his cameras caught an opponent calling herself "the best Republican in the Democratic Party"—an unwise appeal in a primary race. The campaign of Gray Davis, the eventual winner, responded with deception. "We psyched [one taper] out a couple of times by feeding disinformation to him," said Davis's campaign director. "We let out the word that we were going to Santa Barbara when we really weren't, so he wasted his whole day."[27]

Political intelligence has gained enormously from the "sunshine" movement. Congress passed the Freedom of Information Act (FOIA) in 1966 to open federal records for scholars, reporters, and average citizens, but the law has served other purposes as well. It is likely, though hard to prove, that foreign agents use FOIA to obtain data on American military and technological capabilities. What is certain is that corporations file FOIA requests to get information about their competitors; so do political figures. In 1999, Senator Conrad Burns (R-MT) protested when he learned that the Democratic Senatorial Campaign Committee (DSCC) had filed a FOIA request with several agencies, seeking their correspondence with him, Senator Olympia Snowe (R-ME), and other GOP senators up for reelection. A Republican researcher belittled the complaint. "With great respect for Senator Burns and Senator Snowe, this is how the game is played," said the researcher. "This is Oppo Research 101. The DSCC is within their rights and the Republican campaign committees should of course follow suit."[28]

Many official sources are available without FOIA requests. Some have clear political uses: congressional debates and voting records, campaign finance data, and financial disclosure statements. Others are less obvious. Securities and Exchange Commission filings may provide leads to a politician's business activities and possible conflicts of interest.[29] Presidential libraries may seem an unlikely source because their main subjects have left active politics, but their archival collections contain many documents by people who go on to run for office. In the early days of the 1996 presidential campaign, when former Governor Lamar Alexander (R-TN) attacked Governor Pete Wilson (R-CA) for not being a Reaganite, the Wilson camp released a 1976 letter in which Alexander had promised to support President Ford against Reagan for the GOP nomination. Wilson researcher Joe Rodota had found the letter in the Gerald R. Ford Library.[30]

"Sunshine" and cyberspace make a potent mix. More and more information is both open to the public and available on the Internet, so anyone with a personal computer can gather intelligence that would have been prohibitively costly just a few decades ago. By tapping sources such as the Federal Election Commission and the Center for Responsive Politics, an armchair researcher can get detailed intelligence on the political finances of any member of Congress.

Despite easy access, few people use open sources effectively. A consultant with experience in the intelligence community says: "Open sources are just as complex as clandestine sources. It's a discipline in its own right."[31] Online information is so vast that it takes an experienced searcher to sift the desired information from thousands of sites. Yet this material also has limits. Most electronic collections go back only a few years, and many documents and publications are not online at all. Researchers still have to know their way around libraries and archives. This skill is scarce, as we saw with the RNC operative who did not know how to find the Dinkins speech.

TRADECRAFT

Another form of intelligence consists of watching, talking, and listening—often without any effort at concealment. "Contact" people undertake this activity, which may sound simple but which requires talent and expertise.

Intelligence agents spend years learning which sources know which things and how to get the information from them. In some cases, it is merely a matter of asking. In others, an indirect approach is more appropriate, such as eavesdropping on chatter at embassy receptions. Political operatives act much the same way. They, too, cultivate sources, whom they catalog in their Rolodexes and call when they need information. They, too, attend social functions more for business than pleasure. Jack Watson, an aide to President Carter, described Washington parties: "You're learning, listening, picking up perceptions, frequently given the opportunity to correct misimpressions. Washington is an immense rumor mill. . . . It's very important to be in that information flow, to take advantage of it. It's just the way things work. Not only that, you'll get back very helpful intelligence."[32]

Whether chatting with friendly sources or questioning prisoners, intelligence officers watch for nonverbal communication. Reportedly, manuals on interrogation technique include detailed instructions on how to read facial expressions and body language for clues to deception.[33] Congressional vote-counters would probably like to study these handbooks because lawmakers often hide their intentions. Commenting on a vote count in a leadership election, House Republican whip Tom DeLay said: "Unless I get to see the lists and ask the questions and see the members, look them in the eye, I can't tell."[34]

Political figures also observe body language during legislative hearings and official inquiries. At dramatic confrontations such as the Clinton impeachment, much of the debate focuses on the witnesses' demeanor. Aware of the scrutiny, witnesses act accordingly. As chair of the Council of Economic Advisers, Laura Tyson recalled that Federal Reserve Chairman Alan Greenspan warned her to control her expressions and gestures. "If you're trying to— 'hide' is the wrong word—trying to give an on-the-one-hand, on-the-other-hand answer, but you're also nodding your head, you're sort of undermining your point."[35]

EVALUATION

Many people believe that intelligence is about the silver bullet or the magic key—the one item that will expose the opposition's fatal weakness. Silver bullets and magic keys are rare. Good intelligence is about patiently amassing details and discerning patterns. Even before analysts can assemble a mosaic of information, they must be able to tell which material is usable. As Clausewitz said, "Many intelligence reports in war are contradictory; even more are false, and most are uncertain." An officer thus needs good judgment, "which he can gain only from knowledge of men and affairs and from common sense."[36] Besides technical skill, intelligence analysts need worldly wisdom and a profound background knowledge of their subject.

On this point, the national security community is well ahead of the political community. Consultant Joseph Gaylord says that campaigns often delegate research to college students, with only cursory instructions that they find votes that would be unpopular. A student might spend weeks focusing on trivial issues while missing usable bits of information. "Maybe the opponent voted for a bill that he had specifically promised to oppose in the last campaign, . . . but the inexperienced researcher passed right over that bill because he failed to research the past newspaper articles of the last campaign that reported the opponent's promise. . . . The campaign might have saved money using that well-meaning college student but at what cost to winning?"[37]

Just as important as identifying opponents' vulnerabilities is anticipating their behavior. As Sun Tzu wrote, "Therefore, determine the enemy's plans and you will know which strategy will be successful and which will not."[38] Aside from reckoning what adversaries aim to do, good intelligence aims to see the world through their eyes, to grasp how they view relative strengths and weaknesses. As the Marines remind us, "The enemy will do what he thinks is possible, not what we think he can do."[39] A smart leader will act as Defense Secretary Dick Cheney did when he told intelligence briefers just before the Gulf War, "I want to know how this looks from the Iraqi side."[40]

This process entails studying the leader's character. Unlike popular "psychobiographies" that account for public action by attributing it to childhood trauma, solid analyses focus on the leader's decisions, perceptions, and work habits. Such studies begin by "placing" leaders in time and space, that is, by explaining the circumstances that shaped their worldview.[41] One can gain insights by learning when and where leaders came of age and what lessons they drew from their experiences. In the case of the Gulf War, intelligence analysts studied Saddam Hussein's violent past and told Cheney that he was a tough, cold-blooded survivor—an assessment that the 1990s would bear out.

Political leaders may do at least some of this work on their own. As Senate majority leader, Johnson formed mental pictures of all his colleagues—Republican and Democrat alike—and appraised their strengths, weaknesses, tastes, and aspirations. Thus he knew just how far he could push each one, and by what means.[42]

Good intelligence analysis also looks at organizations. A military commander needs to know the other side's internal power structure and standard operating procedures. How does the chain of command work? Who answers to whom? Who listens to whom? What kinds of actions bring promotion or punishment? How does each component part define its mission? By answering these questions, the analyst can help the commander see patterns that transcend personalities. Political figures need similar intelligence. In a legislature, one can rarely assume that the other side's leader wields absolute power; more often, a caucus has various power centers that the leader must satisfy. An examination of rosters, organization charts, and procedural rules will cast light on how the caucus makes decisions.

Making sense of individuals or organizations requires an understanding of their cultural background. This task is hard when their society is radically different from one's own. In the Pacific theater of World War II, in the Vietnam conflict, and in the 1993 Somalia mission, American forces got nasty surprises from adversaries whose beliefs and values were genuinely foreign. Not fully comprehending the role of nationalism and revolutionary communism in Vietnam, Johnson thought that he could get Hanoi to end the war by promising massive economic aid, just as he could switch a senator's vote by dangling a pork-barrel project in front of him.[43]

Cultural and ideological differences do not run as deep in domestic politics, yet they still hinder sound intelligence. As James Carville has pointed out, nothing is harder in politics than thinking as you do not think naturally.[44] In the 1994 midterm campaign, national Democratic leaders had a tough time figuring out the new Republican congressional leadership, with its ties to Christian conservatives, firearms enthusiasts, and libertarian activists—groups that most top Democrats seldom consulted. Underestimating the seriousness of the GOP's strategy and the political strength of its coalition, they got a shock when their party lost the House.

President Clinton then made a smart move by seeking advice from Dick Morris. Unlike most other Democratic consultants, Morris had a long record of working with conservative Republicans. As we saw in chapter 4, Morris had a thorough understanding of the strengths and weaknesses of GOP campaign doctrine: for instance, he knew that Republicans would be slow to catch on to the value of early advertising. And as the discussion of enmity in chapter 5 made clear, Morris knew how just how to exploit the GOP's ties to the gun lobby. By the start of the 1996 campaign, Clinton was consistently out-thinking and out-maneuvering his opponents.

Intelligence evaluation has to be comparative, because a weakness for one side represents an opportunity for its enemy. If military leaders know that their harbor X has much weaker defenses than harbor Y, then they should expect that the enemy will attack the former rather than the latter, all other things being equal. Military forces, then, routinely conduct "vulnerability assessments." Political operatives undertake similar exercises, called "defensive audits" or "vulnerability studies."[45] "Any good researcher will tell you the first target of his research is his own candidate, because you've got to know what you are going to get hit on," a veteran Democratic researcher in Georgia said during the 1998 campaign.[46] Perhaps the most famous vulnerability study occurred in 1992, when Clinton confidant Betsey Wright listed women who might accuse the candidate of sexual misconduct—an episode that appeared in lightly fictionalized form in the novel and movie *Primary Colors*.

Whether the subject is friend or foe, any intelligence evaluation should be dispassionate. In military or political conflict, the need for such objectivity may clash with the need to build up morale. One side can hardly whip up enthusiasm in the ranks by airing clear-eyed assessments of its own faults and the other side's virtues. Consequently, these analyses tend to be closely held secrets. Conversely, efforts to stoke negative feelings toward opponents may spoil intelligence. Depictions of cunning monsters may prompt an overestimation of opposition strength, just as images of a weak and cowardly foe may result in a serious underestimation.[47] Good analysis requires detachment, a willingness to discount one's own propaganda. For this job, it helps to be a cynic.

USING IT

Intelligence is not knowledge for its own sake but a means to more effective action. It has little value if it reaches decisionmakers too late or if they choose to ignore it.

Well-managed storage, retrieval, and distribution are all essential to military and political intelligence. "Battlefield information systems became the ally of the warrior," said General Colin Powell of the years before the Gulf War. "Efficient management of information increased the pace of combat operations, improved the decision-making process, and synchronized various combat capabilities."[48] Computers can make information simultaneously more abundant and more usable. The National Security Agency says that potential foes make use of hardware and software available on the open market. "On-line search engines, and other Internet tools allow intelligence collectors and analysts to rapidly sort through massive quantities of information and extract information pertinent to their area of interest."[49]

In politics, a foretaste of info-war came with the Republican National Committee's 1984 opposition research operation. RNC aides gathered some seventy-five thousand items about Walter Mondale, including forty thousand quotations, the largest such collection of any campaign up to that time. Computer technology now allowed researchers to handle such a volume of material, which would have overwhelmed the customary filing methods of folders, binders, and index cards.[50] Wherever Mondale was speaking, and whatever subject he was addressing, the research team could cross-check his remarks against whatever he had said before in that place or on that topic.

The Southern Poverty Law Center has adapted these techniques to the monitoring of hate groups. Researchers for the Center's Intelligence Project collect about a thousand newspaper articles each week and read many hate publications, which they get through disguised addresses. The researchers then enter the data into sophisticated databases for later reference. "What's garbage today is gold years later," the director of the Intelligence Project told *U.S. News & World Report*. "The trick is to catalog it, retrieve it, and collect the dots."[51]

Despite all the technological advances, some things do not change. In war and politics, decisionmakers still resist intelligence that conflicts with existing assumptions. Up to a point, such resistance is healthy, because it would be disastrous to go back to the drawing board every time a scrap of discrepant information came in. But assumptions can be blinders. Before Pearl Harbor, the American military assumed that the main threat to Hawai'i consisted of sabotage, so decisionmakers gave too little attention to signs of an impending air attack.[52] In the 1988 presidential race, the Dukakis camp had clear signs of the candidate's vulnerability on crime and other social issues. "We picked up the furlough thing very early," said one aide. But Dukakis, a product of the socially liberal Boston suburbs, assumed that these issues would have little impact. "In retrospect," said another aide, "I don't think he took them seriously enough."[53] As long as human beings are fallible and information is limited, such mistakes are a danger. Nevertheless, there are ways to reduce the chance of error.

First, by spelling out critical assumptions, leaders can make sure they are using the intelligence they have gathered to test their assumptions, instead of unconsciously using the assumptions to screen intelligence.[54]

Second, leaders have a better chance of getting good advice from those who have the standing to bring them bad news and who do not have a stake in prior decisions. Without a direct role in setting policy, the theory goes, the CIA has no incentive to bias its estimates in favor of the administration line. (Things have not always worked out that way, however.) In domestic politics, leaders need devil's advocates who can challenge their assumptions without fear of reprisal. A small circle of outsider advisers, or "kitchen cabinet," may serve this function.[55] A shrewd prince, said Machiavelli, should constantly question a select group of counselors, "and he should listen patiently to the truth regarding what he has inquired about. Moreover, if he finds that anyone for some reason holds the truth back he should show his wrath."[56]

Finally, leaders should remember that even perfect information about past events cannot supply a perfect forecast of the future. Whether in war or politics, no two battles are exactly alike: what worked in the past may fail in a slightly different setting. The other side learns from history, too, and may change its behavior accordingly. In conflict, said Clausewitz, "the will is directed at an animate object that *reacts*."[57] We return to this point in chapter 9. In the meantime, we shift our attention to the grittier topics of geography and logistics.

8

Geography and Logistics

In war, the victory does not always go to those having the largest army or the most sophisticated equipment. At the beginning of the Second World War, both the French and the British had tanks superior to those used by the Panzer Divisions. However, the Germans knew how to employ their weapons, while the Allied Forces did not. This lesson applies to political conflict as well.

—Fred Smith, "Learning the Washington Game" in Robert Rector and Michael Sanera, *Steering the Elephant*

In discussions of war or politics, it is tempting to consider only the grand sweep of great plans, overlooking the details that render them workable. Military scholar Martin Van Creveld says: "On the pages of military history books, armies frequently seem capable of moving in any direction at almost any speed and to almost any distance once their commanders have made up their minds to do so. In reality, they cannot, and failure to take cognizance of the fact has probably led to many more campaigns being ruined than ever were by enemy action."[1]

One day in 1959, Senator John F. Kennedy could have adapted these thoughts to his fledgling presidential campaign. Just before a speech in Superior, Wisconsin, he found that he was competing with a local high-school football game and that the hall was only one-third full. "Whenever you plan any appearances," he scolded his advance man, "make absolutely sure of the details. Don't ever, ever schedule another appearance until you know all the facts and you make sure every detail's been completed."[2] Things got better. Traveling with Kennedy in the fall of 1960, Theodore H. White described "the same complete efficiency that one remembers of the American bomber crews flying out of Tinian and Saipan against Japan in the concluding July and August weeks of the Pacific war."[3]

Those American crews, like successful warriors throughout history, won because of attention to geography and logistics. Geography consists of natural features such as rivers, climatic circumstances such as temperature, and artificial structures such as roads and buildings. It also includes human circumstances—that is, where different kinds of people live and work. Knowledge of geography, wrote Frederick the Great, "is to a general what a rifle is to an infantryman and what the rules of arithmetic are to a geometrician. If he does not know the country he will do nothing but make gross mistakes. . . . Therefore study the country where you are going to act!"[4]

Logistics concerns movement and supply: getting forces to the right places at the right times, and ensuring that they have the resources they need.[5] Everything else depends on logistics, because combat cannot happen unless the military provides troops with food, uniforms, and weapons, and then moves them to the battleground on time. Such tasks have a close relationship to geography. As Napoleon's troops learned during the Russian winter of 1812–13, different locales require different kinds of equipment and pose different challenges to supply lines.

Like warriors, political figures must heed geography and logistics. Recall from chapter 2 that political strategy depends on matching ends and means. Geography mingles with both. Our physical location often corresponds to the issues we care about and the outcomes we want; hence the old saw, "Where you stand depends on where you sit." As in the military, geography shapes logistics, for each locale has its own peculiar mix of problems and resources—what Roger Davidson and Walter Oleszek call "the political equivalent of microclimates."[6] It is costly to adapt to these varied settings, but it is costlier to ignore them, as JFK's advance man learned when he belatedly discovered the importance of high school football in small-town Wisconsin.

THE LOCUS OF CONFLICT

War always involves the movement of people and materiel across space: armies invade lands, navies take sea lanes, and air forces bomb targets. Political consultant Charles Lindauer draws a comparison to his field of work: "Every war room contains vital instruments for planning offensive and defensive tactics. The most important tool for any plan of attack is a map. At the onset of any military campaign, decision-makers are constantly reviewing maps to develop strategy, evaluate performance, identify strengths and compensate for weaknesses. Campaigns, polling and political analysis are no different."[7]

This observation holds true in ways both plain and subtle. Obviously, the basis of American political jurisdiction is territorial. As opposed to countries with centralized, unitary political systems, the United States has some eighty-five thousand governments, including states, counties, cities, towns, and various districts. Each has its own boundaries, which determine who joins which political battles, and which themselves cause conflict. Annexation is a hot local issue, because many a cash-strapped city craves the suburbs' tax base, just as Russian czars coveted a warm-water port. Suburbanites often balk, viewing urban politicians as the modern equivalent of Cossacks. Elsewhere, neighborhoods want to secede from cities or counties as a way of rejecting bureaucratic leviathans.[8] Annexations and secessions always affect the power of groups and individuals. Politicians can "capture" friendly voters by shifting municipal lines, as Indianapolis Mayor Richard Lugar did in 1969, when he persuaded the Indiana Legislature to consolidate the city and its Republican suburbs. The purported goal was to broaden the city tax base, but the consolidation also strengthened the GOP's grip on City Hall.

Every ten years, new census figures mean new district boundaries for the U.S. House and the state legislatures, as well as many city councils and county boards. According to Rob Richie, executive director of the Center for Voting and Democracy, "If you control the process of drawing the lines, if you have the power to shape the map to your party's advantage, you have an opportunity to control the outcome of elections for the next decade."[9] Although scholars disagree on whether or not redistricting systematically favors either party, it surely has a profound impact on local voting blocs such as minority communities.[10] Accordingly, voting-rights litigation usually arises, forcing judges to immerse themselves in political map-making.

Presidential races have a territorial basis, too. All the states have their own primaries or caucuses, and candidates set up organizations for each. In the fall campaign, nominees fight for electoral votes state by state, choosing which to target and which to concede. Democratic strategist David Wilhelm explained how these considerations drove the Clinton 1992 bus tour: "The line that I was drawing on the map was the Mississippi River and the Ohio River. It always seemed to me that this region was our key for electoral college strategy, that we could win states along both sides of both rivers. . . . [The bus trip] allowed us to go to key showdown states. . . . And as it turned out, we won every single state along the bus trip."[11]

From the presidential level on down, candidates and campaign operatives use military language to describe political territory. Areas in doubt are "battlegrounds," while those that favor one side are "strongholds," "fortresses," or "the high ground." An organizational presence in hostile country is a "beachhead" or "bridgehead." When the fighting is hard and the likely gains are meager, there is talk of "trench warfare."

Policy issues have a geography of their own, for many decisions are mainly about location. Residents of a town or city work with their elected officials to attract "pork barrel" projects, such as parks and post offices, that bring local benefits at the expense of the larger public. Conversely, they fight "bile barrel" projects, such as landfills and toxic-waste treatment plants, that serve the general good but distress their immediate neighborhoods.[12] Bile-barrel politics is fierce. People in the affected area will fight the project with every possible weapon, including restrictive zoning ordinances, environmental-impact challenges, and Alinsky-inspired civil disobedience.

More generally, the politics of environment and natural resources is a politics of place. Regulations on smog are vital in the Los Angeles basin, whereas acid rain is a more pressing concern in the Adirondacks. The Bureau of Land Management looms large in Nevada, 80 percent of which belongs to the federal government, but has only a trifling presence in Iowa, where federal land covers less than 1 percent of the state.[13]

Natural disasters become political crises, and each part of the country has its own catalog of catastrophe. In the Frost Belt, the careers of elected executives may hinge on their response to winter weather emergencies. Mayor Michael Bilandic of Chicago failed to clear the city streets after a major snowstorm, so Democratic primary voters rejected him in 1979. Tornadoes in the Plains states, hurricanes in the Gulf region, heat waves in Texas, and earthquakes in California have all created political problems and opportunities unique to their regions.

Such linkages seem clear. What is less obvious is that most other issues have geographic components. Whatever the subject matter, the impact of public policies will vary from place to place, and so will their base of political support.[14] Except for gender, no important demographic characteristic has a uniform geographical spread, so states and localities differ in their distributions of age, income, education, occupation, and ethnicity. Policies to benefit poor people will concentrate expenditures in rundown areas and provide little direct help to affluent districts. Education assistance will flow to places with numerous children and bypass retirement communities.

Even the politics of foreign policy and national security has a local accent.[15] Policies on international economics meet with diverse reactions, ranging from the protectionism of the Rust Belt to the free-trade enthusiasm of Midwestern farmlands. Support for the armed forces runs high in areas surrounding large military bases. And ethnic communities will take a strong interest in policy toward their ancestral countries: Chicago's Poles supported Solidarity, Cleveland's Serbs questioned the Kosovo bombing, and Miami's Cubans continue to oppose Castro.

Those who make major decisions on campaign strategy or public policy need to consider geography. They should beware of stereotypes, though, because few places are completely homogeneous in their physical, human, or political geography.[16] New Jersey may seem the quintessential Northeastern urban state, but agriculture is important in its southern counties, which reach below the Mason-Dixon line. Political figures have to understand such nuances, adjusting their plans accordingly.

TERRAIN AND TECHNIQUE

Geography shapes combat. It is hard to wage war on tundras, high mountain ranges, and wastelands far from the sea, so with few exceptions (e.g., Kashmir), generals avoid such terrain.[17] They prefer battlegrounds that lie within range of a friendly base, allow for mobility and resupply, and have bearable weather.

Eisenhower had such things on his mind when drafting strategy for the invasion of Europe during World War II. Though reasonably close to Britain, Holland would have made a poor choice for landings because its rivers and canals could have blocked an Allied advance.[18] The Pas de Calais offered the shortest sea route, but it also featured heavy German defenses and flat beaches unsuitable for landing craft. Eisenhower decided that Normandy was a better site, even though it posed daunting challenges of its own.

In politics, strategic and tactical decisions often pertain to points in space. When planning demonstrations, protest movements give careful thought to which location will send the most vivid image to the greatest number of people. As mentioned in chapter 5, the leaders of the Southern Christian Leadership Conference targeted Birmingham, Alabama, in 1963 because they knew that city government would overreact and bare its segregationist teeth.

Locational choices are especially crucial in election campaigns. Consultant Charles Lindauer says: "Detailed routes of Tomahawk cruise missiles are pre-programmed to optimize a successful target hit. Without these guidance systems, the bombs may stray off course. One can exercise the same logic with campaign walking maps."[19] By using detailed maps showing the likely location of supporters, opponents, and undecideds, a campaign can find the most effective target areas for door-to-door canvasses and get-out-the-vote efforts. On a larger scale, campaigns use maps to decide where to buy advertising. Not only can they focus on swing voters, but they can tailor their message to specific audiences. They must use this technique with care, however, lest a message for one constituency stray off course and offend another. In his 1998 reelection campaign, Senator Alfonse D'Amato (R-NY) bombarded upstate New York television market with ads that morphed New York City Democrats into sharks swimming north to devour the upstaters' tax money. Democrats turned the ad against D'Amato by denouncing it in the downstate news media.[20]

Candidates spend much of their time traveling from one place to another to make appearances. Even when these events serve mainly as a backdrop for news coverage, choice of location still matters because campaigns want to pick places where their supporters can turn out friendly crowds. Representative Morris Udall (D-AZ), running for the 1976 Democratic presidential nomination, wanted to have a campaign event in Philadelphia's inner city. His advance woman later described what happened: "A walk into a ghetto and then a rally. The local person who was going to run the routes or give us the directions gave us the wrong directions. We were out of money but we didn't want to tell the press so we billed it as a day of local transportation. We took the wrong subway and then got on the wrong bus and wound up in the wrong ghetto. The rally was not there."[21]

This example leads to the next point: failure to anticipate the terrain can have harmful consequences. Once the Allies started to make headway after D-Day, they found that their planners had not prepared them for the Normandy hedgerows. Earthen dikes averaging about four feet high and covered with hedges and trees, the hedgerows sprawled over much of the countryside, providing cover to the Germans and slowing the invasion.[22] The

Allies eventually developed tactics and equipment for hedgerow fighting, but only after taking many casualties.

Problems such as the botched Philadelphia rally are practically inevitable in the chaos of a campaign, a phenomenon discussed further in chapter 9. Other errors are less forgivable. Political operatives often proffer advice without even the most basic knowledge of the terrain. In the 1960s, an East Coast consulting firm urged a California candidate to walk out onto a freeway on a smoggy morning. The consultants said that he "can carry a flashlight as he approaches voters to ask for their votes; he can campaign on the Freeways passing out literature while the cars are stalled bumper to bumper."[23] These consultants did not know that:

- California law bans pedestrians from freeways;
- California motorists hate solicitations;
- California smog is different from Northeastern fog.

If the smog were thick enough to require flashlights, people would be dying in droves.

Like campaign consultants, policymakers need to check their geography, because programs that work in one place may run aground elsewhere. In the 1960s, the Economic Development Administration carried out an ambitious program to create jobs for the hard-core unemployed in Oakland, California. The agency's experience, however, mainly involved depressed areas such as Appalachia, where need was so widespread that bureaucrats did not have to worry about targeting. Oakland, in contrast, was a depressed city in an otherwise prosperous region. Instead of going to Oakland's poorest, the new jobs went to middle-class commuters with attractive résumés.[24]

Nowhere in public policy is knowledge of the terrain more vital than in bile-barrel politics. Without a thorough knowledge of the social and physical lay of the land, policymakers will probably fail in any attempt to site an obnoxious facility. One might think, for instance, that sparsely populated deserts would make ideal locations for nuclear waste. Yet whenever such proposals come up, it quickly becomes evident that small desert towns can become effective political opponents, especially when they join forces with outside activists to document risks to the desert ecosystem.

"THE TRADITION IS THE TERRAIN"

In a 1940 book called the *Small Wars Manual*, the Marine Corps reminded expeditionary forces to look beneath the surface and learn about "the traits peculiar to the persons with whom we are dealing. The individual characteristics as well as the national psychology are subjects for intensive study." It stressed that human geography is full of landmines: "A failure to use tact when required or lack of firmness at a crucial moment might readily precipitate a situation that could have been avoided had the commander been familiar with the customs, religion, morals, and education of the people with whom he was dealing."[25] Faced with low-intensity conflicts around the world, the Marines continue to apply these lessons. In 1995, Lieutenant General Anthony Zinni listed key questions to ask in unfamiliar territory: "Who makes decisions in this culture? What is the power of religious leaders? Of political people? Of professionals?"[26]

Saul Alinsky asked similar questions, teaching radical organizers to learn the local power structure, get a feel for local sentiment, and speak the vernacular of the people they were seeking to rally. "Just as knowledge of the terrain is of utmost importance for military tactics in actual warfare," he wrote, "so too is the knowledge, the full understanding and appreciation of the power of local traditions. The first maxim in conflict tactics to all leaders of People's Organizations is that *the tradition is the terrain*" (emphasis in original).[27]

In the United States, that terrain is complex. Each state and locality has a unique political culture that molds attitudes toward government ethics, party competition, campaign style, and the appropriate role of public policy. In New York State, party organizations still matter, and remnants of old-style patronage have survived legal challenge. Politicians wield power with a bluntness verging on ruthlessness, and they tolerate practices that would elsewhere seem corrupt.[28] In California, parties exist mainly on paper, and patronage is scarce. With a huge and mobile population, the state's distinguishing mark is anonymity. As one politician put it in 1964: "Out here our people are lost. In California they read about their neighbors only in the papers."[29] Alinsky organizers, who do their best work with well-established neighborhoods, have a rough time in such terrain.[30]

TO KNOW THE GROUND

The "terrain walk" or "staff ride" is a common military training practice. Officers will study a past engagement and then visit the battlefield for firsthand knowledge of its geographical context. During the Cold War, American commanders in West Germany would undertake terrain walks of potential battlegrounds, places where they thought the Soviet Union might strike. They would then write "battle books" telling exactly how they would defend the ground in question.[31]

Radical political activists also believe in good reconnaissance. The Ruckus Society, which aids direct-action causes, has an online "scouting manual" that tells leaders how to assess the physical and social characteristics of potential action sites. The manual advises protesters to stock up on measuring tape for factory-gate blockades and on light meters "for those real early morning actions."[32]

Ron Faucheux, editor of *Campaigns & Elections*, urges similar exercises for political candidates. His emphasis is less on the physical characteristics of the terrain than on the social characteristics that should inform the candidate's strategy and message: "Ride the roads and streets; check out the neighborhoods and businesses; learn where parks, playgrounds, churches, schools and shopping areas are located. Have someone drive you around for several days, or longer if necessary, with map and notebook in hand. Jot down your observations about the residents and landmarks. Give some flesh to polling and demographic data."[33]

This course of study is useful even for those who have lived in the constituency for a long time. During day-to-day life, one will ignore a multitude of details that become vital during a political campaign. In 1985, Edd Hargett, a Republican candidate in a special election for the House from Texas, inflicted a fatal wound on himself by saying, "I don't know what trade policies have to do with bringing jobs to East Texas."[34] Had he spent more time walking around, he would have known that local unemployment was high and that many residents blamed foreign competition.

Legislative leaders need to know their members' constituencies, and chairing a campaign committee is an excellent way to gain such familiarity. House Speaker Tip O'Neill (D-MA) recalled his experience as the Democratic campaign chief: "I had to learn about every congressional district in America, the ethnic, economic and party characteristics of each and the strength of our candidates in each." Visiting the districts, he said, helped him understand his colleagues: "On these trips, I learned what made these members tick and how secure they were, so when I asked them to support a Democratic Party position, I knew how far I could ask them to go. I could handle them."[35]

Though he had not headed a campaign committee, Speaker Sam Rayburn (D-TX) intimately knew his members' districts and understood their political needs. When one colleague falsely claimed that he could not support a party position because of district pressure, the Speaker erupted: "You could have voted with me. I've known that district since before you were born, and that vote wouldn't have hurt you one bit. Not one bit. You didn't vote with me because you didn't have the guts to."[36] Rayburn then drove him out of politics.

Sun Tzu wrote, "Those who do not use local guides are unable to obtain the advantages of the ground."[37] Armies make use of friendly locals, and so do political campaigns. In presidential nomination politics, governors are especially important as local guides, for three reasons. First, they usually have a stronger political organization than any other state figure. Second, they have access to the local news media and can serve as spokespeople for the campaign. Third, as Lee Atwater said, governors "know the bends in the river" and can guide candidates to places where they can gain advantage while steering them away from trouble spots.[38] At a crucial moment in the 1988 New Hampshire primary, the Bush campaign produced an attack ad accusing rival candidate Bob Dole of "straddling" on the tax issue. Bush worried that the ad might backfire, but Governor John Sununu convinced him that it would appeal to the state's anti-tax sentiment. Sununu then used his close relationship with the operators of a local television station to substitute this ad for other Bush spots that were already on the schedule.[39]

Interest groups use local guides, too. When they deal with a state government, they need employees or contract lobbyists who know the folkways and formal procedures of the state capital. That lore is important because no two states are alike. In Texas, the lieutenant governor dominates the state senate, while in New Jersey the office does not even exist. In some states, the legislative leaders are the key combatants, whereas in others the committee chairs are more powerful. Lobbyists have to know such things, along with the personal and political histories of the people with whom they deal.

Local help is essential in influencing legislators, both in the states and in Congress. Interest groups often engage in "grass-roots lobbying" by peppering lawmakers with letters, phone calls, and emails from their constituencies. "Grasstops lobbying," an increasingly frequent tactic, involves persuading influential figures within the district to approach the member directly.[40] Either approach will fail if the lawmaker sees it as contrived "astroturf." The sentiments must be real—and to mobilize people with these sentiments, the interest group needs professionals who know the territory.

S. L. A. Marshall said that "the reason why action does not always conform to logic is that many headquarters people become strangers to the front and cannot speak its language or understand its tribulations."[41] Local guides will do little good if the headquarters people ignore them. In 1976, when the leaders of Gerald Ford's election campaign tried to run the New Hampshire primary effort from Washington, a local operative said: "I guess you might say we're trying here to win the hearts and minds of people. . . . As in Vietnam, the generals aren't always the ones who know the most about local pacification."[42]

LOGISTICS

"Military officers like to say that amateurs study strategy—experts study logistics," wrote reporter John Broder after Bob Dole's poor early showings in the 1996 primary season. Even though the opposition had won some ground, Dole was ready to fight for delegates in every state, and his foes were not. "The logistic challenges of the coming battles favor Dole virtually everywhere."[43]

Logistics is about getting and using scarce resources. The Marine Corps says that it includes "any action that serves to transport a military force from one place to another, provide it with the physical means of waging war, or preserve its combat power for subsequent employment."[44] Logistics alone cannot win a war: one can point to many armies that lost in spite of strong material advantages. But failure to take account of logistics can ensure defeat. Without adequate food, fuel, and equipment, military forces simply lack the means to fight.

Logistics begins with time and money. "In military operations," said the Duke of Wellington, "time is everything."[45] Leaders have a fighting chance only if they have time to assemble the necessary troops and equipment. Movements have to match weather and lighting. If they occur at the wrong moment, conditions will be too dark (if the forces need visibility), too bright (if they need cover), too dry (if they need high tides for amphibious landing), or too wet (if they need to use dirt roads). If forces reach the battlefield too late, the enemy can destroy them "in detail"— that is, one by one. Accordingly, officers always watch the calendar and the clock.

Political figures share this concern. Senator Jacob Javits (R-NY) often drew upon his Army training, which taught him the method of "backtiming," which consists of "deciding where you wanted to be at what date and hour, and with what forces and equipment, and planning back from that objective."[46] Though major political leaders are sometimes tardy about their appointments, they need subordinates who make sure that important tasks (e.g., the filing of papers) take place on schedule. But timing matters in a more basic way. Just as there are certain moments when lighting, weather, and tides combine to make an invasion possible, so there are times when public opinion and the other elements of politics open a window of opportunity for passing a bill or launching a candidacy. Able leaders seize such opportunities, as LBJ did when he passed Great Society legislation in the aftermath of his 1964 landslide victory.

As for money, King Archidamus of Sparta put it best in 432 B.C.E.: "And war is not so much a matter of armaments as of the money which makes armaments effective."[47] In politics, many observers equate money with armaments, referring to the competition for campaign funds as an "arms race." When a reporter asked President Clinton why he continued to raise soft money while seeking to ban it, he replied: "I do. I plead guilty to that. I don't believe in unilateral disarmament."[48] Budgets supply power in public policy issues as well, and agencies fight constant battles to maintain their warchests.

FIGHTING WASTE AND HASTE

Aggregate spending levels, however, supply an incomplete picture of logistics. In every realm of human endeavor, individuals and organizations manage to snatch defeat from the jaws of victory by squandering resources. Although many tales of Pentagon waste have turned out to be inaccurate, there is little question that much of the defense budget has gone to pork instead of readiness. In domestic politics, similarly, there is no reason to expect that money always means results. Although few scholars have systematically studied the subject, it seems likely that the pressures of political campaigns lead to waste.

Occasionally, the waste consists of failure to use resources. An electoral battle differs from combat in one crucial respect: it ends at a certain date. Therefore, although it makes sense for a general to keep a reserve, a campaign should spend everything by election day. In 1964, the Goldwater campaign and the Republican committees finished with a huge surplus. In 1976, the Ford campaign was so scrupulous about not exceeding its $21.8 million federal allotment that it left about $1 million unspent.[49]

More frequently, though, campaigns go too far in the other direction. "A candidate cannot experiment," wrote Stimson Bullitt. "He must act promptly on limited information, as though he were an officer in battle, taking his troops over a hill when he does not know what is on the other side." There is pressure to use everything at once, from broadcast ads to billboards: "No one dares omit any approach. Every cartridge must be fired because among the multitude of blanks one may be a bullet."[50]

Amid the haste and uncertainty, politicians may fire their cartridges at the wrong targets. In his 1960 presidential campaign, Richard Nixon promised to campaign in all fifty states. The basic premise seemed sensible at the time, because every electoral vote could count in a close race. But Nixon overlooked the logistical costs of taking a campaign entourage to all fifty states—especially the new states of Alaska and Hawai`i. In keeping his promise, he diverted time and money from places where campaigning might have had much more impact, especially Illinois and Texas.

In the military, headquarters staffs may take resources that would go to better use at the front. The same thing happens in politics. Edward N. Costikyan, a leader of New York City's Reform Democrats, once wrote: "Beware of large headquarters. Don't spend money just because you have it, or because someone says 'we need it,' or because it's traditional. Above all, keep your mind on one question: 'How many votes do you think *that* expenditure, *that* program, *that* office, *that* mailing will produce?'"[51]

S. L. A. Marshall wrote: "When forces are committed to combat, it is vital that not one unnecessary pound be put on any man's back. Lightness of foot is the key to speed of movement and the increase of firepower."[52] In electoral politics, lightness of foot can help an underfunded cause outmaneuver bigger, slower opponents. But as Gary Hart explained, it is difficult to sustain this edge. An insurgent campaign for a party nomination, he said, can move "like a guerrilla army," but once the campaign moves into the general election, it "requires heavy machinery and an unwieldy apparatus, particularly when the campaign must perform healing, ministerial, and ambassadorial functions within the party itself while trying to win an election."[53]

Attention to detail can yield psychological benefits. According to the Marine Corps, "By displaying economy, adaptability, fairness, flexibility, and innovation, a logistics system can foster the sense that those in charge know what they are doing. In other words, good logistics reinforces the moral authority of leaders."[54] As we saw chapter 3, generals can bolster their troops' loyalty by tending to their needs. Political leaders also find that morale improves when the operation works as efficiently as possible. Even if there are not enough funds, computers, or copiers to go around, the troops will appreciate knowing that their leaders are doing their best with whatever they have.

CUTTING OFF THE ENEMY'S SUPPLIES

Machiavelli wrote that it is better to subdue the enemy "by famine than by sword."[55] Politicians, like warriors, must disrupt the opposition's logistics.

Political figures have many ways to follow this advice. One rests on the assumption that there is a finite pool of money available for campaign contributions, so a dollar that goes to one campaign is a dollar that is not available to its opponents. Presidential candidates may start running early not only to fill their own warchests but to deny those funds to potential rivals. As Democratic consultant Bob Beckel said in 1987, "The front-runner should be using this time to pick up endorsements, raise money and cut off the supply lines for his opponents."[56] Texas Governor George W. Bush used that approach in the early days of the race for the 2000 Republican presidential nomination. Said fundraiser and Bush supporter Wayne Berman, "It basically means that the air supply has been shut off to all the second-tier candidates."[57]

Intimidation is another variation on the theme. The power to reward friends and punish foes is also the power to deter others from backing opponents. In 1986, Democratic Congressional Campaign Committee chair Tony Coelho (D-CA) put it baldly: "We're going to be the majority party for a long time, so it doesn't make good business sense to give to Republicans."[58] When the House GOP took the majority in the 1990s, Republican whip Tom "The Hammer" DeLay sent similar messages to the PAC community.

The 1998 California "paycheck protection" initiative illustrates two other ways of attacking opposition supplies. This ballot measure would have forbidden unions in the state from using a member's dues for political purposes unless he or she had given express permission. Although its ostensible aim was to protect worker rights, Republicans and business groups supported it as a way of reducing the unions' campaign contributions, most of which went to Democrats. "This is a war for them, and they are following the admonition of the old Zulu warrior battle cry: Leave your enemies dead behind you," said Art Pulaski, executive secretary-treasurer of the California Labor Federation, AFL-CIO. "That is their purpose, and that is their goal."[59] Supporters also hoped that their initiative would force unions to spend vast sums in an effort to defeat it, thereby diverting their resources from Democratic coffers. In the end, the measure lost. As it turned out, Democratic fundraising was so strong that year that the diversion of resources had little effect.

Office-holders have also used the government's power of the purse. For years, conservative activists have argued that many liberal individuals and groups use federal money for political purposes, both directly and indirectly. In the mid-1990s, conservative activists such as Grover Norquist called on Republican lawmakers to target purportedly left-leaning agencies such as the National Endowment for the Arts. That way, said Norquist in 1995, the GOP would be "making its opponents on the left a little smaller and poorer."[60] Although these agencies survived the attack, they left the battlefield with less money than a Democratic majority would have appropriated.

Within legislative bodies, majorities may seek to deny resources either to the minority party or to rival factions. In New York, mutual partisan gerrymandering has given Republicans a lock on the State Senate and Democrats a lock on the State Assembly. In each chamber, the majority has routinely refused to supply basic office necessities to the minority. In 1999, the research staff of the Assembly Republicans had to make do with mid-1980s computers that could not use up-to-date software, much less access the Internet.[61] And when Republicans took control of the House in 1994, incoming Speaker Newt Gingrich moved to stop official funding for more than two dozen congressional caucuses. Though Gingrich defended the cut as a management-efficiency move, it just happened to strike at groups that were critical of the GOP, such as the Congressional Black Caucus. It also wiped out the Republican Study Committee, an in-house think tank that could have supplied staff support for anti-Gingrich conservatives.

In short, political figures try to make life difficult for their opponents. As we shall see in chapter 9, political life is difficult enough.

9

Friction and Finality

Rely on planning but never trust plans.
—Dwight Eisenhower
in Fred I. Greenstein, *The Hidden-Hand Presidency*

Thoughtless use of military metaphors can encourage certain myths about American politics. One is the "Desert Storm" myth—namely, that if political figures only had the skill and grit of a Norman Schwarzkopf, they could carry out their plans with the effectiveness that U.S. forces showed in the Persian Gulf War. Right after the conflict, GOP lawmakers bought into this notion when they called on President Bush to launch an Operation "Domestic Storm."

The "V-E Day" myth holds that it is always possible to win a "final" victory, to settle major issues "once and for all," just as the United States did at the end of World War II. Party leaders often succumb to this myth in the aftermath of a major election victory, thinking that they will make a "new beginning" and usher in a golden age.

Study of Carl von Clausewitz can help us see through both myths. "Everything in war is very simple, but the simplest thing is difficult," he wrote. "The difficulties accumulate and end by producing a kind of friction that is inconceivable unless one has experienced war."[1] Friction, he stressed, sets real war apart from war on paper. On a battle map, getting from point A to point B merely requires the drawing of a straight line. On a battlefield, countless problems get in the way: jammed weapons, flooded roads, and misunderstood orders. It is fitting that one term for such events—"snafu"—is an informal army acronym for "Situation normal: All fouled up." Sometimes friction can supply the stuff of military comedies, but it can also cause military catastrophe. American unreadiness at Pearl Harbor resulted from a long chain of botches, the last of which came when a radar operator mistook the Japanese attack force for U.S. aircraft.

What of winning "conclusive" victory? Clausewitz taught that "even the ultimate outcome of a war is not always to be regarded as final."[2] Victory in a military struggle often creates the conditions for further conflict, and possibly future defeat. Among other things, the winning side may face internal divisions over the spoils while the losing side nurses its resentments and draws lessons for the future. "Never again" is a common battle cry for those who have just lost a war.

Wise political veterans understand how these ideas work in their world. While valuing diligence and forethought, they know that they must live with friction. Having witnessed cycles of triumph and disaster, they resist both exaltation and depression. Longtime Kennedy aide and Democratic National Committee chair Lawrence O'Brien thus entitled his memoirs *No Final Victories*.

There are many reasons why political war is so messy and open-ended. Some of these reasons reflect human nature, whereas others stem from the peculiar features of American political institutions.

THE FOG OF WAR

Clausewitz taught that military action takes place "in a kind of twilight, which, like fog or moonlight, often tends to make things seem grotesque and larger than they really are."[3] Despite the most careful intelligence operations, each side may surprise the other (and itself) by showing unexpected courage or by seizing a sudden opportunity. So many things happen so fast that a commander cannot digest them all. For the ground troops, there is no "big picture," just noise, smoke, and explosions that spray blood and body parts. In the chaos, warriors may have only the vaguest sense of place and direction. Frequently, they lose their way and find themselves in enemy hands.

Political wars may lack physical terror, but they can be just as confusing. Large operations such as running for national office or passing a comprehensive budget plan may involve too many components for leaders to keep in sight. During his 1981 fight for President Reagan's economic plan, Budget Director David Stockman said: "None of us really understands what's going on with all these numbers. You've got so many different budgets out and so many different baselines and such complexity now in the interactive parts of the budget between policy action and the economic environment and all the internal mysteries of the budget, and there are a lot of them. People are getting from A to B and it's not clear how they're getting there."[4]

Political leaders often run short of time and energy to clear their own minds. Serious policy arguments "tend to get lost in the fog of war on Capitol Hill," wrote journalist Richard E. Cohen in 1984. "Many lawmakers complain that they have little time to think or to talk constructively with their colleagues during their often overscheduled three-day Washington workweek. And weary staffers use their Fridays and Mondays to catch their breath and to prepare for the next battle."[5]

In both war and politics, the fog may give rise to "friendly fire." It seems obvious that soldiers should refrain from firing their weapons in certain places, lest they hit their own comrades. Yet nothing is so clear in combat. General H. Norman Schwarzkopf says: "The very chaotic nature of the battlefield, where quick decisions make the difference between life and death, has resulted in numerous incidents of troops being killed by their own fires in every war that this nation has fought."[6] At the Civil War battle of Chancellorsville, Confederate General Stonewall Jackson was riding in semi-darkness when his own troops mistook him for an enemy cavalryman and shot him.

The political equivalent occurs when a verbal attack on the opposition ends up spilling one's own blood. In 1884, a prominent Republican minister failed to get the word that GOP presidential nominee James G. Blaine was courting Irish Catholics in New York. At a public meeting, the minister greeted Blaine by damning the Democrats as the party of "Rum, Romanism, and Rebellion" (alcoholism, the Roman Catholic Church, and the Confederacy). Blaine missed the comment, so he made no effort to control the damage. When the news got out, so many Irish voters switched sides that Blaine lost the state and the election.

LACK OF GENIUS

Through sheer instinct, a leader with the quality of *coup d'oeil* (see chapter 3) may overcome the fog. Churchill explained why the fog usually prevails: "Nothing but genius, the daemon in man, can answer the riddles of war. . . . In default of genius, nations have to make war as best they can, and since that quality is much rarer than the largest and purest diamonds, most wars are mainly tales of muddle."[7] The Crimean War was one such tale. Heading British forces was Field Marshal Lord Raglan, a rich and well-connected man who did not have the experience to command such a large effort. At a crucial point during the Battle of Balaklava (1854), Raglan gave the order for a reckless cavalry charge. Misunderstanding the order, his subordinates made things worse by attacking the Russians at their strongest point. The result was an appalling British death toll and an enduring catch-phrase for futility: the Charge of the Light Brigade.[8]

In politics, key jobs may fall to mediocre people because of wealth, seniority, inertia, or bad judgment on the part of those who choose them. President Eisenhower probably thought of Churchill's "tales of muddle" whenever he dealt with his party's leadership on Capitol Hill. In the House, GOP leader Joe Martin of Massachusetts had lingered on past his prime. Though Eisenhower respected Martin's integrity, he privately complained that "it was almost impossible to get him to understand any subtle suggestions."[9] On the Senate side, William Knowland of California irked Eisenhower with his strident support for the Nationalist Chinese and his insensitivity to public opinion. "In his case," Eisenhower wrote in his diary, "there seems to be no final answer to the question, 'How stupid can you get?'"[10]

After losing majorities in 1954 and failing to recapture them in the Eisenhower landslide of 1956, the congressional GOP suffered massive setbacks in 1958. Frustrated House Republicans sacked Martin. Knowland had left the Senate voluntarily, figuring that he could win the governorship of California as a launching pad for a presidential candidacy. Characteristically, he bungled the move. First, he forced incumbent Republican governor Goodwin Knight to step aside and run for the Senate seat he himself was vacating, a job swap that struck many voters as crass. Second, he supported an anti-union ballot measure that created a backlash among pro-union voters. The ensuing surge in Democratic turnout helped defeat both Knowland and Knight.

ILLNESS AND FATIGUE

The most commonplace human experiences—falling ill and get-ting tired—have had a significant impact on history. Until this century, disease often killed more warriors than combat. Sick-ness has also claimed lives by impairing commanders. Historians speculate that hemorrhoids distracted Napoleon at Waterloo and that Robert E. Lee suffered mental lapses at Gettysburg because of undiagnosed heart disease.

A more common cause of military error, especially in recent decades, is fatigue. War has always been an exhausting affair, even more so since technology has allowed for round-the-clock combat. At all levels, warriors feel pressure to stay awake nearly all the time. Beyond a certain point, the resulting fatigue can lead to lethargy, loss of emotional control, and failure of judgment. In the 1942 naval battle of Savo Island, Japanese warships off Guadalcanal sank one Australian and three American cruisers. Few Americans fired weapons, so the Japanese sustained little damage. Although anyone on deck could have seen the Japanese vessels, sleep-deprived sailors failed to spot them in time, and then reacted hesitantly. More than a thousand died.[11]

Presidents get sick and tired, too. During his 1961 Vienna summit with Nikita Khrushchev, John Kennedy was in pain from his chronic back problems, and he may also have been taking mood-altering drugs.[12] In face-to-face meetings, he came across as shallow and unprepared, an impression that encouraged Khrushchev to become more aggressive toward the United States. A dozen years later, Richard Nixon was recovering from viral pneumonia just as the Watergate tapes became public. Though some advisers urged him to burn the tapes, Nixon heeded others who assured him that the courts would take his side: "Most of my friends and even some of my critics agree that I made the wrong decision. If I had been up to par physically, there is certainly a chance that I would have stepped up to the issue and ordered the tapes destroyed."[13] In 1991 and 1992, George Bush suffered from Graves' disease, a thyroid ailment that left him worn out and moody—feelings that spread throughout his reelection campaign.[14]

In politics, the hours can be long and punishing. George Stephanopoulos remembers the Clinton White House: "A lot of the mistakes we made in the first weeks were because we were so tired."[15] Sleep deprivation is abundant at the end of congressional and state legislative sessions, when lawmakers work late to make their last-minute deals. Petty arguments break out. More significantly, the bleary-eyed lawmakers may overlook important legislative details that they would otherwise catch.

MADISONIAN FRICTION

The constitutional system makes political warfare more difficult than politicians would like. With words that recall Clausewitz, Justice Louis Brandeis once explained: "The purpose was not to avoid friction, but, by means of the inevitable friction incident to the distribution of governmental powers among three departments, to save the people from autocracy."[16] James Madison knew that good government required thoughtful deliberation and virtuous officials, but he also understood that ambitious politicians would try to grab too much power. The separation of powers, he argued, would thwart them. In *The Federalist*, he built his case with military metaphors:

> The provision for defense must in this, as in all other cases, be made commensurate to the danger of attack . . . that the private interest of every individual, may be a centinel [*sic*] over the public rights. . . . But it is not possible to give each department an equal power of self-defense. . . . As the weight of the legislative authority requires that it

should be thus divided, the weakness of the executive may require, on the other hand, that it should be fortified.[17]

Each branch has its own institutional perspectives, which cause friction between the president and members of Congress, even if they belong to the same party. Political analysts often refer to lawmakers of the party currently in the White House as "the president's troops on Capitol Hill." The phrase is inaccurate. Although the president has some leverage over lawmakers, the Founders denied him the power to dismiss or demote them. A better term would be "the president's uneasy allies."

When the president's party has a majority in Congress, the party's lawmakers may feel some accountability for results. But this sentiment is no guarantee of unified action. When the president's partisans are in the congressional minority, additional problems crop up. In this case, the president's party on Capitol Hill is like a superpower's weak ally, simultaneously fearing the common opponent and worrying that the bigger country will sell it out. (Think of the United States and South Vietnam.) The smaller country will often turn uncooperative, if only to show its independence. When the GOP was in the minority during the 1980s, Representative Jerry Lewis (R-CA) said, "As for influencing what happens inside the House, we have just enough votes to be irresponsible."[18] Such an attitude brings the minority into direct conflict with the president, who must cooperate with the majority party in order to pass legislation. As Representative Vin Weber (R-MN) explained, "What is good for the president may well be good for the country, but it is not necessarily good for congressional Republicans."[19]

A president's quest for a second term may worsen the friction. The president and the congressional party might be employing different strategies in different wars with different purposes. In the 1996 campaign, a top Democratic congressional staffer complained to the Clinton White House: "Forget winning forty-nine states, even forty-four states, and reallocate your money into states that'll help us."[20] The Clinton forces took the advice too late and too lightly, so Republicans held the House.

Discussing multilateral alliances, Clausewitz said that "political unity is a matter of degree. The question then is whether each state is pursuing an independent interest and has its own independent means for doing so, or whether the interests and forces of most of the allies are subordinate to those of the leader."[21] In the constitutional structure, friction arises not just because the House and Senate are independent of the president, but also because they are independent of each other. As Newt Gingrich said in 1980, "Just electing a party in both branches is not enough. . . . They can all wear the same uniform, and run in opposite directions."[22] Clinton learned this lesson when his 1993 economic-stimulus package went down to defeat. "The stimulus debacle also intensified friction between House and Senate Democrats, whose cooperation Clinton must have to pass his program," the *Washington Post* reported. "House members accused senators of succumbing too easily to Republican tactics of obstruction and Senate Democrats said House members set the stage for obstruction by demanding too much."[23]

A party may have a majority in one chamber and a minority in the other. In this case, philosophical kinship will often give way to the conflict between a majority outlook, which emphasizes governance, and a minority outlook, which emphasizes position-taking. This is what happened to congressional Republicans between 1981 and 1987. In a 1984 interview, Senator Bob Dole (R-KS) explained: "In the Senate, where we have a majority, we have less freedom to run around and stake out positions of our own. We're supporting the president's position; we have to think of votes. . . . While we're passing the legislation, they're [the House's Gingrich faction] looking around for new ideas."[24] The *Washington Post* described this conflict as a "verbal civil war."

Internal conflict may roil each party caucus in each chamber. Unlike systems in which national parties can pick candidates for Parliament, the American electoral system has a local basis. Members answer to their constituents and supporters first, and to legislative leaders second. From this angle, American parties sometimes look like the armies of medieval Europe.

Soldiers of the Middle Ages obviously had a stake in victory, since defeat would mean death or captivity. But in this pre-firearm era, a battle usually turned into a set of individual fights as men-at-arms met their enemies with swords, daggers, maces, and battleaxes. More than that, warriors engaged in "single combat" in order to show off their prowess and grab their share of the loot.[25] Like the soldiers of Agincourt, American politicians go to battle with mixed motives. They want their side to win, all other things being equal, but must also fight their own "single combats" for their own interests. As a result, discipline suffers.

Because of the multiple sources of friction built into the constitutional system, legislative and electoral battles are confusing and messy. The example of the tax issue underscores the point.

TAX WARFARE

"If there is an area without the possession of which one cannot risk an advance into enemy territory," wrote Clausewitz, "it may correctly be designated as the key to the country."[26] During the 1980s, most Republicans agreed that the core of a GOP appeal— "the key to the country"—consisted of opposition to tax increases. Friction, however, kept them from maintaining a united front on this issue.

Faint hints of clashing agendas showed up as early as 1981, when President Reagan was trying to pass his original tax-cut plan. To achieve a legislative success—and not merely keep an issue alive for the 1982 midterm—he needed Democratic votes. Throughout the debate, he shunned partisan rhetoric and quietly passed the word that he would not campaign against Southern Democrats who backed him on the issue. The bill passed, but House Republicans worried about losing the electoral advantage.

Meanwhile, the economy slumped and the deficit grew. A number of Senate Republicans were willing to consider new taxes, but the House Republicans balked. Budget Director David Stockman recalled: "The internecine warfare over taxes and the budget had become so severe that House and Senate Republicans were invited to separate meetings."[27] President Reagan initially sided with the House Republicans, but White House aides persuaded him to work with Senate leaders to craft a massive tax increase.

Intraparty friction heated up as Reagan's legislative strategy scraped against the House GOP's electoral plans. The White House had earlier offered cover to anti-tax Democrats; now, Reagan aides were warning House Republicans that the President would refuse to raise money for them if they voted against his tax hike. To complete the irony, the Republican National Committee launched an ad campaign in support of the tax increase. Congress narrowly passed the measure, and soon followed by hiking the gasoline tax. The recession was already hurting House Republicans, and without the tax issue, they became vulnerable. In the 1982 elections, they gave up most of the ground they had gained two years before. Blaming White House aides, Gingrich later said: "The Administration has had no capacity to launch a strategic offensive on behalf of Reagan's vision."[28]

In 1984, Reagan sought another deficit-reduction package and ended up signing a bill containing more tax increases than spending cuts. Most Republican senators backed the plan, while most House Republicans voted against it. This split showed up again that summer, during debates on the party platform. Jack

Kemp (R-NY), chair of the House Republican Conference, argued for a no-new-taxes-period plank, while Senator Robert Dole (R-KS) took the President's position by saying that the party should keep all options open. Though Kemp's side won the platform fight, there was no partywide offensive on the tax issue. President Reagan concentrated on his opponent Walter Mondale, leaving congressional Republicans to fight for themselves.

The 1984 election caused Republican celebrations—but not in the House. Amid Reagan's landslide reelection, House Republicans gained only a handful of seats. They quietly seethed at Reagan, who had given them so little support and who had done so much since 1982 to blur the partisan lines on taxes.

In 1985, President Reagan proposed a tax reform that would reduce tax rates and make up the lost revenue by closing loopholes. Looking to the end of his presidency, Ronald Reagan wanted a legislative achievement, not just a hot issue. To pass a bill, he had to work with House Democrats, who in turn rebuffed House Republican efforts to help draft the legislation. When the bill came to the House floor, resentful Republicans backed a successful effort to block consideration. Over the objections of the party's conservative wing, Reagan quickly rounded up enough support to return the bill to the House floor. The second time around, the House Republicans were confused and disorganized, like a retreating army. After the bill passed by voice vote, the Republicans were so dazed that no one on their side remembered to ask for a recorded roll call. "We screwed up," said Representative Vin Weber (R-MN).[29]

Following the 1987 stock-market break, Reagan agreed to another budget summit that seemed likely to produce another tax increase. Conservative commentator Patrick Buchanan wrote: "'Know thy enemy, know thyself; in a thousand battles, a thousand victories,' wrote Sun Tzu centuries ago. The central failing of the moderate Republicans [is that] they do not understand the philosophical struggle on-going in America." Buchanan denounced the typical moderate Republican who shied away from political brawls with the Democrats: "He does not like to fight them; and he does not really know how. And, unfortunately, you cannot make an attack dog out of a cocker spaniel."[30] The tax increase passed.

Within a couple of years, many Republicans had forgotten these battles. They believed that George Bush's "no new taxes" pledge had won him the White House and would help them gain ground in Congress. President Bush enjoyed high approval ratings, and Republicans had matched Democrats in party identification for the first time in decades. Republicans could hope for extraordinary achievements only if their usual friction did not set in. It did. In May 1990, Bush announced that he was agreeing to a budget summit with "no preconditions," and a few weeks later, Democrats got him to agree that "tax revenue increases" would be necessary. GOP strategists lamented the breaking of the tax pledge, together with Bush's willingness to yield on other issues. Ed Rollins, co-chairman of the House GOP's campaign committee, said that, unlike Bush, the House Republicans were in a war and "there are going to be some casualties."[31]

House Republicans passed a resolution opposing the tax increase, and the President's top aides bickered with them. The *Washington Post* summed up the party's plight with two headlines for Evans and Novak columns: "The GOP Divided and Demoralized" (August 6) and "Friction in the GOP" (August 20).

During the budget summit, the President had to compromise with House Democrats because of their overwhelming strength in the chamber. Summit participant Senator Phil Gramm (R-TX) observed that this strength forced the President "to compromise much further than House Republicans have any desire of going. That's what produces the friction."[32] The friction worsened when the summit produced an agreement to raise taxes.

Once again, the GOP was groping in the fog of tax warfare. At the state level, some governors stuck to the no-taxes messages while others, such as Bob Martinez of Florida, had to defend their own Bush-like reversals. From his sickbed, Lee Atwater sent a letter to House Republicans asking them not to turn their backs on President Bush. Meanwhile, House GOP campaign chief Ed Rollins told the same lawmakers that they should not hesitate to oppose Bush for the sake of their own political survival. Rollins's message had more impact than Atwater's. In the hand-to-hand combat of individual House elections, many Republicans did not want to face the same "flip-flop" charges that Democrats were firing at Bush.

After some fluctuation in the battle lines, Congress eventually passed a budget agreement with tax increases. In November, House Republicans lost seats for the third election in a row. Bush's standing on domestic issues sustained permanent damage, and in the 1992 election, both Bill Clinton and Ross Perot used the "read my lips" line to great effect. In language reminiscent of Clausewitz's "key to the country" analysis, Democratic pollster Celinda Lake said in 1993: "Controlling the Republicans' advantage on taxes was key to the 1992 victory."[33]

CRISIS AND OVERCONFIDENCE

Military success brings some respite from the fatigue and stress of combat. This relief makes for a mixed blessing. "Success is disarming," wrote S. L. A. Marshall. "Tension is the normal state of mind and body in combat. When the tension suddenly relaxes through the winning of a first objective, troops are apt to be pervaded by a sense of extreme well-being and there is apt to ensue laxness in all its forms and with all its dangers."[34] Nixon applied almost identical words to politics. Describing the phases of political crisis and conflict, he wrote: "The most dangerous period is the aftermath. It is then, with all resources spent and his guard down, that an individual must watch out for dulled reactions and faulty judgment."[35]

Nixon could well have been describing the first year of the Clinton administration. In the aftermath of victory, the new president and his aides made many political misjudgments on military policy, health care, and other issues. (As we saw in the observation earlier in this chapter from George Stephanopoulos, fatigue dulled their instincts even further.) Perhaps the most serious error consisted of proposing a major tax increase without seeking GOP support. Nervous congressional Democrats defected, leaving the measure with one-vote margins in both the House and the Senate. Republicans now had a powerful issue, because in each case where a Democrat had supported the measure, the GOP challenger could accuse the incumbent of casting the deciding vote for tax increases.

In 1994, Republicans won both chambers of Congress—and, almost instantly, victory led them into trouble. On election night, an ecstatic Newt Gingrich stayed up to answer press questions about the GOP's unexpected success. Reporters from the *New York Times* and *Washington Post* asked if he thought Clinton was too liberal and if the election was a repudiation of Clinton policies. Years later, Gingrich reflected that he should have sidestepped the questions. Instead, he talked about Clinton's background as a liberal student activist. "Naturally the next day both papers ran front-page stories under headlines that read 'Gingrich Lobs a Few More Bombs' . . . and 'GOP's Rising Star Pledges to Right Wrongs of the Left.' . . . And there went all my effort to reach out and establish a good working relationship with the President."[36]

Over the longer run, success can have intellectual drawbacks. Once a military force scores a major win, its leaders may come to believe that they have found the formula for success, or that good luck will forever be on their side. Consequently, they may forgo the difficult intellectual process of rethinking strategy and anticipating potential weaknesses. As Charles de Gaulle wrote, "Every great victory is usually followed by this kind of mental decline."[37]

Successful politicians, like successful warriors, frequently forget that the conditions of initial success may be fleeting. By the late 1980s, Republicans had won five of the last six presidential elections. Consequently, high-ranking officials in the Bush administration did not feel any need to develop a serious domestic agenda. They failed to notice that the end of the Cold War had rendered moot the GOP's advantage on national security issues, and that serious economic distress had undercut its status as the party of prosperity.

LOSERS LEARN

If winning can be debilitating, losing can be educational. Armies that suffer major defeat will often undergo a period of reflection and come out with new doctrine and reformed leadership. The Vietnam War and its aftermath inflicted great pain on the American armed services, but it also led them to reform policies on drugs and race relations. Most important, it caused them to rethink strategy—and to study Clausewitz. Colin Powell recalls his studies at the National War College, where he learned that *On War* was "like a beam of light from the past," illuminating what went wrong in Vietnam.[38] Clausewitz taught that a war required a clear national purpose, steady political leadership, and support from the people. The Vietnam War flunked all three tests. Powell and other military figures of his generation vowed that if they ever ran a war, they would do it right. The result was Desert Storm.

Political losers learn, too. In the late 1980s, just as top national Republicans were getting complacent, national Democrats were finally coming to grips with the problems that had brought down

Walter Mondale in 1984 and Michael Dukakis in 1988. Two leading strategists, William Galston and Elaine Ciulla Kamarck,
wrote an influential study that debunked excuses for Democratic
defeat and forthrightly called for a new approach based on "middle-class values—individual responsibility, hard work, equal
opportunity—rather than the language of compensation."[39]
Those brief lines became Bill Clinton's message in 1992.

The Clinton team also learned how to foil Republican campaign tactics. Learning from the 1984 GOP opposition-research
operation (see chapter 7), the operatives in the Clinton war room
were ready to counter every statement from the Bush camp. When
Republicans attacked Clinton's character, he turned the attacks
against them by denouncing "the politics of personal destruction." The Republicans should have read Alinsky, who warned that
once you use a specific tactic, it stops being outside the experience of your enemy, who will start working on countermeasures.

Alinsky offered this example: "Recently the head of a corporation showed me the blueprint of a new plant and pointed to a large
ground-floor area: 'Boy, have we got an architect who is with it!' he
chuckled. 'See that big hall? That's our sit-in room! When the sit-
inners come they'll be shown in and there will be coffee, TV, and
good toilet facilities—they can sit here until hell freezes over.'"[40]

OVERSTRETCH

Even if a military force avoids the pitfalls of overconfidence and
predictability, success still bears the seeds of failure. The Marine
Corps explains the process succinctly: "We advance at a cost—
lives, fuel, ammunition, physical and sometimes moral
strength—and so the attack becomes weaker over time. Eventually, the superiority that allowed us to attack and forced our
enemy to defend in the first place dissipates and the balance tips

in favor of the enemy."[41] In a wider context, historian Paul Kennedy explains how world powers eventually decline. By over-stretching themselves strategically—by conquering vast territories or running costly wars—nations run the risk that the cost of expansion will outweigh the benefits.[42]

We see a similar cycle in domestic politics. Candidates and parties advance at the cost of making commitments to supporters. After victory, the supporters expect something. In 1832, one congressman said: "The country is treated as a conquered province, and the offices distributed among the victors, as the spoils of the war."[43] Whether the spoils consist of jobs or policy initiatives, there are never enough to go around. Those who get their way are often ungrateful, and sometimes bitter that they did not get more. Those who fail to get a share grow resentful, and then form the nucleus for an internal opposition. In 1997, the House GOP underwent a "civil war" when dissatisfied junior members tried to oust Gingrich from the speakership. Though the attack fizzled, it further weakened his political standing and contributed to his resignation at the close of the following year.[44]

In politics, the more one wins, the more one must defend. Just as conquered territory is vulnerable at the rim, so are large political gains: most electoral "sweeps" bring in weak candidates who would not have won otherwise. An unusually large majority in a legislative body is thus a target-rich environment for the minority. After scoring historic congressional gains in 1964, Democrats suffered major losses two years later. The Reagan victory of 1980 helped elect dozens of GOP House members, many of whom were not strong enough to survive their first reelection battle. The 1980 election also gave control of the Senate to the Republicans, who lost it in 1986, in part because several of their first-termers were unusually inept.

Similarly, the more policy changes you can make, the more political ammunition your opponents will have when problems arise, as they invariably do. Republicans benefited in 1966 from the perceived failures of Lyndon Johnson's Great Society program, just as Democrats scored in 1982 because they could blame a deep recession on the Reagan economic program.

ENABLING THE ENEMY

B. H. Liddell Hart wrote: "The more brutal your methods the more bitter you will make your opponents, with the natural result of hardening the resistance you are trying to overcome; thus, the more evenly the two sides are matched the wiser it will be to avoid extremes of violence which tend to consolidate the enemy's troops and people behind their leaders."[45] Dave Grossman calls this phenomenon "enabling the enemy."[46] When soldiers of one side hear atrocity stories about the other, they are less likely to surrender, thinking that it is safer to make a last-ditch stand than to become the prisoners of a murderous adversary.

Recall from chapter 5 that political figures rally their troops by roundly denouncing their opponents. The latter then rally against the attacker, and so on. This cycle of mutual antagonism can lead to harsh politics. With each side hearing atrocity stories about the other, members are less likely to compromise. In the 1980s and early 1990s, Gingrich's tough attacks against congressional Democrats helped energize his own party. These attacks also made Democrats hate him. When he became Speaker, they were reluctant to work with him and eager to battle him on policy, procedure, and ethics. Their common hostility to Gingrich became a great source of party unity.

In describing what Senator Paul Coverdell told him in 1995, Gingrich suggested the atmosphere of the contemporary House: "We have not won the war, we are simply on the beach at Normandy and now we have to fight our way through the hedgerows and across Europe. The Left is not about to ask for an armistice or negotiate their own surrender. They are going to do everything they can to throw us back into the minority and end our threat to their values and their power structure."[47]

The "enabling of the enemy" reached a particularly severe point during the Clinton impeachment. Republicans accused the President of perjury, and suggested that the congressional Democrats were covering for him. Democrats charged Republicans with attempting a "coup." When Clinton launched air strikes against Iraq during the impeachment proceedings, Democrats used military rhetoric in a harsher, more direct way. Said Representative Martin Frost (D-TX): "By starting this proceeding against President Clinton today, we are sending the ultimate mixed message to Saddam about our national resolve. We may be encouraging him to resist longer by our actions in the midst of war. Starting this proceeding today may wind up costing American lives. The majority may well have blood on its hands by starting this proceeding today."[48] Because of mutual distrust, Republicans and Democrats found no common ground on impeachment. Each side's attacks made the other side more stubborn.

MADISON AND CLAUSEWITZ

Newcomers may suffer "shell shock" when they first encounter the discord, confusion, and wasted effort that always surround political life. Just as veterans of World War I bitterly recalled the slogan, "The War to End All Wars," so political novices may feel bewilderment when they find that each battle begets new ones. As we saw at the outset of this chapter, the presence of friction and the absence of finality have roots in human nature.

The constitutional system does not make things any easier. The Founders knew very well that a national movement or party could become as powerful as a well-disciplined army, which is exactly what they wanted to prevent. They apportioned power between the national government and the states, then divided the national government into three branches and split the legislative branch into two chambers. Politicians in each corner of this fragmented system would have their own particular interests, and thus would have less incentive to cooperate in building disciplined national organizations. Whether or not they wore the same party label, their institutional interests would inevitably grate against one another.

Friction creates light as well as heat. Zealous advocates of a particular policy may feel frustration when they must fight on many battlegrounds, making their case over and over, battling objection after objection. But the whole process helps produce thorough debate, so what is bad for the smooth execution of political strategy is good for deliberative democracy. Reflecting on his experience in all three branches—as House member, federal judge, and White House counsel—Judge Abner Mikva said that the best thing about American government is the "marvelous friction between the three branches. Occasionally one gains an ascendancy, as Congress did after the '94 landslide election. But that didn't last long."[49]

10

Scholars and Metaphors

All metaphor breaks down somewhere. That is the
beauty of it. It is touch and go with the metaphor, and
until you have lived with it long enough you don't
know where it is going. You don't know how much
you can get out of it and when it will cease to yield. It
is a very living thing. It is life itself.
— Robert Frost, "Education by Poetry"
in Hyde Cox and Edward Connery,
Selected Prose of Robert Frost

By this point, readers may have more questions
than answers. Here are a few:

- How far can the military model go?
- How does it work in settings that the book does not address?
- What other military concepts might shed light on politics?
- What additional qualifications and refinements does this form
  of analysis require?

To the extent that this book has provoked such questions, it has
succeeded. Its aim has not been to settle any empirical issue but

to make an initial foray into new intellectual territory, in the hope that others will follow. In one sense, its perspective is familiar: everybody uses military metaphors, including academicians. In another sense, it is unusual. One seldom meets Carl von Clausewitz and Sun Tzu in the endnotes of a book about American politics. And more than that, we have seen a common thread in the thoughts of Richard Nixon, Saul Alinsky, Gary Hart, Newt Gingrich, Hillary Clinton, Lee Atwater, and Martin Luther King. That is a rare thread indeed.

Political scientists may note the book's departure from the discipline's dominant metaphor—namely, the market. As chapter 1 explained, nothing here belittles studies that assume the market metaphor and use the analytical tools of economics. This body of work has lent clarity and rigor to the study of politics. The economic frame of mind has displayed an impressive subtlety, for it has not reduced all political phenomena to smooth exchanges but has instead pointed out paradoxes and market failures.[1]

As Robert Frost reminds us, however, one can take a metaphor only so far. Market imagery explains some things very well, but it has overlooked others. A new approach, such as the one that this books suggests, can show us some things we had not noticed.

What, then, would we get from a political science that starts with military metaphors? Such an approach would not necessarily contradict any established findings. For instance, where existing studies have found that affluent people tend to vote Republican, a military approach would not claim that they vote Democratic. Rather, it would have a distinct research agenda, posing new questions in different ways. It would draw on the literature but would take various strands of this material and weave them together with military thought to create new patterns, as this study has done. A brief review of this book's topics illustrates the point.

STRATEGY

When formal theorists write of strategy, they usually refer to courses of action that lend themselves to diagrams. Adapting a method by which economists explain the location of businesses, one school of thought analyzes party strategy as a matter of choosing issue positions along a left-right scale.[2] Another uses decision trees to break strategy down into a series of moves, each with its own likely payoff.[3] These approaches have driven countless books and articles, many with genuine insights. This perspective has the defect of its elegance, however, because it limits the strategist to picking a point on a graph or following a set of rules.

Military analysis confronts a messier reality—namely, the fact that effective strategists often go "outside the box" and actually break the rules. Instead of playing the "find-the-optimal-position" game, a candidate may surprise the opponent by reframing the terms of debate. A customary way of explaining the 1972 election is that Nixon positioned himself closer to the center than McGovern, thereby winning a bigger market share.[4] Nixon indeed took moderate issue positions, but there is another part of the story as well. For decades, a major source of the Democratic Party's power had been its image as the party of the "little guy," the party that cared about waitresses and construction workers. In 1972, Nixon reversed that image.[5] He outflanked the Democrats by casting the election as a choice between left-wing elites and the "silent majority" of working Americans.

Also consider President Clinton's impeachment. One might look at the conflict as a series of moves along a flowchart, but such an analysis would miss a great deal. Clinton essentially redefined the conflict by going on the offensive, shifting the terms of debate from his own conduct to that of the independent counsel and congressional Republicans. This response confounded his foes, who had expected him to behave like other tarnished politicians and slink away from the battlefield. Clinton was not like other politicians. According to George Stephanopoulos, "Clinton's shamelessness is a key to his political success."[6] Here, military analysis would remind us how leaders may surprise their opponents by shifting from defense to offense, and doing so in creative ways.

LEADERSHIP

Using the market metaphor, scholars have written of leaders as brokers, bargainers, entrepreneurs, salespeople, and even products.[7] Leaders surely talk about "marketing" themselves, and haggle with colleagues in transactions that have the pungent aroma of business deals. But politics is more than a big blob of bargains. Scholars of the market school have a hard time dealing with leaders who really lead, who move attitudes by educating the public.[8] "Transformational" leaders change minds, reshape lives, and make history.

Military analysis can give us greater insight into crusaders such as Martin Luther King. Although it may sound paradoxical, even blasphemous, to apply military metaphors to an apostle of nonviolence, King himself saw their value. Like a general, he had to get masses of people to make sacrifices for a larger cause, and in many cases that sacrifice involved physical danger. King met this challenge by deploying what he called "the sword that heals," that is, "the peaceable weapon of nonviolent direct action."[9] He inspired his followers, as many military leaders have, by invoking a shared cultural heritage. African-American religious tradition, he said, had shown that "the nonviolent resistance of the early Christians had constituted a moral offensive of such overriding power that it shook the Roman Empire."[10] Charles de Gaulle said that a leader must respond to those who seek perfection in the ends they serve. King put it this way:

> In order to be somebody, people must feel themselves part of something. In the nonviolent army, there is room for everyone who wants to join up. . . . There is no examination, no pledge, except that, as a soldier in the armies of violence is expected to inspect his carbine and keep it clean, nonviolent soldiers are called upon to burnish their greatest weapons—their heart, their conscience, their courage and their sense of justice.[11]

King, like other great leaders, showed political and physical courage, a subject that political science has ignored. A search of the journals turns up scores of articles about economic influences on congressional elections but almost none about political courage.[12] Military analysis would start to fill this gap.

COORDINATION

In explaining coordination, a military style of analysis would share some ground with the economic style. Both would talk about standard operating procedures, for instance. But military analysis would pay more attention to the development of doctrine. It would also build on James Q. Wilson's insight that "whereas economics is based on the assumption that preferences are given, politics must take into account the efforts made to change preferences."[13] Instead of looking only at incentives—offering people what they want—a military approach to politics would ask how organizations persuade people to want different things.

Playing off the example of "basic training" or "boot camp," this style would examine the process of indoctrination. Gingrich's use of GOPAC seminars would make a good case study of explicit indoctrination and its unanticipated consequences. The literature to date includes few such studies. Although there is a good deal of work on childhood socialization, there is much less on the training of political elites.

Likewise, scholars need to give more attention to the technology of political "command and control." Here, the rapid growth of the Internet points to another area for the application of military analysis. The Mexican Zapatistas and other guerrilla movements around the world are using email messages and websites to coordinate their followers and keep in touch with potential allies. Analysis of such developments can tell us much about how American direct-action groups could fight their battles in cyberspace. If Saul Alinsky were still alive, he would be writing about strategy and tactics for the World Wide Web.

RALLYING THE TROOPS

On the topic of building morale, the existing literature does tell us a good deal about the effects of mass communication.[14] Military analysis would differ in emphasis, focusing more on implementation. How can a party leader rally the faithful? What specific appeals will build individual loyalty? How do political figures try to demonize their opponents? As for the latter question, it is hard to understand contemporary Washington without probing the idea of enmity. As we all saw during the impeachment proceedings of 1998 and 1999, many lawmakers really hate each other. With few exceptions, the literature on Congress has not captured the depth of this ill will.[15] Studies of enmity, such as Richard Holmes's *Acts of War*, can furnish a starting point for understanding the emotional minefield of Capitol Hill.

Pride is another emotion that political scientists tend to disregard, except perhaps during tenure reviews. In the military, pride helps drive people to seek honors such as promotions and decorations. It also fuels the concern for "honor" (in the singular), or fidelity to right conduct under all circumstances, regardless of the consequences. Honor in this sense is different from what social scientists would call "peer approval" because it can involve actions that take place when peers are not looking. In studying political behavior, then, we should ask why the desire for "honors," or signs of recognition, can influence people far out of proportion to the accompanying material benefits. We should also think about the concept of "political honor," which is a willingness to do the right thing even though it does not serve one's own cost-benefit calculus.

Serious study of passions such as enmity and pride can remedy a shortcoming in the literature. Contemporary theory is very good at explaining rational behavior in pursuit of self-interest, but it strains to account for the sacrifices that people make in the service of collective goals. One can stretch the definition of "rational choice" to cover heroism in the face of Hitler's machine guns or Bull Connor's police dogs, but that would be a silly contrivance, as if "saving Private Ryan" were essentially the same thing as saving mortgage interest. Often, scholars see political figures as what C. S. Lewis called "Men without Chests." Academic treatments ponder the base desires that come from the belly and the rational calculations that come from the head, but miss the sentiments and habits of the heart. Lewis said that "it is by this middle element that man is man: for by his intellect he is mere spirit and by his appetite mere animal." Heartfelt passions, both positive and negative, are what bind people to something larger than themselves. That is, one fights the enemy to avenge a wrong to the group or to preserve a sense of duty and honor. "In battle it is not syllogisms that will keep reluctant nerves and muscles to their post in the third hour of the bombardment," wrote Lewis. "The crudest sentimentalism . . . about a flag or a country or a regiment will be of more use."[16]

DEMORALIZATION, DECEPTION, AND STEALTH

Many works in political science take rationality as the norm. But a major point of demoralization is to get those on the other side to think and behave irrationally, to make their passions wrest the scepter from reason. In this light, military analysis would examine the various "mind games" that political figures use against one another.

As mentioned earlier, current formal theory does admit the possibility of "deceptive moves." A military approach would consider deception not just as a move in an artificial game but as an elaborate effort to mislead others about intentions, feelings, and loyalties. Similarly, the military concept of distraction can help explain media politics. Right after David Maraniss released an unflattering biography of him, President Clinton decided to intervene in the baseball strike. "He knew he'd fail," writes Dick Morris. "But the baseball strike story was a whole lot better than letting the Maraniss book dominate the weekend's coverage."[17]

Researchers have sometimes noted "stealth tactics" by interest groups but have rarely studied why and how these tactics work. This neglect is unfortunate. Attention to stealth would help us understand, for instance, why the House passed legislation in 1999 imposing penalties for harm to a fetus during the commission of a federal crime. "The bill was in drafting stage for months, but there was no public discussion, in order to avoid tipping off the pro-abortion lobby," said the National Right to Life Committee in a statement that it quickly deleted from its website. One abortion-rights lobbyist said that the bill had "definitely caught us off-guard."[18]

INTELLIGENCE

Some scholars have examined how policymakers make use of expert knowledge, but on the larger question of political

intelligence, the cupboard is bare. Military analysis would empha-
size such topics as opposition research, which has received no systematic attention. This topic should interest students of the
media as well as election specialists. As already discussed, opposition researchers sometimes supply investigative reporters with
source material.

As mentioned in chapter 7, political intelligence also encompasses such activities as monitoring news broadcasts and check-
ing information online. How do intelligence-gatherers use this
information to anticipate what adversaries might do? Although
there is some literature on the public-opinion effects of broadcast debates, it is skimpy on debate preparation, including the
ways in which public political figures gain intelligence about
their opponents' tactics.

Except for Eugene Bardach's splendid essay on "subformal
warning systems,"[19] phenomena such as "grapevines" and "old
boy/old girl intelligence networks" have stayed off the discipline's
radar. Here, the ways in which military officers gather their
"human intelligence" in foreign capitals may offer some pointers
to the informal intelligence process in Washington. The study of
political intelligence should also prompt scholars to ponder ethical questions about the line between legitimate information-
gathering and intrusive spying.

GEOGRAPHY AND LOGISTICS

Almost every book about military conflict features maps that
show how the fighting unfolded. Scholars of American politics
often slight political geography. Many works on elections pay
only glancing attention to differences among districts or regions,
instead relying on nationwide survey data or aggregate voting
figures. A surprisingly large share of books in this field do not
contain a single map.

With its strong geographical orientation, military analysis would offer us a healthy reminder that people live in cities and towns, not aggregates. It would also encourage us to follow Richard Fenno's example and take some "terrain walks" of the constituencies that we normally see only as data points.

Similarly, works on the logistical side of politics tend to focus on aggregate levels of spending. Many scholars have examined where contributions come from and have tried to correlate overall spending levels with election outcomes. But warfare warns us that aggregate spending levels bear only a loose relationship to results: the United States outspent North Vietnam but still lost the war. What matters is how leaders use the resources they have. The campaign literature, however, offers candidates little guidance on how they can most effectively allocate their scarce campaign resources.[20] Military analysis would lead us to ask a key question: what works?

The "bombing of supply lines" also deserves attention. Edward Schneier and Bertram Gross say that "the military advantage conferred by superior arms has no close analogy in the legislative arena."[21] As we have seen, however, there is another way of looking at the matter: lawmakers do try to gain advantages in information and staff support, and to deny these resources to their opponents. With this point in mind, we can ask additional questions. For instance, what are the informal "rules of engagement" for logistical warfare? And what happens to the capabilities of the members who are its targets?

FRICTION

The 1970s literature on public policy implementation certainly had a feel for friction, as do certain case studies of the legislative process.[22] But such observation-based work has fallen into disfavor within large parts of the world of political science. Journal articles have a regrettable tendency to miss the glitches and frustrations of the flesh-and-blood world. Writes Donald Kettl: "In the early '80s some scholars developed elaborate theoretical models to explain and predict the decisions of Federal Reserve officers. Although they showed an impressive knowledge of the Fed's decisions and an undeniable analytical elegance, as a predictive tool the models were useless and, to the Fed officials who saw them, laughable."[23]

Some very important measures have slipped into the lawbooks amid the political fog of war. In 1980, a House-Senate conference committee added a last-minute provision to a banking bill that greatly increased federal insurance of savings and loan deposits. Time-pressed lawmakers failed to anticipate that the measure would encourage risky speculation by thrift operators, who now had an assurance that Washington would cover most of their losses. The 1990 Budget Enforcement Act, in a similar manner, became part of a major budget deal even though most members were barely aware of it. In this case, a combination of stealth and congressional fatigue conspired to restructure fiscal policy-making in the federal government. Because of its strong emphasis on friction, a military approach would draw scholarly attention to such muddy patches of the political process.

ADVANTAGES AND DISADVANTAGES

As the preceding pages suggest, military analysis should shift some of our scholarly labor from overtilled to undertilled fields.[24] That shift would be all to the good: too many of us are toiling in the zone of boredom, doing endless iterations on the same survey data.

Another advantage is that political practitioners could read the material and apply it in their work. Says Kettl, "The abstract approach favored in much cutting-edge scholarship offers little help to people out in the trenches," who must seek their lessons from the accounts of journalists and entrepreneurs, "and from their own front-line battles."[25] Written for people who literally work in the trenches and on the front lines, military scholarship has a practical bent: even in histories of ancient campaigns, lessons for the present seldom lurk far from the surface. Edward N. Luttwak's *Grand Strategy of the Roman Empire* foreshadowed his *Grand Strategy of the Soviet Union*. Some scholars might dismiss this argument, contending that practical utility is an unworthy criterion for judging political science. Such an attitude is foolish. We need not expect that all scholarship should have immediate applications, but all other things being equal, practicality is a virtue. Politics, after all, is not some abstract concern that we can take or leave at whim, for it affects everything else that we do. John Adams famously observed that he had to study politics and war so that his children could study mathematics and commerce, so that their children could study painting, poetry, and music.

There are, of course, some difficulties. Economics brings us some precise analytical tools, whereas military analysis tends to be more qualitative. By itself, this difference does not necessarily work to the latter's disadvantage. As Alexis de Tocqueville said, "Where statistics are not based on strictly accurate calculations, they mislead instead of guide. The mind easily lets itself be taken in by the false appearance of exactitude which statistics retain even in their mistakes, and confidently adopts errors clothed in the forms of mathematical truth. Let us abandon figures then, and try to find our proofs elsewhere."[26]

When we extend our studies beyond the comfortable confines of data tables, we have to overcome some practical challenges. "Terrain walks" require travel to local constituencies. Studies of opposition research mean attempting to interview people who are notoriously tight-lipped. Such projects would require money, and the traditional funding sources might hesitate to support this style of research. Nevertheless, the benefit is worth the effort.

Another, more substantive potential drawback relates to Robert Frost's caution that all metaphors are limited. The market metaphor fails to capture every possible aspect of politics, and so does the military metaphor. Conflict is crucial, but there is more to politics than battles and stratagems: there are also occasions for growth, deliberation, and compromise. Just as a given lens works better under certain lighting conditions than others, so the applicability of the military style of analysis varies across places and institutions. For example, it applies more precisely to the Hobbesian politics of New York State than to the neighborly politics of Vermont. And as we saw earlier, the U.S. Senate is less "warlike" than the House, in part because of the possibility of "mutually assured destruction." Military analysis can still tell us quite a bit about political life in Vermont and the Senate—it just cannot tell us everything.

But who says we have to base political analysis on a single metaphor? This book has explored one alternative. There are others, which might not be as elaborate as the military model but which could still serve as auxiliary lenses. The sharp-eyed reader will have noted that some of these metaphors have already cropped up within this book. In chapter 3, we saw the political leader as general, but we also saw the general as both teacher and actor—metaphors within a metaphor. In a book on models and metaphors, Phillip Gianos identifies such multiple perspectives as "complementary ways of looking at the same things, and each of which, if used well, may help us understand more about political life."[27]

PHYSICS AND MECHANICS

Political thinkers have long derived imagery from the world of mechanics. Hence we often refer to political procedures as "mechanisms" and use such ideas as "the balance of power" and "checks and balances."[28] Fascination with the physical world was especially strong during the Enlightenment. "The Declaration's opening is Newtonian," writes Garry Wills, explaining that its line about "the course of human events" is a scientific proposition: "In the flow of things there is perceivable necessity, a fixity within flux."[29] These metaphors teach us about equilibrium and direct us to look for patterns and regularities. They also encourage us to be optimistic about our ability to "fix" things, or, as Ross Perot likes to say, to "get under the hood." Some degree of friction may be inevitable, but that knowledge just tells us where to put the lubricant.

Traditional mechanics and Newtonian physics are not the only metaphorical options from the hard sciences. In a reader entitled *Quantum Politics*, scholars from various fields attempt to apply quantum physics to contemporary issues. Laurence Tribe's essay on "The Curvature of Constitutional Space" offers a sample: "Just as space cannot extricate itself from the unfolding story of physical reality, so also the law cannot extract itself from social structures; it cannot 'step back,' establish an 'Archimedean' reference point of detached neutrality."[30]

ECOLOGY

Woodrow Wilson said that previous scholars had described government as a machine subject to laws resembling those of physics, noting that "the trouble with the theory is that government is not a machine, but a living thing. It falls, not under the theory of the universe, but under the theory of organic life. It is modified by its environment, necessitated by its tasks, shaped to its functions by the sheer pressure of life."[31] James Q. Wilson continues in this vein: "An organization is like a fish in a coral reef. To survive, it needs to find a supportive ecological niche."[32] This metaphor reminds us of another figure of speech: people in politics often speak of their place on "the food chain," with the big fish eating the little fish. How do enough little fish survive to keep the ecosystem going? The answer is that they make themselves inconspicuous, or hidden—which may suggest clues for survival in bureaucratic life.

Like the military metaphor, the ecological metaphor points to the phenomenon of deception. One kind of orchid has a picture of a bee's head on its flower. When a wasp sees the image, it attacks by plunging its stinger though the bee image into a pollen pod, which sticks to it. Repeating this exercise with the next orchid, the wasp pollinates it.[33] CIA official James Jesus Angleton made a lifelong study of orchids, believing they would help him reflect on the role of deception in his own profession.

Different political persuasions can apply the ecological perspective. Virginia Postrel, former editor of the libertarian magazine *Reason*, has outlined a point of view called "dynamism," which emphasizes the value of social and economic change unfettered by government: "Dynamists are often drawn to biological metaphors, symbols of unpredictable growth and change, of variety, of experiment, feedback, and adaptation."[34] One such dynamist is Michael Rothschild, whose *Bionomics: The Inevitability of Capitalism* puts the matter thus: "Organisms and organizations are nodes in networks of relationships. As time passes, and evolution proceeds, some nodes are wiped out and new ones crop up, triggering adjustments that ripple across each network."[35]

At the other end of the spectrum, one socialist writer uses the "tragedy of the commons" as a metaphor for the danger of unfettered change: the tragedy is not public ownership of the commons but private ownership of the sheep.[36]

MEDICINE

Closely related to ecological metaphors are medical ones, which depict political problems as illnesses and enlightened leaders as physicians. Medical metaphors have become increasingly common in recent years, perhaps reflecting a broader "therapeutic culture."[37] Nevertheless, they have a long history. In *The Federalist*, James Madison likened the United States to a patient getting sicker. One set of physicians unanimously prescribed a remedy, while another set warned against that prescription without offering an alternative. Would it not be better, he asked, to side with the former than with "those who could neither deny the necessity of a speedy remedy, nor agree in proposing one?"[38] The two groups, of course, represented the Federalists and Anti-Federalists, respectively.

Medical metaphors deal with health and healing, so to the extent that they influence political science, they may lead to a stronger focus on problem-solving. Yet such seemingly benign figures of speech also have their critics. One major objection to military metaphors—that they encourage harsh thoughts and actions—applies with equal force here. As Susan Sontag says, "To liken a political event or situation to an illness is to impute guilt, to prescribe punishment."[39]

GAMES

As mentioned earlier, a large body of social science literature deals with "game theory." But this work is abstract, largely incomprehensible to non-specialists, and almost totally unrelated to the games that human beings actually play in their leisure time. Though sports metaphors are nearly as pervasive as military ones, no one has yet tried to draw systematic lessons from players and coaches. There is much to learn. Serious athletes, like political figures, often have to make split-second decisions under conditions of intense stress and public scrutiny, while trying to out-think opponents who are trying to out-think them. And like major politicians (but unlike most military leaders), athletes find that the temptations of celebrity may cloud their judgment and alter their behavior.

Many people liken politics to a board game. Lenin insisted that chess was an invaluable mental exercise for leaders, while Mao Zedong had his generals study Go, the ancient and complex Chinese game in which players move hundreds of stones on a grid. Nevertheless, American foreign policy expert Michael Ledeen argues that we can actually learn more from cards. In chess and Go, each player starts with the same strength and can always see the other side's forces, whereas "in card games, each player sees only a small percentage of the cards around the table; he must discover the balance of power by listening carefully to the communications from other players and watching their moves."[40]

Using this metaphor, political science research would look not just at probability tables but at the various tricks of the poker trade. As we saw in chapter 7, nonverbal communication is an important part of politics—and poker has much to teach us about it. Poker players look for "tells," the gestures of body language that reveal whether competitors are holding good hands or are merely bluffing.

Does skill at poker carry over into politics? Perhaps. Serving in the South Pacific during World War II, young Richard Nixon made somewhere between $3,000 and $10,000 from poker games.[41] The money helped finance his first congressional race.

THEATER

Leaders, as we know, consciously play roles. More generally, one can depict politics as a grand theatrical enterprise, complete with lead actors and aides who act as stagehands.[42] From this perspective, government activity does not just confer benefits but placates or arouses spectators. Murray Edelman offered this example: "Even the FBI has consistently concentrated on the dramatic capture of the Dillingers while making little headway against national organized gambling and other crime syndicates. The 'ten most wanted criminals' device has been the dramaturgical core of FBI publicity and claims of effectiveness in its law enforcement work."[43]

As with the military metaphor, the theatrical metaphor can shade into literal truth. Since FDR's time, Hollywood celebrities have advised political figures on stagecraft and lent their production expertise to campaigns. In the Clinton campaign, veteran motion-picture producer Mort Engelberg assisted with the advance work, saying: "It's like doing three movies a day."[44]

Happily, some political scientists have begun to work with this metaphor. Herbert F. Weisberg and Samuel C. Patterson have edited *Great Theater*, a collection of essays analyzing Congress as a place where political actors entertain, enlighten, and bamboozle their audiences.[45] In *The Comedy of Democracy*, James E. Combs and Dan Nimmo "take a comic stance toward the institutions, processes, rituals, and policies of contemporary democracy in the United States."[46]

EDUCATION

Chapter 3, on leadership, quoted military commanders describing their work as a form of teaching. One may extend the metaphor. Drawing on the work of John Stuart Mill, William K. Muir says: "A legislature is like a school. It educates its members in the science of public policy and the arts of politics. Through its subject-matter committees it exposes legislators to a wealth of knowledge about human affairs. Through the bill-carrying responsibilities it imposes on authors of legislation, it teaches the art of negotiation."[47]

Tocqueville wrote in a similar vein: "Local institutions are to liberty what primary schools are to science; they put it within the people's reach; they teach people to appreciate its peaceful enjoyment and accustom them to make use of it."[48] From this perspective, an especially important institution is the jury, "a free school which is always open in which each juror learns his rights, comes into daily contact with the best-educated and most-enlightened members of the upper classes, and is given practical lessons in the law."[49]

One could argue that the entire political process is a school for citizens, with political speeches serving as lectures, and newspapers and ballot pamphlets as homework reading. The point is that democracy is not just about balancing interests but involves deliberating about the common good—a process that requires reflection and study by all citizens. A political science resting on this metaphor would look much more closely into deliberation, the process by which people learn about issues and then reason about the merits of public policy.[50]

One could elaborate on any of these metaphors, or identify many others. The point, however, is not to indulge in metaphorical overload but to return to the idea with which we started: that there is more than one perspective on American politics. In some ways, politics does resemble market exchange, but in others, it resembles military conflict. This book has suggested a form of analysis that will help us understand the political battlefield. The picture may not always be pretty, but we can learn much from appreciating the art of political warfare.

Notes

CHAPTER 1: Introduction

1. William Safire, *Safire's New Political Dictionary* (New York: Random House, 1993), 454–455.

2. George Lakoff and Mark Johnson, *Metaphors We Live By* (Chicago: University of Chicago Press, 1980), 79. The authors discuss war as a metaphor for argument, but their observations apply to the political context. One may also apply military metaphors and ideas to the judicial system. See, for instance, Guyora Binder, "On Critical Legal Studies as Guerrilla Warfare," *Georgetown Law Journal* 76 (October 1987): 1–36. For the sake of space and simplicity, however, this study focuses on the political branches and electoral campaigns.

3. Ibid., 4.

4. "Conflict" derives from the Latin *com-* (with) and *fligere* (to strike). Similarly, "combat" comes from *com-* and *battuere* (to fight).

5. President Bill Clinton, Remarks to the Community at Robert Taylor Homes in Chicago, June 17, 1994, 30 *Weekly Compilation of Presidential Documents*, 1296.

6. Paul Seabury and Angelo Codevilla, *War: Ends and Means* (New York: Basic Books, 1989), 28.

7. "Crusade" comes from the Latin *crux* (cross). The original Crusades, of course, were the Christian expeditions of the eleventh-thirteenth centuries to drive Muslims from the land where Jesus died on the Cross.

8. Harry S Truman, Address in the Chicago Stadium, October 25, 1948, *American Freedom Library* [CD-ROM] (Western Standard Publishing, 1997).

9. Anonymous [Joe Klein], *Primary Colors* (New York: Random House, 1996), 365.

10. Quoted in Steven F. Hayward, *Churchill on Leadership* (Rocklin, Calif.: Forum/Prima, 1997), 29.

11. Quoted in John F. Harris, "The Man Who Squared the Oval Office," *Washington Post*, January 4, 1997, A11.

12. Gary Hart, *Right from the Start: A Chronicle of the McGovern Campaign* (New York: Quadrangle, 1973), 60–61.

13. *Compact Oxford English Dictionary*, Vol. I (Oxford: Oxford University Press, 1971), 53.

14. Letter of Jesse A. Pearson to John Steele, July 30, 1809, in H. M. Wagstaff, ed., *The Papers of John Steele*, Vol. II (Raleigh: Edwards and Broughton, 1924), 601.

15. Abraham Lincoln, "Circular from Whig Committee," January 1840, in John G. Nicolay and John Hay, eds., *The Complete Works of Abraham Lincoln*, Vol. I (New York: Lamb, 1905), 145.

16. Robert J. Dinkin, *Campaigning in America: A History of Election Practices* (New York: Greenwood Press, 1989), 64.

17. For an explanation of why the "army style" of rallies and parades disappeared in the 1890s, see Richard Jensen, *The Winning of the Midwest: Social and Political Conflict 1888–1896* (Chicago: University of Chicago Press, 1971), 165–167.

18. Quoted in Matthew Josephson, *The Politicos* (New York: Harcourt, Brace and World, Harvest Books, 1938), 693.

19. Ibid., 695.

20. William E. Leuchtenberg, "The New Deal and the Analogue of War," in John Braeman, Robert H. Bremner, and Everett Walters, eds., *Change and Continuity in Twentieth-Century America* (Columbus: University of Ohio Press, 1964), 81–143, at 109, 114.

21. Franklin D. Roosevelt, Inaugural Address, Washington, D.C., March 4, 1933, at New Deal Network, http://newdeal.feri.org/speeches/1933a.htm, accessed August 27, 1999.

22. Franklin D. Roosevelt, radio address on party primaries, Washington, D.C., June 24, 1938, at New Deal Network, http://newdeal.feri.org/chat/chat13.htm, accessed August 27, 1999.

23. Michael S. Sherry, *In the Shadow of War: The United States Since the 1930s* (New Haven, Conn.: Yale University Press, 1995).

24. Michael Kelly, "The 1992 Campaign: The Democrats; Clinton's Staff Sees Campaign as a Real War," *New York Times*, August 11, 1992, A16.

25. Evan Thomas et al., *Back from the Dead: How Clinton Survived the Republican Revolution* (New York: Atlantic Monthly Press, 1997), 94.

26. Mary Matalin and James Carville, with Peter Knobler, *All's Fair: Love, War, and Running for President* (New York: Random House, 1994).

27. EMILY's List, at http://www.emilyslist.org/eljoin/campaigns.html, accessed August 27, 1999.

28. Pat Buchanan, speech in Manchester, New Hampshire, February 20, 1996, at http://www.buchanan.org/nhspch.html, accessed August 27, 1999.

29. Robert Michels, *Political Parties*, trans. Eden and Cedar Paul (New York: Free Press, 1962 [1915]), 80.

30. Hart, *Right from the Start*, 183 (see note 12 above).

31. For a provocative explanation of the defensive hypothesis, see Barbara Ehrenreich, *Blood Rites: Origins and History of the Passions of War* (New York: Henry Holt and Company, Metropolitan Books, 1997).

32. Quoted in Lee Smith, "New Ideas from the Army (Really)," *Fortune*, September 19, 1994, 204.

33. Quoted in Peter Goldman and Tony Fuller, *The Quest for the Presidency 1984* (New York: Bantam, Newsweek Books, 1985), 422–423.

34. Ibid., 315.

35. Peter J. Boyer and Stephen Talbot (writers), "The Long March of Newt Gingrich," *Frontline*, PBS, January 16, 1996, at http://www.pbs.org/wgbh/pages/frontline/newt/newtscript.html, accessed August 27, 1999.

36. Quoted in Howard Fineman, "The Warrior," *Newsweek*, January 9, 1995, 28. Mao wrote: "It can therefore be said that politics is war without bloodshed while war is politics with bloodshed." Mao Tse-Tung, *Quotations from Chairman Mao Tse-Tung*, ed. Stuart R. Schramm (New York: Bantam, 1967), 32.

37. Quoted in Damon Chappie, "General Gingrich Ices the 104th Congress," *Roll Call*, September 20, 1996, 26.

38. David Rogers, "General Newt," *Orange County Register*, December 30, 1995, G6 (reprint from the *Wall Street Journal*).

39. William Green, "It's Time for the Democrats to Party," *Newsday*, January 8, 1995, A41.

40. Quoted in Richard Fly, "The Guerrilla Fighter in Bush's War Room," *Business Week*, June 6, 1988, 92.

41. Quoted in Dan Sewell, "'The Art of War': Learning How to Fight, According to the Book," *Los Angeles Times*, November 23, 1989, E20.

42. Quoted in David Runkel, ed., *Campaign for President: The Managers Look at '88* (Dover, Mass.: Auburn House, 1988), 32–33.

43. Sun Tzu, *The Art of War*, trans. Samuel B. Griffith (New York: Oxford University Press, 1971), 84.

44. Quoted in Runkel, *Campaign for President*, 109 (see note 42 above).

45. Sun Tzu, *The Art of War*, 67 (see note 43 above).

46. Ibid., 96.

47. Ibid.

48. Ibid., 69.

49. Quoted in James Pinkerton, "Life in Bush Hell," *The New Republic*, September 14, 1992, 22.

50. Carl von Clausewitz, *On War*, ed. and trans. Michael Howard and Peter Paret (Princeton, N.J.: Princeton University Press, 1984), 191.

51. Maureen Dowd, "Guns and Poses," *New York Times Magazine*, August 16, 1992, 10.

52. James F. Childress, *War as Reality and Metaphor: Some Moral Reflections* (Boulder, Colo.: United States Air Force Academy, 1992), 20.

53. Quoted in Elizabeth Drew, *Showdown: The Struggle Between the Gingrich Congress and the Clinton White House* (New York: Simon and Schuster, 1996), 55–56.

54. Ibid., 76.

55. U.S. Marine Corps, *Warfighting* (New York: Doubleday, Currency, 1995), 10–11.

56. Quoted in Molly Moore, "General Describes Emotions of War; 'Agonizingly Difficult Decisions' Abound, Schwarzkopf Says," *Washington Post*, February 5, 1991, A1.

57. Quoted in William C. Rempel and Alan C. Miller, "First Lady's Aide Solicited Check to DNC, Donor Says," *Los Angeles Times*, July 27, 1997, A1.

58. Formal political theory, write Lalman, Oppenheimer, and Swistak, "resembles economic analysis which is concerned with rational behaviors in market contexts. In other words, the two fields share the same set of assumptions concerning individual choice." David Lalman, Joe Oppenheimer, and Piotr Swistak, "Formal Rational Choice Theory: A Cumulative Science of Politics," in Ada W. Finifter, ed., *Political Science: The State of the Discipline II* (Washington, D.C.: American Political Science Association, 1993), 77.

59. J. McIver Weatherford, *Tribes on the Hill* (South Hadley, Mass.: Bergin and Garvey, rev. ed., 1985).

60. Murray Edelman, *The Symbolic Uses of Politics* (Urbana: University of Illinois Press, 1964), 12.

61. E. E. Schattschneider, *The Semi-Sovereign People* (Hinsdale, Ill.: Dryden, 1960), 18.

62. On the incompleteness of metaphors, see Lakoff and Johnson, *Metaphors We Live By*, chap. 3 (see note 2 above). On the lens metaphor, see Graham Allison, *Essence of Decision: Explaining the Cuban Missile Crisis* (Boston: Little, Brown, 1971), 251.

63. "In becoming bewitched by greater power or rigor in what is explained, the political scientist may focus too much attention on those aspects of human behavior amenable to this type of analysis." James W. Ceaser, *Liberal Democracy and Political Science* (Baltimore: The Johns Hopkins University Press, 1990), 84. For different critical perspectives on the market metaphor in political science, see: Andries Hoogerwerf, "The Market as a Metaphor of Politics: A Critique of the Foundations of Economic Choice Theory," *International Review of Administrative Sciences* 58 (March 1992): 23–42; Mark K. Landy and Henry A. Plotkin, "Limits of the Market Metaphor," *Transaction/Society* 19 (May-June 1982): 8–17; and E. Spencer Wellhofer, "Contradictions in Market Models of Politics: The Case of Party Strategies and Voter Linkages," *European Journal of Political Research* 18 (January 1990): 9–28.

64. Bertram M. Gross, *The Legislative Struggle: A Study in Social Combat* (New York: McGraw-Hill, 1953), 4.

65. Ross K. Baker, *Friend and Foe in the U.S. Senate* (New York: Free Press, 1980), 248.

66. Matalin and Carville, *All's Fair*, 471 (see note 26 above).

CHAPTER 2: Strategy

1. U.S. Marine Corps, "Strategy," Marine Corps Doctrine Publication 1–1, 1997, at http://www.quantico.usmc.mil/docdiv/1-1/chap2.htm, accessed August 29, 1999.

2. Arthur F. Lykke, Jr. "Defining Military Strategy," *Military Review*, May 1989, 3; B. H. Liddell Hart, *Strategy* (New York: Penguin/Meridian, 2nd ed., 1991 [1967]), 322.

3. Ron Faucheux, "Strategies That Win!" *Campaigns & Elections*, December-January 1998, 25.

4. Robert Humphreys, "How to Plan a Political Campaign," in James Cannon, ed., *Politics U.S.A.* (Garden City, N.Y.: Doubleday, 1960), 192.

5. Frank Kent attributed the line to FDR aide Harry Hopkins, who denied saying it. Michael Barone, *Our Country: The Shaping of America from Roosevelt to Reagan* (New York: Free Press, 1990), 118.

6. Bernard Brodie, *War and Politics* (New York: Macmillan, 1973), 1.

7. U.S. Marine Corps, "Strategy," chap. 2 (see note 1 above).

8. Quoted in Lynda V. Mapes, "Gay-Marriage Ban Coasts into Law—Harried Democrats Help Override Veto," *Seattle Times*, February 7, 1998, A1.

9. James M. McPherson, "Lincoln and the Strategy of Unconditional Surrender," in idem, *Abraham Lincoln and the Second American Revolution* (New York: Oxford University Press, 1990), 65–91; James MacGregor Burns, *Roosevelt: The Soldier of Freedom 1940–1945* (New York: Harcourt Brace Jovanovich, 1970), 323.

10. Harry G. Summers, Jr., *On Strategy: A Critical Analysis of the Vietnam War* (New York: Dell, 1984), 147; Philip A. Crowl, "The Strategist's Short Catechism: Six Questions Without Answers," in George Edward Thibault, ed., *The Art and Practice of Military Strategy* (Washington, D.C.: National Defense University, 1984), 31.

11. The Eddie Mahe Company, "Our Approach," at http://www.temc.com/html/approach.asp, accessed August 29, 1999.

12. Quoted in Robert Dallek, *Lone Star Rising: Lyndon Johnson and His Times 1908–1960* (New York: Oxford University Press, 1961), 518.

13. Quoted in Richard F. Fenno, Jr., *Home Style: House Members in Their Districts* (Boston: Little, Brown, 1978), 13.

14. R. Douglas Arnold, *The Logic of Congressional Action* (New Haven, Conn.: Yale University Press, 1990), 117–118.

15. Eugene Bardach, *The Implementation Game: What Happens After a Bill Becomes a Law* (Cambridge, Mass.: MIT Press, 1977).

16. Quoted in Curt Suplee, "The Man Behind the GOP's Economic Revolution," *Washington Post*, August 11, 1981, C1.

17. 1 Corinthians 14:8, King James Version.

18. George Silver, "Topics for Our Times: Clausewitz v. Sun Tzu—The Art of Health Reform," *American Journal of Public Health* 85 (March 1995): 308.

19. Saul David, *Military Blunders: The How and Why of Military Failure* (New York: Carroll and Graft, 1998), 272.

20. Robert Jervis, *Perception and Misperception in International Politics* (Princeton, N.J.: Princeton University Press, 1976), 410–417.

21. James H. Rowe, "The Politics of 1948," September 18, 1947, at http://www.ksg.harvard.edu/case/3pt/rowe.html, accessed August 29, 1999.

22. Grady McWhiney and Perry D. Jamieson, *Attack and Die: Civil War Military Tactics and the Southern Heritage* (University, Ala.: University of Alabama Press, 1982), 56–58.

23. Newt Gingrich, *Lessons Learned the Hard Way: A Personal Report* (New York: HarperCollins, 1998), 49.

24. Dick Morris, *Behind the Oval Office: Getting Reelected Against All Odds* (Los Angeles: Renaissance Books, 1999), 185.

25. U.S. Marine Corps, "Campaigning," Marine Corps Doctrine Publication 1–2, 1997, at http://www.quantico.usmc.mil/docdiv/1-2/ch2.htm, accessed August 31, 1999.

26. Murray Chotiner, "Managing the Campaign," in James Cannon, ed., *Politics U.S.A.* (Garden City, N.Y.: Doubleday, 1960), 211.

27. Ibid.

28. Edward V. Schneier and Bertram Gross, *Legislative Strategy: Shaping Public Policy* (New York: St. Martin's, 1993), chap. 1.

29. Lykke, "Defining Military Strategy," 4 (see note 2 above).

30. Sun Tzu, *The Art of War*, trans. Samuel B. Griffith (New York: Oxford University Press, 1971), 82.

31. Quoted in Nicol C. Rae, *Conservative Reformers: The Republican Freshmen and the Lessons of the 104th Congress* (Armonk, N.Y.: M. E. Sharpe, 1998), 120.

32. Quoted in Public Broadcasting Service, "The People and the Power Game," 1996, at http://www.pbs.org/powergame/files/panetta.html, accessed August 33, 1999.

33. Liddell Hart, *Strategy*, 335 (see note 2 above).

34. Victor Kamber, "How to Win and Really Lose in Washington," *Public Relations Quarterly*, Winter 1993–1994, 5, 7.

35. See the discussion of 1972 strategy in Ripon Society and Clifford Brown, Jr., *Jaws of Victory: The Game-Plan Politics of 1972, the Crisis of the Republican Party, and the Future of the Constitution* (Boston: Little, Brown, 1974), chaps. 1–2.

36. William Harris, "Heraclitus: The Philosophical Fragments," at http://www.middlebury.edu/~harris/Philosophy/Heracleitus.html, accessed August 31, 1999.

37. James W. Ceaser and Andrew E. Busch, *Losing to Win: The 1996 Elections and American Politics* (Lanham, Md.: Rowman and Littlefield, 1997).

38. Liddell Hart, *Strategy*, 330 (see note 2 above).

39. Paul Gigot, "Gingrich Plots a Comeback," *Wall Street Journal*, April 26, 1996, A14.

40. Carl von Clausewitz, *On War*, ed. and trans. Michael Howard and Peter Paret (Princeton, N.J.: Princeton University Press, 1984), 357.

41. Jeff Spencer, quoted in Lorene Hanley Duquin, "Door-to-Door Campaigning," in Larry J. Sabato, ed., *Campaigns and Elections: A Reader in Modern American Politics* (Glenview, Ill.: Scott, Foresman, 1989), 42.

42. Quoted in Leanne Bernstein, "Permanent Guerrilla Government: Legal Services Corporation," in Robert Rector and Michael Sanera, eds., *Steering the Elephant: How Washington Works* (New York: Universe Books, 1987), 222.

43. Ibid., 231.

44. U.S. Marine Corps, *Warfighting* (New York: Doubleday, Currency, 1995), 31.

45. Gingrich, *Lessons Learned the Hard Way*, 188 (see note 23 above).

46. Clausewitz, *On War*, 357 (see note 40 above).

47. Quoted in Thomas "Doc" Sweitzer, "Kill or Be Killed: Military Strategies Can Help Win Campaigns," *Campaigns & Elections*, September 1996, 46.

48. U.S. Marine Corps, *Warfighting*, 35 (see note 44 above).

49. Clausewitz, *On War*, 194 (see note 40 above).

50. Faucheux, "Strategies That Win!" 32 (see note 3 above).

51. U.S. Marine Corps, *Warfighting*, 76 (see note 44 above).

52. Liddell Hart, *Strategy*, 325–326 (see note 2 above).

53. Ibid., 327.

54. Sun Tzu, *The Art of War*, 134 (see note 30 above).

55. Quoted in William Safire, *Safire's New Political Dictionary* (New York: Random House, 1993), 181–182.

56. David A. Stockman, *The Triumph of Politics: How the Reagan Revolution Failed* (New York: Harper and Row, 1986), 79.

57. Saul D. Alinsky, *Rules for Radicals* (New York: Random House, Vintage, 1972), 127.

58. Ibid.

59. Martin Luther King, Jr., *Why We Can't Wait* (New York: Harper and Row, 1964), 30.

60. J. McIver Weatherford, *Tribes on the Hill* (South Hadley, Mass.: Bergin and Garvey, rev. ed., 1985), 233–235.

61. Quoted in Louis Jacobson, "The Rise, Fall and Rise of a Think Tank," *National Journal*, August 22, 1998, 1991.

62. Sun Tzu, *The Art of War*, 77 (see note 30 above).

63. David A. Vise, "Fannie Mae Lobbies Hard to Protect Its Tax Break," *Washington Post*, January 16, 1995, A1.

64. Crowl, "The Strategist's Short Catechism," 35 (see note 10 above).

CHAPTER 3: Leadership

1. Quoted in Richard E. Neustadt, *Presidential Power and the Modern Presidents* (New York: Free Press, 1990), 10.

2. Ibid., 40. Here I paraphrase Neustadt's definition of the president's persuasive task.

3. Kevin S. Donohue and Leonard S. Wong, "Understanding and Applying Transformational Leadership," *Military Review*, August 1994, 25.

4. Paul Seabury and Angelo Codevilla, *War: Ends and Means* (New York: Basic Books, 1990), 93.

5. Quoted in Donohue and Wong, "Transformational Leadership," 26 (see note 4 above).

6. Charles de Gaulle, *The Edge of the Sword*, trans. Gerard Hopkins (New York: Criterion, 1960), 31.

7. Newt Gingrich, *Lessons Learned the Hard Way: A Personal Report* (New York: HarperCollins, 1998), 142.

8. U.S. Army, *Military Leadership*, Field Manual 22–100, Washington, D.C., 31 July 1990, at http://155.217.58.58/cgi-bin/atdl.dll/fm/22-100/PAR2CH6.HTM, accessed September 11, 1999.

9. Quoted in Peter G. Tsouras, *Warriors' Words: A Dictionary of Military Quotations* (London: Cassell, Arms and Armour Press, 1992), 236.

10. U.S. Department of Defense, *The Armed Forces Officer* (Washington, D.C.: Government Printing Office, 1960), 178.

11. Forrest McDonald, *Novus Ordo Seclorum: The Intellectual Origins of the Constitution* (Lawrence: University Press of Kansas, 1985), 193–194.

12. Erving Goffman, *The Presentation of Self in Everyday Life* (New York: Doubleday Books, Anchor Books, 1959), 15–16.

13. McDonald, *Novus Ordo Seclorum*, 195–199 (see note 11 above).

14. Frederick the Great, "The Instruction of Frederick the Great for His Generals, 1747," trans. Thomas R. Phillips, in Thomas R. Phillips, ed., *Roots of Strategy*, Book 1 (Harrisburg, Pa.: Stackpole, 1985), 346.

15. De Gaulle, *The Edge of the Sword*, 59 (see note 6 above).

16. John Keegan, *The Mask of Command* (New York: Penguin, 1988), 11.

17. De Gaulle, *The Edge of the Sword*, 58 (see note 6 above).

19. Peggy Noonan, *What I Saw at the Revolution: A Political Life in the Reagan Era* (New York: Random House, 1990), 150.

19. Al Kaltman, *Cigars, Whiskey and Winning: Leadership Lessons from General Ulysses S. Grant* (Paramus, N.J.: Prentice Hall Press, 1998), 6.

20. U.S. Department of Defense, *The Armed Forces Officer*, 70 (see note 10 above).

21. George S. Patton, "Speech to Third Army," at http://www.1918.com/phil/patton.shtml, accessed September 12, 1999. George C. Scott's famous opening speech in the movie *Patton* is a tamer version of the obscenity-laced address that Patton delivered at various times in 1944.

22. Quoted in James M. McPherson, *For Cause and Comrades: Why Men Fought in the Civil War* (New York: Oxford University Press, 1997), 58.

23. Warren Rudman, *Combat: Twelve Years in the U.S. Senate* (New York: Random House, 1997), 274.

24. Stimson Bullitt, *To Be a Politician* (New Haven, Conn.: Yale University Press, rev. ed., 1977), 36.

25. Dave Grossman, *On Killing: The Psychological Cost of Learning to Kill in War and Society* (Boston: Little, Brown and Company, Back Bay Books, 1996), 79.

26. Bullitt, *To Be a Politician*, 45 (see note 24 above).

27. Norma M. Riccucci, *Unsung Heroes: Federal Execucrats Making a Difference* (Washington, D.C.: Georgetown University Press, 1995), 42–45; U.S. Congress, House, Committee on Standards of Official Conduct, *Report of the Special Outside Counsel in the Matter of James C. Wright, Jr.* (Washington, D.C.: Government Printing Office, 1989), 255–259, 274–277.

28. Survey for the Campaign Assessment and Candidate Outreach Project, University of Maryland and *Campaigns & Elections*, supported by a grant from the Pew Charitable Trusts, at http://www.campaign-line.com/survey.cfm, accessed September 12, 1999.

29. Carl von Clausewitz, *On War*, ed. and trans. Michael Howard and Peter Paret (Princeton, N.J.: Princeton University Press, 1984), 192.

30. Quoted in James M. McPherson, *Battle Cry of Freedom: The Civil War Era* (New York: Ballantine, 1989), 726.

31. Bill Clinton and Al Gore, *Putting People First: How We Can All Change America* (New York: Random House, Times Books, 1992), 222.

32. Clausewitz, *On War*, 193 (see note 29 above).

33. Quoted in Keegan, *The Mask of Command*, 168 (see note 16 above).

34. Stephen E. Ambrose, *Eisenhower: Soldier, General of the Army, President Elect 1890–1952* (New York: Simon and Schuster, 1983), 555.

35. Quoted in Stephen E. Ambrose, "Eisenhower's Legacy," *Military Review*, October 1990, 5.

36. Quoted in Herbert M. Baus and William B. Ross, *Politics Battle Plan* (New York: Macmillan, 1968), 19.

37. Quoted in Kaltman, *Cigars, Whiskey and Winning*, 220 (see note 19 above).

38. Richard Nixon, *In the Arena: A Memoir of Victory, Defeat and Renewal* (New York: Pocket Books, 1991), 20.

39. U.S. Army, *Military Leadership*, Field Manual 22–100, Washington, D.C., October 31, 1983, 121.

40. Ibid., 90.

41. John F. Kennedy, *Profiles in Courage* (New York: Harper and Brothers, 1961), 20.

42. Quoted in Tsouras, *Warriors' Words*, 204 (see note 9 above).

43. William L. Riordon, *Plunkitt of Tammany Hall* (New York: E. P. Dutton, 1963), 25.

44. James MacGregor Burns, *Leadership* (New York: Harper and Row, Harper Colophon, 1979), 19.

45. Quoted in Donohue and Wong, "Transformational Leadership," 29 (see note 3 above).

46. Baus and Ross, *Politics Battle Plan*, 269 (see note 36 above).

47. Aubrey "Red" Smith, *Follow Me III: Lessons on the Art and Science of High Command* (Novato, Calif.: Presidio, 1997), 62.

48. Omar N. Bradley, "Leadership," *Military Review*, September 1966, 49.

49. Douglas Southall Freeman, "Leadership," *Naval War College Review*, March-April 1979, 4 (reprint of a lecture at the Naval War College, May 11, 1949).

50. U.S. Marine Corps, *Warfighting* (New York: Doubleday, Currency, 1995), 67.

51. Donald J. Devine, "Political Administration: The Right Way," in Robert Rector and Michael Sanera, eds., *Steering the Elephant: How Washington Works* (New York: Universe, 1987), 130.

52. William K. Muir, Jr., *Legislature: California's School for Politics* (Chicago: University of Chicago Press, 1985), chaps. 7–8.

53. Clausewitz, *On War*, 102 (see note 29 above).

54. Quoted in Keegan, *The Mask of Command*, 200 (see note 16 above).

55. Colin Powell, with Joseph Persico, *My American Journey* (New York: Random House, 1995), 117.

56. James B. Stockdale, "Taking Stock," *Naval War College Review*, June-July 1979, 2. See also Perry M. Smith, *Taking Charge: A Practical Guide for Leaders* (Washington, D.C.: National Defense University Press, 1986), 4.

57. Thomas E. Ricks, *Making the Corps* (New York: Simon and Schuster, Touchstone, 1998), chap. 7.

58. U.S. Marine Corps, *Warfighting*, 66 (see note 50 above).

59. Newt Gingrich, Remarks to Mortgage Bankers Association of America, Washington, D.C., March 4, 1992 (Federal News Service transcript).

60. Newt Gingrich, *To Renew America* (New York: HarperCollins, 1995), 40.

61. De Gaulle, *The Edge of the Sword*, 64 (see note 6 above).

62. Franklin D. Roosevelt, Inaugural Address, Washington, D.C., March 4, 1933, at New Deal Network, http://newdeal.feri.org/speeches/1933a.htm, accessed September 13, 1999.

63. Freeman, "Leadership," 9 (see note 49 above).

64. Bradley, "Leadership," 52 (see note 48 above).

65. William Niskanen, Jr., "Lessons for Political Appointees," in Robert Rector and Michael Sanera, eds., *Steering the Elephant: How Washington Works* (New York: Universe, 1987), 58.

66. Quoted in Porter B. Williamson, *Patton's Principles* (New York: Simon and Schuster, Touchstone, 1979), 102.

67. De Gaulle, *The Edge of the Sword*, 59–60 (see note 6 above).

68. Quoted in William F. Connelly, Jr. and John J. Pitney, Jr., *Congress' Permanent Minority? Republicans in the U.S. House* (Lanham, Md.: Rowman and Littlefield, 1994), 163.

69. Gordon R. Sullivan, "Leadership, Versatility and All That Jazz," *Military Review*, August 1994, 5.

CHAPTER 4: Coordination

1. Herbert Kaufman, *The Forest Ranger: A Study in Administrative Behavior* (Baltimore: The Johns Hopkins University Press, 1967), 87.

2. John Keegan, *A History of Warfare* (New York: Random House, Vintage, 1994), 342.

3. Flavius Vegetius Renatus, "The Military Institutions of the Romans," trans. John Clarke, in Thomas R. Phillips, ed., *Roots of Strategy*, Book 1 (Harrisburg, Pa.: Stackpole, 1985), 80.

4. Min Chen, "Sun Tzu's Strategic Thinking and Contemporary Business," *Business Horizons*, March-April 1994, 47.

5. U.S. Army, Operations, FM 100–5, June 1993, at http://155.217.58.58/cgi-bin/atdl.dll/fm/100-5/100-5c1.htm accessed September 14, 1999.

6. U.S. Marine Corps, *Warfighting* (New York: Doubleday, Currency, 1995), 80–81.

7. Ibid., 75–76.

8. Ibid., 92.

9. Ralph P. Hummel, "Toward a New Administrative Doctrine: Governance and Management for the 1990s," *American Review of Public Administration* 19 (September 1989): 175. Hummel notes that civilians prefer not to speak directly of "doctrine."

10. Kaufman refers to these decisions as "preformed." See his *The Forest Ranger*, 91 (see note 1 above).

11. Martha Derthick, *Policymaking for Social Security* (Washington, D.C.: Brookings, 1979), 23–31.

12. Philip A. Klinkner, *The Losing Parties: Out-Party National Committees 1956–1993* (New Haven, Conn.: Yale University Press, 1994), 200–215.

13. Dick Morris, *Behind the Oval Office: Getting Reelected Against All Odds* (Los Angeles: Renaissance Books, 1999), 271.

14. "Gingrich Marshaled GOP Revolution with Help from Fort Monroe," *Virginian-Pilot* (Norfolk, Virginia), December 25, 1995, A1.

15. Quoted in Damon Chappie, "General Gingrich Ices the 104th Congress," *Roll Call*, September 30, 1996, 26.

16. U.S. House Republican Conference, "A Framework for House Republicans," November 20, 1996 (photocopy).

17. Newt Gingrich, *Lessons Learned the Hard Way: A Personal Report* (New York: HarperCollins, 1998), 4.

18. Robert K. Barnhart, ed., *The Barnhart Dictionary of Etymology* (New York: H. H. Wilson, 1988), 897–898.

19. Brian R. Reinwald, "Retaining the Moral Element of War," *Military Review*, January-February 1998, at http://www-cgsc.army.mil/milrev/english/janfeb98/reinwald.htm, accessed September 14, 1999.

20. Anthony Downs, *Inside Bureaucracy* (Boston: Little, Brown, 1967), 229.

21. Derthick, *Policymaking for Social Security*, 28–30 (see note 11 above).

22. Kaufman, *The Forest Ranger*, 161–162 (see note 1 above).

23. Quoted in Jonathan Lash, *A Season of Spoils* (New York: Pantheon, 1984), 11.

24. Quoted in Pete Yost, "Starr Comes Under Fire as He Pursues His Criminal Investigation," Associated Press, April 19, 1996.

25. Quoted in Howard Kurtz, "The Defenders," *Washington Post Magazine*, November 1, 1998, W10.

26. Gloria Borger, "Between the Ideals and the Reality," *U.S. News & World Report*, July 1, 1996, 42.

27. Michael Weisskopf, "Replenishing the Troops for a Revolution: House GOP's Top Recruiter Is Part Proselytizer, Part Broker," *Washington Post*, April 30, 1996, A1.

28. Quoted in Gil Troy, *Affairs of State: The Rise and Rejection of the Presidential Couple Since World War II* (New York: Free Press, 1997), 59.

29. Thomas E. Ricks, "The Widening Gap Between the Military and Society," *Atlantic Monthly*, July 1997, at http://www.theatlantic.com/issues/97jul/milisoc.htm, accessed September 15, 1999.

30. Public Broadcasting System, Frontline Online, "The Choice '96," interview with Larry O'Donnell, Former Chief of Staff for Senate Finance Committee, interviewed July 14, 1996, at http://www2.pbs.org/wgbh/pages/frontline/shows/choice/bill, accessed March 13, 1999.

31. Jennifer Warren, "'Boot Camp' Gets New Lawmakers Up to Speed in Term Limits Era," *Los Angeles Times*, January 17, 1999, A3.

32. U.S. Marine Corps, *Warfighting*, 60 (see note 6 above). See also Gwynne Dyer, *War* (New York: Crown, 1985), 109.

33. U.S. Department of Defense, *The Armed Forces Officer* (Washington, D.C.: Government Printing Office, 1960), 145.

34. Michelle Kodis, "New Eco-Forces: Green Corps," *Earth Journal*, November 1993, 76.

35. Downs, *Inside Bureaucracy*, 235–236 (see note 20 above).

36. Antonio Olivo, "A New Latino School for Politics Takes a Wider View," *Los Angeles Times*, August 28, 1999, A1.

37. Quoted in Derthick, *Policymaking for Social Security*, 30–31 (see note 11 above).

38. Richard Nathan, *The Administrative Presidency* (New York: John Wiley & Sons, 1983), 75.

39. Quoted in Damon Chappie, "Gingrich Enlists Army," *Roll Call*, October 3, 1996, 24.

40. Dan Balz and Ronald Brownstein, *Storming the Gates: Protest Politics and the Republican Revival* (Boston: Little, Brown, 1996), 145.

41. Thomas E. Ricks, *Making the Corps* (New York: Simon and Schuster, Touchstone, 1998), 38.

42. Hugo Martin, "Language Barrier: Jargon-Laden City Hall Parlance Could Drive Listeners BANANAS," *Los Angeles Times*, March 17, 1994, B3.

43. Quoted in Donn Esmonde, "Power Training: Political Workshops Offer Women Candidates a Running Start," *Buffalo News*, March 1, 1998, 1A.

44. Nonviolence Web, Training for Change, at http://www.nonviolence.org/training, accessed September 16, 1999.

45. Marjorie Randon Hershey, *Running for Office: The Political Education of Campaigners* (Chatham, N.J.: Chatham House, 1984), 140.

46. Jo Mannies, "Democrats Gird for Battle—Campaign '96," *St. Louis Post-Dispatch*, June 19, 1996, 5B.

47. Peter Wendel and David Rabinow, "Political Education's Coming of Age," *Campaigns & Elections*, December 1998–January 1999, 22 ff.

48. Quoted in Hershey, *Running for Office*, 64 (see note 45 above).

49. Ricks, *Making the Corps*, 146 (see note 41 above).

50. Balz and Brownstein, *Storming the Gates*, 318 (see note 40 above).

51. Quoted in Rebecca S. Weiner, "Many Groups Look for Candidates to Run in '96," *St. Louis Post-Dispatch*, December 18, 1994, 4A.

52. James A. Muarry, ed., *A New English Dictionary on Historical Principles*, Vol. 6 (Oxford: Clarendon Press, 1908), 562.

53. Martin van Creveld, *Command in War* (Cambridge, Mass.: Harvard University Press, 1985), 55–56.

54. Ibid., 107–109.

55. Davis Homer Bates, *Lincoln in the Telegraph Office* (Lincoln, Nebr.: University of Nebraska Press, 1995 [1907]).

56. Don E. Fehrenbacher, *Prelude to Greatness: Lincoln in the 1850s* (Stanford, Calif.: Stanford University Press, 1962), 8.

57. Richard J. Jensen, *Grass Roots Politics: Parties, Issues and Voters, 1854–1983* (Westport, Conn.: Greenwood Press, 1983), 35.

58. Van Creveld, *Command in War*, 193 (see note 53 above).

59. Quoted in Bob Woodward, *The Agenda: Inside the Clinton White House* (New York: Simon and Schuster, 1994), 255.

60. Quoted in Rich Lowry, "Fax Populi: Armed with Computers and Fax Machines, Grass-Roots Organizations Are Shaking Up the Liberal Establishment," *National Review*, November 7, 1994, 50.

61. Quoted in Philippe Shepnick, "Tobacco Foes Create 'War Room' to Devise Lobbying Strategies," *The Hill*, June 17, 1998, 1.

62. Quoted in Joel Garreau, "Point Men for a Revolution: Can the Marines Survive a Shift from Hierarchies to Networks?" *Washington Post*, March 6, 1999, A01.

63. Quoted in Rebecca Fairley Raney, "Former Wrestler's Campaign Got a Boost From the Internet," *New York Times*, November 6, 1998, at http://www.politicsonline.com/coverage/nytimes2/06campaign.html, accessed September 17, 1999.

64. Ibid.

65. Quoted in Garreau, "Point Men" (see note 62 above).

66. National Security Archive, "The Cuban Missile Crisis: A Chronology of Events," at http://www.gwu.edu/~nsarchiv/nsa/cuba_mis_cri/cmcchron4.html, accessed September 17, 1999.

CHAPTER 5: Rallying the Troops

1. Quoted in Peter G. Tsouras, *Warriors' Words: A Dictionary of Military Quotations* (London: Cassell, Arms and Armour, 1992), 266.

2. Carl von Clausewitz, *On War*, ed. and trans. Michael Howard and Peter Paret (Princeton, N.J.: Princeton University Press, 1984), 184.

3. Edward L. Bernays, *Propaganda* (New York: Horace Liveright, 1928), 27.

4. Clausewitz, *On War*, 137 (see note 2 above).

5. Sun Tzu, *The Art of War*, trans. Samuel B. Griffith (New York: Oxford University Press, 1971), 75.

6. Niccolo Machiavelli, *The Art of War*, trans. Ellis Farneworth (New York: Da Capo, 1990 [1521]), 127.

7. Quoted in Jeff Greenfield, *Playing to Win: An Insider's Guide to Politics* (New York: Simon and Schuster, 1980), 50.

8. Quoted in Larry Sabato, *The Rise of Political Consultants: New Ways of Winning Elections* (New York: Basic, 1981), 241.

9. James Q. Wilson, *The Moral Sense* (New York: Free Press, 1993).

10. S. L. A. Marshall, *Men Against Fire* (New York: William Morrow, 1968 [1947]), 50.

11. Ibid, 79.

12. Dave Grossman, *On Killing: The Psychological Cost of Learning to Kill in War and Society* (Boston: Little, Brown and Company, Back Bay Books, 1996), 35.

13. Richard Holmes, *Acts of War: The Behavior of Men in Battle* (New York: Free Press, 1985), 146–147.

14. Kathleen Hall Jamieson, *Dirty Politics: Deception, Distraction, and Democracy* (New York: Oxford University Press, 1992), 41.

15. Sam Keen, *Faces of the Enemy: Reflections on the Hostile Imagination* (New York: Harper and Row, 1986), 39.

16. Grossman, *On Killing*, 157 (see note 12 above).

17. Stephen G. Shadegg, *How to Win an Election* (New York: Taplinger, 1964), 71–72.

18. Quoted in Stephen E. Ambrose, *Nixon: The Triumph of a Politician 1962–1972* (New York: Simon and Schuster, 1989), 307.

19. William Safire, *Before the Fall: An Inside View of the Pre-Watergate White House* (New York: Ballantine, 1977), 396.

20. Richard M. Nixon, Remarks in Anaheim, California, October 30, 1970, *American Freedom Library* [CD-ROM] (Western Standard Publishing, 1997).

21. Dick Morris, *Behind the Oval Office: Getting Reelected Against All Odds* (Los Angeles: Renaissance Books, 1999), 418–419.

22. James A. Aho, *This Thing of Darkness: A Sociology of the Enemy* (Seattle: University of Washington Press, 1994), 15.

23. Harry S Truman, Citation Accompanying the Legion of Merit Presented to President de Gaulle of France, August 24, 1945, *American Freedom Library* [CD-ROM] (Western Standard Publishing, 1997).

24. Harry S Truman, Statement by the President Upon Issuing Order Modifying the Wage-Price Policy, February 14, 1946, *American Freedom Library* [CD-ROM] (Western Standard Publishing, 1997).

25. Harry S Truman, Address in Philadelphia on Accepting the Democratic Presidential Nomination, July 15, 1948, *American Freedom Library* [CD-ROM] (Western Standard Publishing, 1997).

26. Quoted in "Clinton Jokes He Did His Part to Help Democrats in November with His Lewinsky Affair," *The White House Bulletin*, September 29, 1998.

27. Richard Hofstader, *The Paranoid Style in American Politics and Other Essays* (New York: Alfred A. Knopf, 1965), 29, 31.

28. David Zarefsky, *Lincoln, Douglas and Slavery: In the Crucible of Public Debate* (Chicago: University of Chicago Press, 1990), chap. 3.

29. Bruce L. Felknor, *Political Mischief: Smear, Sabotage and Reform in U.S. Elections* (New York: Praeger, 1992), 87.

30. Bruce L. Felknor, *Dirty Politics* (New York: W. W. Norton, 1966), 35.

31. Franklin D. Roosevelt, Campaign Address at Brooklyn, New York, November 1, 1940, *American Freedom Library* [CD-ROM] (Western Standard Publishing, 1997).

32. Quoted in Hofstader, *Paranoid Style*, 7 (see note 27 above).

33. Quoted in Howard Kurtz, *Spin Cycle: Inside the Clinton Propaganda Machine* (New York: Free Press, 1998), 298.

34. "'Some Folks Are Going to Have a Lot to Answer For'" [interview transcript], *Washington Post*, January 28, 1998, A21.

35. Quoted in Paul F. Boller, Jr., *Presidential Campaigns* (New York: Oxford University Press, 1984), 12.

36. Quoted in James M. McPherson, *For Cause and Comrades: Why Men Fought in the Civil War* (New York: Oxford University Press, 1997), 21.

37. Newt Gingrich, "Building the Conservative Movement after Ronald Reagan," Remarks to Heritage Foundation Resource Bank, Chicago, Illinois, April 21, 1988 (Heritage Lecture 167).

38. Quoted in Tsouras, *Warriors' Words*, 275 (see note 1 above).

39. Vito Russo, "Why We Fight," excerpts from a speech at the headquarters of the Department of Health and Human Services during a demonstration on Monday, October 10, 1988, at http://www.actupny.org/documents/whfight.html, accessed September 18, 1999.

40. Barbara Ehrenreich, *Blood Rites: Origins and History of the Passions of War* (New York: Henry Holt, Metropolitan Books, 1997), chap. 10.

41. Wayne Andrews, ed., *The Autobiography of Theodore Roosevelt* (New York: Octagon, 1975), 345.

42. Franklin D. Roosevelt, Nomination Address, Chicago, Illinois, July 2, 1932, at New Deal Network, http://newdeal.feri.org/speeches/1932b.htm, accessed September 18, 1999.

43. William Todd Baker, "Symbolism and Substance: Imagery in the Why We Fight Series," *Old Dominion University Historical Review* 1994, at http://www.odu.edu/~hanley/history1/Baker.htm, accessed September 18, 1999.

44. Aho, *This Thing of Darkness*, 11–14 (see note 22 above).

45. Quoted in Maralee Schwartz, "Losing Incumbent Says Using Religion Was Impolitic," *Washington Post*, August 8, 1986, A4.

46. Franklin D. Roosevelt, First Inaugural Address, March 4, 1933, at http://www.bartleby.com/124/pres49.html, accessed September 18, 1999.

47. "'We Must Turn Pain to Partnership" (excerpts from Jesse Jackson speech), *U.S.A. Today*, July 15, 1992, 3A.

48. Franklin D. Roosevelt, "We Have Only Just Begun to Fight," campaign address at Madison Square Garden, October 31, 1936, *Public Papers and Addresses of Franklin D. Roosevelt*, Vol. 5 (New York: Random House, 1938), 568.

49. Wyatt Walker, quoted in David J. Garrow, *Bearing the Cross: Martin Luther King, Jr. and the Southern Christian Leadership Conference* (New York: Random House, Vintage, 1988), 251.

50. Harold D. Lasswell, *Propaganda Technique in the World War* (New York: Alfred A. Knopf, 1927), 102, 113.

51. Paul Fussell, *Wartime: Understanding and Behavior in the Second World War* (New York: Oxford University Press, 1989), 149.

52. Quoted in Samuel Kernell and Samuel L. Popkin, eds., *Chief of Staff: Twenty-Five Years of Managing the Presidency* (Berkeley: University of California Press, 1986), 135–136.

53. Quoted in James M. McPherson, *Drawn With the Sword: Reflections on the American Civil War* (New York: Oxford University Press, 1996), 115.

54. Richard Nixon, Remarks to White House Staff, August 9, 1974, at http://vcepolitics.com/wgate/090874.htm, accessed September 18, 1999.

55. Mick Underwood, "Cultural Studies," at http://www.cultsock.ndirect.co.uk/MUHome/cshtml/nvc/nvc.html, accessed September 18, 1999.

56. Francis X. Clines, "Act I, Scene I: Crying Babies, Raw Anger, and a Showdown," *New York Times*, January 8, 1997, A1.

57. Holmes, *Acts of War*, 28 (see note 13 above).

58. J. McIver Weatherford, *Tribes on the Hill* (South Hadley, Mass.: Bergin and Garvey, rev. ed., 1985), chap. 8.

59. James Bryce, *The American Commonwealth*, Vol. 2 (Indianapolis, Ind.: Liberty Fund, 1995 [1910]), 856.

60. Robert A. Dahl, *Who Governs? Democracy and Power in an American City* (New Haven, Conn.: Yale University Press, 1961), 113.

61. *Official Report of the Proceedings of the Thirty-Second Republican National Convention* (Washington, D.C.: Republican National Committee, 1980), 506.

62. Fussell, *Wartime*, 48–49 (see note 51 above).

63. Mary Matalin and James Carville, with Peter Knobler, *All's Fair: Love, War, and Running for President* (New York: Random House, 1994), 464.

64. Stephen E. Pease, *Psywar: Psychological Warfare in Korea 1950–1953* (Harrisburg, Pa.: Stackpole, 1992), 11.

65. Ronald Brownstein, "Parties Defined by Where They See the Enemies," *Los Angeles Times*, September 1, 1996, A1.

66. Saul D. Alinsky, *Rules for Radicals* (New York: Random House, Vintage, 1972), 133.

67. Ibid., 134.

CHAPTER 6: Demoralizing, Deception, and Stealth

1. Carl von Clausewitz, *On War*, ed. and trans. Michael Howard and Peter Paret (Princeton, N.J.: Princeton University Press, 1984), 231.

2. Harry G. Summers, Jr., *On Strategy: A Critical Analysis of the Vietnam War* (New York: Dell, 1984), 21.

3. Quoted in Center of Military History, *American Military History* (Washington, D.C.: United States Army, 1989), at http://www2.army.mil/cmh-pg/books/amh/AMH-10.htm, accessed June 2, 1999.

4. Sun Tzu, *The Art of War*, trans. Samuel B. Griffith (New York: Oxford University Press, 1971), 67.

5. Quoted in Peter Goldman and Tony Fuller, *The Quest for the Presidency 1984* (New York: Bantam, 1985), 432.

6. Ibid., 442.

7. Calvin Trillin, "Ending the War: Just Say the Word," *St. Louis Post-Dispatch*, March 10, 1991, 2C.

8. J. McIver Weatherford, *Tribes on the Hill* (South Hadley, Mass.: Bergin and Garvey, rev. ed., 1985), 33.

9. Quoted in Karen Ball, "Democrats May Target Gingrich's House Seat," Associated Press, December 9, 1993.

10. Paul Seabury and Angelo Codevilla, *War: Ends and Means* (New York: Basic Books, 1990), 161–162.

11. Ed Rollins, with Tom DeFrank, *Bare Knuckles and Back Rooms: My Life in American Politics* (New York: Broadway Books, 1996), 103–104.

12. Barbara Sinclair, *The Transformation of the U.S. Senate* (Baltimore: The Johns Hopkins University Press, 1989), 172–173.

13. Quoted in Sarah A. Blinder and Steven S. Smith, *Politics or Principle? Filibustering in the United States Senate* (Washington, D.C.: Brookings Institution Press, 1997), 151.

14. Jacob E. Cooke, ed., *The Federalist* (Middletown, Conn.: Wesleyan University Press, 1961), no. 73, p. 494.

15. Cooke, ed., *The Federalist*, no. 58, p. 394 (see note 14 above).

16. Quoted in Robert A. Caro, *The Years of Lyndon Johnson: The Path to Power* (New York: Alfred A. Knopf, 1982), 399.

17. Saul D. Alinsky, *Reveille for Radicals* (New York: Random House, Vintage, 1989 [1946]), 144–145.

18. Saul D. Alinsky, *Rules for Radicals* (New York: Random House, Vintage, 1972), 142–143.

19. Dan Balz, "Bush Launches His Presidential Exploratory Panel," *Washington Post*, March 8, 1999, A4.

20. Harold D. Lasswell, *Propaganda Technique in the World War* (New York: Alfred A. Knopf, 1927), 164.

21. Ardant du Picq, "Battle Studies: Ancient and Modern Battle," trans. John N. Greely and Robert C. Cotton, in Thomas R. Phillips, ed., *Roots of Strategy*, Book 2 (Harrisburg, Pa.: Stackpole, 1987), 147.

22. Quoted in Ronald Brownstein and Bob Sipchen, "Dole, Forbes Look Ahead to NY Showdown," *Los Angeles Times*, March 5, 1996, A1.

23. Mark Lloyd, *The Art of Military Deception* (London: Leo Cooper, 1997), 160.

24. Eleanor Clift and Tom Brazaitis, *War Without Bloodshed: The Art of Politics* (New York: Scribner, 1996), 90–91.

25. "How He Won the War," *60 Minutes* transcript, May 25, 1997.

26. Quoted in Linda Feldmann, "GOP Stalks Democrats Who May Switch Parties," *Christian Science Monitor*, October 7, 1994, 1.

27. Quoted in "Deal Announces He Is Switching to Republican Party," *National Journal's Congress Daily*, April 10, 1995.

28. Stephen Ansolabehere and Shanto Iyengar, *Going Negative: How Attack Ads Shrink and Polarize the Electorate* (New York: Free Press, 1995), 9. Some scholars disagree with their analysis, arguing that the evidence for "demobilization" is weak. See Darrell M. West's aptly titled *Air Wars: Television Advertising in Election Campaigns 1952–1996* (Washington, D.C.: CQ Press, 2nd ed., 1997), 63–64.

29. David Beiler, *The Classics of Political Television Advertising: A Viewer's Guide* (Washington, D.C.: Campaigns & Elections, 1987), 37.

30. Pascale Combelles Siegel, "Target Bosnia: Integrating Information Activities in Peace Operations. NATO-Led Operations in Bosnia-Herzegovina, December 1995–1997," C4ISR Cooperative Research Program, April 1998, at http://www.dodccrp.org/tartoc.htm, accessed October 3, 1999.

31. Matthew Cooper, Gloria Borger, and Michael Barone, "Dirty Tricks? Cheap Shots? Says Who?" *U.S. News & World Report*, July 6, 1992, 41.

32. Paul Fussell, *Wartime: Understanding and Behavior in the Second World War* (New York: Oxford University Press, 1989), 46.

33. Quoted in Larry J. Sabato, *Feeding Frenzy: How Attack Journalism Has Transformed American Politics* (New York: Free Press, 1991), 141.

34. "FDR Discusses the Uses of Political Scandal," *American Heritage*, February-March 1982, 21.

35. Larry J. Sabato and Glenn R. Simpson, *Dirty Little Secrets: The Persistence of Corruption in American Politics* (New York: Random House, Times Books, 1996), 253.

36. Quoted in James MacGregor Burns, *Roosevelt: The Lion and the Fox* (New York: Harcourt Brace & World, 1956), 286.

37. Ken Khachigian, "Dividing the Democrats in 1972 (and before then)," September 22, 1971, Ken Khachigian Files, White House Special Files, Nixon Presidential Materials Staff, National Archives, College Park, Maryland.

38. Quoted in Sam Dealey, "GOP and Dems Exploit Divisions in Other's Ranks," *The Hill*, July 21, 1999, 1.

39. Sun Tzu, *The Art of War*, 66 (see note 4 above).

40. Donald C. Daniel and Katherine L. Herbig, "Propositions on Military Deception," in Donald C. Daniel and Katherine L. Herbig, eds., *Strategic Military Deception* (New York: Pergamon Press, 1982), 4–5.

41. Sissela Bok, *Lying: Moral Choice in Public and Private Life* (New York: Vintage, 1979), 14.

42. Andrea Cozad, "Deception," Center for Army Lessons Learned Newsletter 3–88, 1997, at http://call.army.mil/call/newsltrs/388/toc9.htm, accessed October 3, 1999.

43. Quoted in David Maraniss, *First in His Class: A Biography of Bill Clinton* (New York: Simon and Schuster, 1995), 238.

44. Philip Weiss, "The Senator Cannot Help Being Himself," *New York Times Magazine*, March 3, 1996, 50.

45. Laurie Goodstein, "Coalition's Woes May Hinder Goals of Christian Right," *New York Times*, August 2, 1999, A1.

46. Hugh Gregory Gallagher, *FDR's Splendid Deception* (New York: Dodd, Mead, 1985), 195.

47. Jill Lawrence, "Behind the Angry Walkout That Wasn't ," *U.S.A. Today*, September 23, 1998, 4A.

48. Robert A. Caro, *The Power Broker: Robert Moses and the Fall of New York* (New York: Random House, Vintage Books, 1975), 612.

49. J. Barton Bowyer, *Cheating: Deception in War & Magic, Games & Sports, Sex & Religion, Business & Con Games, Politics & Espionage, Art & Science* (New York: St. Martin's, 1982), 50–52.

50. Quoted in Michael Rezende, "Massachusetts GOP Tries to Rattle Dukakis," *Washington Post*, October 21, 1988, A4.

51. Mary Matalin and James Carville, with Peter Knobler, *All's Fair: Love, War, and Running for President* (New York: Random House, 1994), 349–350.

52. Sun Tzu, *The Art of War*, 98 (see note 4 above).

53. Quoted in James Gerstenzang and David Lauter, "Clinton Talks Like a Winner, But Warns Against Overconfidence," *Los Angeles Times*, October 17, 1992, A20.

54. Statement of David Schippers, House Judiciary Committee, December 10, 1998, at http://www.house.gov/judiciary/101338.htm, accessed October 3, 1999.

55. Caro, *The Power Broker*, 174 (see note 48 above).

56. Sissela Bok, *Secrets: On the Ethics of Concealment and Revelation* (New York: Random House, Vintage, 1984), 192–193.

57. Frederick the Great, "The Instruction of Frederick the Great for His Generals, 1747," trans. Thomas R. Phillips, in Thomas R. Phillips, ed., *Roots of Strategy*, Book 1 (Harrisburg, Pa.: Stackpole, 1985), 347.

58. Scott Armstrong, "The War Over Secrecy: Democracy's Most Important Low-Intensity Conflict," in Athan Theoharis, ed., *A Culture of Secrecy* (Lawrence: University Press of Kansas, 1998), 141.

59. Quoted in "The Iran-Contra Hearings," *Los Angeles Times*, July 22, 1987, 12.

60. Quoted in David Herbert Donald, *Lincoln* (New York: Simon and Schuster, Touchstone, 1996), 213.

61. Abraham Lincoln, "Circular from Whig Committee," January 1840, in John G. Nicolay and John Hay, eds., *The Complete Works of Abraham Lincoln*, Vol. I (New York: Lamb, 1905), 142–145.

62. Caro, *The Years of Lyndon Johnson: The Path to Power*, xviii–xix (see note 16 above).

63. Robert A. Caro, *The Years of Lyndon Johnson: Means of Ascent* (New York: Alfred A. Knopf, 1990), 272–277.

64. Lisa Rosenberg, "A Bag of Tricks: Loopholes in the Campaign Finance System," Center for Responsive Politics, 1996, at http://www.open secrets.org/pubs/law_bagtricks/contents.html, accessed October 3, 1999.

65. Paul Richter, "Low-Key California Congressman Wages High-Stakes Battle Over F-22," *Los Angeles Times*, September 30, 1999, A11.

66. Stephen C. Shadegg, *How to Win an Election: The Art of Political Victory* (New York: Taplinger, 1964), 106–107.

67. Quoted in Barry M. Horstman, "Christian Activists Using 'Stealth' Campaign Tactics," *Los Angeles Times*, April 5, 1992, A1.

68. Quoted in Peter Goldman et al., *Quest for the Presidency 1992* (College Station, Texas: Texas A & M University Press, 1994), 563.

69. Quoted in Peter G. Tsouras, *Warriors' Words: A Dictionary of Military Quotations* (London: Cassell, Arms and Armour, 1992), 159.

CHAPTER 7: Intelligence

1. Marine Corps Institute, *Introduction to Combat Intelligence* (Washington, D.C.: United States Marine Corps, 1989), 1–2.

2. Allen Dulles, *The Craft of Intelligence* (New York: Signet, 1965), 145–146.

3. I have very loosely based these questions on the definition of intelligence in U.S. Marine Corps, "Intelligence," Marine Corps Doctrine Publication 2, 1997, at http://www.quantico.usmc.mil/docdiv/2/chp1.htm, accessed October 4, 1999.

4. Quoted in Harold Holzer, "Introduction," in Harold Holzer, ed., *The Lincoln-Douglas Debates* (New York: HarperCollins, HarperPerennial, 1994), 17.

5. This discussion draws on Harold L. Wilensky, *Organizational Intelligence: Knowledge and Policy in Government and Industry* (New York: Basic, 1967), 10–16.

6. Eugene Bardach, "Subformal Warning Systems in the Species *Homo Politicus*," *Policy Sciences* 5 (December 1974), 422–425.

7. Ibid., 421.

8. On the clash of organizational cultures in the CIA and elsewhere, see James Q. Wilson, *Bureaucracy: What Government Agencies Do and Why They Do It* (New York: Basic, 1989), 101–102.

9. Sonni Efron and David Lauter, "Spy vs. Spy: Campaign Dirt Game," *Los Angeles Times*, March 28, 1992, A20.

10. Rowland Evans and Robert Novak, "The Johnson System," in Lawrence K. Pettit and Edward Keynes, eds., *The Legislative Process in the U.S. Senate* (Chicago: Rand McNally, 1969), 194.

11. Quoted in Samuel Kernell and Samuel L. Popkin, ed., *Chief of Staff: Twenty-Five Years of Managing the Presidency* (Berkeley: University of California Press, 1986), 79.

12. Wilensky, *Organizational Intelligence*, 13 (see note 5 above).

13. Maureen Dowd, "The Sniping Begins and All Is Normal," *New York Times*, November 17, 1990, 11.

14. Lawrence F. O'Brien, *No Final Victories: A Life in Politics—from John F. Kennedy to Watergate* (Garden City, N.Y.: Doubleday, 1974), 80.

15. Robert Dallek, *Flawed Giant: Lyndon Johnson and His Times* (New York: Oxford University Press, 1998), 161–162.

16. Lee Edwards, *Goldwater: The Man Who Made a Revolution* (Washington, D.C.: Regnery, 1995), 305–312.

17. Quoted in Herbert M. Baus and William B. Ross, *Politics Battle Plan* (New York: Macmillan, 1968), 295.

18. Quoted in Richard Reeves, *Convention* (New York: Harcourt Brace Jovanovich, 1977), 71.

19. Quoted in Larry J. Sabato and Glenn R. Simpson, *Dirty Little Secrets: The Persistence of Corruption in American Politics* (New York: Random House, Times Books, 1996, 182).

20. Deborah Orin, "GOP Admits Aide Lied to Obtain Dinkins' Speech," *New York Post*, August 31, 1989, 14.

21. Richard Eells and Peter Nehemkis, *Corporate Intelligence and Espionage: A Blueprint for Executive Decision Making* (New York: Macmillan, 1984), 128.

22. National Security Agency, "Operations Security: Intelligence Threat Handbook," April 1996, at http://www.fas.org/irp/nsa/ioss/threat96/part06.htm, accessed October 6, 1999.

23. John Kern, quoted in Amy Keller, "World Wide Web Stole the Show At Annual Consultants Gathering," *Roll Call*, January 18, 1996.

24. National Security Agency, "Operations Security" (see note 23 above). See also H. Norman Schwarzkopf, with Peter Petre, *It Doesn't Take a Hero* (New York: Bantam, 1993), 510.

25. George Stephanopoulos, *All Too Human: A Political Education* (Boston: Little, Brown, 1999), 88.

26. Quoted in "Faster than a Speeding Bullet," *Campaigns & Elections*, August 1996, 8.

27. Quoted in Scott Lindlaw, "California Candidate Uses 'Spy' Tactics," Associated Press, May 29, 1998.

28. Quoted in Amy Keller, "Burns Cries Foul, But Both Parties Exploit FOIA Laws," *Roll Call*, September 30, 1999, 17.

29. Joseph Rodota, "Putting Your Op Research Through a Two-Minute Drill," in Ron Faucheux, ed., *The Road to Victory: The Complete Guide to Winning in Politics* (Dubuque, Iowa: Kendall/Hunt, 1995), 133.

30. William Saletan, "Spy vs. Spy," *George*, December 1995–January 1996, 148.

31. Robert D. Steele, quoted in Vernon Loeb, "Spying Intelligence Data Can Be an Open-Book Test," *Washington Post*, March 22, 1999, A17. See also the website for Steele's consulting firm, Open Source Solutions, at http://www.oss.net.

32. Quoted in Sally Quinn, "Welcome to Washington, But Play by Our Rules," *Washington Post*, November 15, 1992, C1.

33. Using examples from intelligence and law enforcement, Erving Goffman discussed interrogation and deception in *Strategic Interaction* (Philadelphia: University of Philadelphia Press, 1969), 28–46.

34. Quoted in "DeLay: Lighten Up in Speaker Race," *National Journal's Congress Daily*, March 19, 1998.

35. Quoted in Ben Wildavsky, "Atlas Schmoozes," *National Journal*, May 17, 1997, 974.

36. Carl von Clausewitz, *On War*, ed. and trans. Michael Howard and Peter Paret (Princeton, N.J.: Princeton University Press, 1984), 117.

37. Joseph Gaylord, *Flying Upside Down: 88 Truisms to Help Guide Challenger Campaigns* (Washington, D.C.: National Republican Congressional Committee, 1987), 29.

38. Sun Tzu, *The Art of War*, trans. Samuel B. Griffith (New York: Oxford University Press, 1971), 100.

39. U.S. Marine Corps, "Intelligence," Marine Corps Doctrine Publication 2, 1997, at http://www.quantico.usmc.mil/docdiv/2/chp2.htm, accessed October 8, 1999.

40. Quoted in Bob Woodward, *The Commanders* (New York: Simon and Schuster, 1991), 257.

41. This discussion draws on Richard E. Neustadt and Ernest R. May, *Thinking in Time: The Uses of History for Decision Makers* (New York: Free Press, 1986), 157–162.

42. Doris Kearns, *Lyndon Johnson and the American Dream* (New York: New American Library, Signet, 1977), 124–125.

43. Ibid., 278–279.

44. Bob Woodward, *The Agenda: Inside the Clinton White House* (New York: Simon and Schuster, 1994), 178.

45. Howard Kurtz, "Weapon of Choice for Republican Rivals Is 'Opposition Research,'" *Washington Post*, February 25, 1996, A10.

46. Quoted in Frank LoMonte, "'Opposition Research' Is Common Aspect of Politics," *Athens Daily News*, July 18, 1998, at http://www.onlineathens.com, accessed October 1, 1999.

47. U.S. Marine Corps, "Campaigning," Marine Corps Doctrine Publication 1–2, 1997, at http://www.quantico.usmc.mil/docdiv/1-2/ch2.htm, accessed October 8, 1999.

48. Colin L. Powell, "Information-Age Warriors," *Byte*, July 1992, 370.

49. National Security Agency, "Operations Security: Intelligence Threat Handbook," April 1996, at http://www.fas.org/irp/nsa/ioss/threat96/part06.htm, accessed October 6, 1999.

50. Michael J. Bayer and Joseph Rodota, "Computerized Opposition Research: The Instant Parry," *Campaigns & Elections*, Spring 1985, 26.

51. Quoted in Joseph R. Shapiro, "Hitting Before Hate Strikes," *U.S. News & World Report*, September 6, 1999, 57.

52. Roberta Wohlstetter, *Pearl Harbor: Warning and Decision* (Stanford, Calif.: Stanford University Press, 1962), 392–393.

53. Quoted in Jack W. Germond and Jules Witcover, *Whose Broad Stripes and Bright Stars? The Trivial Pursuit of the Presidency 1988* (New York: Warner Books, 1989),358.

54. Neustadt and May, *Thinking in Time*, chap. 8 (see note 42 above).

55. Robert Jervis, *Perception and Misperception in International Politics* (Princeton, N.J.: Princeton University Press, 1976), 415–423.

56. Niccolo Machiavelli, *The Prince*, trans. George Bull (Baltimore: Penguin, 1961), 127.

57. Clausewitz, *On War*, 149 (see note 36 above).

CHAPTER 8: Geography and Logistics

1. Martin Van Creveld, *Supplying War: Logistics from Wallenstein to Patton* (New York: Cambridge University Press, 1977), 2.

2. Quoted in Jerry Bruno and Jeff Greenfield, *The Advance Man* (New York: William Morrow, 1971), 39.

3. Theodore H. White, *The Making of the President 1960* (New York: New American Library, Signet, 1967), 364.

4. Frederick the Great, "The Instruction of Frederick the Great for His Generals, 1747," trans. Thomas R. Phillips, in Thomas R. Phillips, ed., *Roots of Strategy*, Book 1 (Harrisburg, Pa.: Stackpole, 1985), 338–339.

5. U.S. Marine Corps, "Logistics," Marine Corps Doctrine Publication 4, 1997, at http://www.quantico.usmc.mil/docdiv/4/ch1.htm, accessed October 10, 1999.

6. Roger H. Davidson and Walter J. Oleszek, *Congress and Its Members* (Washington: CQ Press, 6th ed., 1998), 135.

7. Charles Lindauer, "Tactical Cartography," *Campaigns & Elections*, April 1999, 48.

8. Alan Ehrenhalt, "Neighborhoods and the L.A. Leviathan," *Governing*, November 1998, 7.

9. Quoted in John Nichols, "Politics '98—What Really Matters: Power to Redistrict Is the True November Prize," *The Nation*, November 2, 1998, at http://www.thenation.com/issue/981102/1102NICH.HTM, accessed October 10, 1999.

10. For a skeptical view of the partisan impact of redistricting, see Mark E. Rush, *Does Redistricting Make a Difference?* (Baltimore: The Johns Hopkins University Press, 1993).

11. Quoted in Charles T. Royer, ed., *Campaign for President: The Managers Look at '92* (Hollis, N.H.: Hollis Publishing, 1994), 203.

12. John J. Pitney, Jr., "Bile Barrel Politics: Siting Unwanted Facilities," *Journal of Policy Analysis and Management* 3 (Spring 1984): 446–448.

13. U.S. Department of Commerce, Bureau of the Census, *Statistical Abstract of the United States 1998* (Washington, D.C.: Government Printing Office, 1998), 236.

14. Kevin R. Cox, *Location and Public Problems: A Political Geography of the Contemporary World* (Chicago: Maaroufa Press, 1979).

15. Stanley D. Brunn, *Geography and Politics in America* (New York: Harper and Row, 1974), 320–321.

16. Richard F. Fenno, Jr., *Home Style: House Members in Their Districts* (Boston: Little, Brown, 1978), 4–8.

17. John Keegan, *A History of Warfare* (New York: Random House, Vintage, 1994), 68–69.

18. In the fall of 1944, Holland's geographical obstacles contributed to the failure of Operation Market-Garden. Harold A. Winters, *Battling the Elements: Weather and Terrain in the Conduct of War* (Baltimore: The Johns Hopkins University Press, 1998), 142–143. I thank Bill Rood for impressing this point on me.

19. Lindauer, "Tactical Cartography," 50 (see note 7 above).

20. Blaine Harden, "Democrats Turn GOP Ads Inside Out," *Washington Post*, September 25, 1998, A19.

21. Quoted in Mark Shields, "What to Do When Your Candidate Goes to the Wrong Ghetto," *Washington Post*, July 8, 1984, D3.

22. Gordon A. Harrison, *Cross-Channel Attack* (Washington, D.C.: U.S. Army Center for Military History, 1993), 284.

23. Quoted in Herbert M. Baus and William B. Ross, *Politics Battle Plan* (New York: Macmillan, 1968), 190.

24. Jeffrey L. Pressman and Aaron B. Wildavsky, *Implementation* (Berkeley: University of California Press, 1974), 148–160.

25. U.S. Marine Corps, *Small Wars Manual* (Manhattan, Kans.: Sunflower University Press, 1996 [1940]), 1–11.

26. Quoted in Thomas E. Ricks, *Making the Corps* (New York: Simon and Schuster, Touchstone, 1998), 186–187.

27. Saul D. Alinsky, *Reveille for Radicals* (New York: Random House, Vintage, 1989 [1946]), 153.

28. For a wonderful impressionistic view of New York politics, see Samuel G. Freedman, *The Inheritance: How Three Families and America Moved from Roosevelt to Reagan and Beyond* (New York: Simon and Schuster, 1996).

29. Los Angeles County Republican chairman Julius Leetham, quoted in Theodore H. White, *The Making of the President 1964* (New York: New American Library, Signet, 1966), 157.

30. Peter Skerry, *Mexican Americans: The Ambivalent Minority* (Cambridge, Mass.: Harvard University Press, 1995), 183–187.

31. Tom Clancy and Fred Franks, Jr., *Into the Storm: A Study in Command* (New York: G. P. Putnam's Sons, 1997), 96.

32. The Ruckus Society, "Scouting Manual," at http://www.ruckus.org/man/scouting_manual.html, accessed October 11, 1999.

33. Ron Faucheux, "The First 25 Steps Every Smart Candidate Should Take," *Campaigns & Elections*, July 1997, 21.

34. Quoted in Paul Taylor, "Anger Over Imports Fuels Texas Campaign," *Washington Post*, August 1, 1985, A4.

35. Tip O'Neill with Gary Hymel, *All Politics Is Local and Other Rules of the Game* (New York: Random House, Times Books, 1994), 79–80.

36. Quoted in Robert A. Caro, *The Years of Lyndon Johnson: The Path to Power* (New York: Alfred A. Knopf, 1982), 329–330.

37. Sun Tzu, *The Art of War*, trans. Samuel B. Griffith (New York: Oxford University Press, 1971), 104.

38. Quoted in David Hoffman, "Strong GOP Governors in Key States Play Crucial Role in Bush Campaign," *Washington Post*, March 12, 1988, A12.

39. Jack W. Germond and Jules Witcover, *Whose Broad Stripes and Bright Stars? The Trivial Pursuit of the Presidency 1988* (New York: Warner Books, 1989), 142.

40. James G. Gimpel, "Grassroots Organizations and Equilibrium Cycles in Group Mobilization and Access," in Paul S. Herrnson, Ronald G. Shaiko, and Clyde Wilcox, eds., *The Interest Group Connection* (Chatham, N.J.: Chatham House, 1998), 105.

41. S. L. A. Marshall, *Men Against Fire* (New York: William Morrow, 1968 [1947]), 101.

42. Sandra Salmans and Tony Fuller, "The Candidates' Men," *Newsweek*, February 23, 1976, 22.

43. John M. Broder, "Logistic Demands of Primaries in Next 2 Weeks Favor Dole," *Los Angeles Times*, February 21, 1996, A5.

44. U.S. Marine Corps, "Logistics," Marine Corps Doctrine Publication 4, 1997, at http://www.quantico.usmc.mil/docdiv/4/ch1.htm, accessed October 11, 1999.

45. Quoted in Peter G. Tsouras, *Warriors' Words: A Dictionary of Military Quotations* (London: Cassell, Arms and Armour, 1992), 434.

46. Jacob K. Javits, with Rafael Steinberg, *Javits: The Autobiography of a Public Man* (Boston: Houghton Mifflin, 1981), 64.

47. Quoted in Thucydides, *The Peloponnesian War*, trans. Rex Warner (New York: Penguin, 1972), 85.

48. Transcript of President Clinton's press conference of August 6, 1997, at http://www.whitehouse.gov, accessed October 11, 1999.

49. Jules Witcover, *Marathon: The Pursuit of the Presidency 1972–1976* (New York: Viking, 1977), 635.

50. Stimson Bullitt, *To Be a Politician* (New Haven, Conn.: Yale University Press, rev. ed., 1977), 110.

51. Edward N. Costikyan, *Behind Closed Doors: Politics in the Public Interest* (New York: Harcourt, Brace and World, 1966), 278.

52. U.S. Department of Defense, *The Armed Forces Officer* (Washington, D.C.: Government Printing Office, 1960), 239.

53. Gary Hart, *Right from the Start: A Chronicle of the McGovern Campaign* (New York: Quadrangle, 1973), 249.

54. United States Marine Corps, "Logistics," Marine Corps Doctrinal Publication 4, 1997, at http://www.quantico.usmc.mil/docdiv/4/ch1.htm, accessed October 12, 1999.

55. Niccolo Machiavelli, *The Art of War*, trans. Ellis Farneworth (New York: Da Capo, 1990 [1521]), 202.

56. Quoted in Bill Peterson and T. R. Reid, "Hart Says His Judgment, Not Conduct Was Flawed," *Washington Post*, May 6, 1987, A1.

57. Quoted in Jill Abramson, "Bush's Big Bankroll and What It Means," *New York Times*, July 2, 1999, A14.

58. Quoted in Paul Houston, "Political Gifts, Fueled by PACs, Continue to Soar," *Los Angeles Times*, April 8, 1986, I8.

59. Quoted in Ed Mendel, "Initiative Targets Political Use of Union Dues," *San Diego Union-Tribune*, April 19, 1998, A3.

60. Grover G. Norquist, *Rock the House* (Fort Lauderdale, Fla.: Vytis, 1995), 303.

61. Clifford J. Levy, "In New York Legislature, Entrenched Majorities Lord It Over the Underdogs," *New York Times*, April 19, 1999, A25.

CHAPTER 9: Friction and Finality

1. Carl von Clausewitz, *On War*, ed. and trans. Michael Howard and Peter Paret (Princeton, N.J.: Princeton University Press, 1984), 119.

2. Ibid., 80.

3. Ibid., 140.

4. Quoted in William Greider, *The Education of David Stockman and Other Americans* (New York: E. P. Dutton, 1982), 33.

5. Richard E. Cohen, "When There's Too Much of a Good Thing," *National Journal*, June 18, 1994, 1476.

6. H. Norman Schwarzkopf, with Peter Petre, *It Doesn't Take a Hero* (New York: Bantam, 1993), 581.

7. Winston S. Churchill, *Marlborough: His Life and Times*, Book One (London: George C. Harrap, 1947 [1934]), 569. I am grateful to Larry Arnn for drawing my attention to this passage.

8. Saul David, *Military Blunders: The How and Why of Military Failure* (New York: Carroll and Graf, 1998), 13–24.

9. Quoted in Stephen E. Ambrose, *Eisenhower the President* (New York: Simon and Schuster, Touchstone, 1985), 412–413.

10. Ibid., 118.

11. Jonathan Shay, "Ethical Standing for Commander Self-Care: The Need for Sleep," *Parameters*, Summer 1998, at http://carlisle-www.army.mil/usawc/parameters/98summer/shay.htm, accessed September 1, 1999.

12. Thomas C. Reeves, *A Question of Character: A Life of John F. Kennedy* (New York: Free Press, 1991), 294–300.

13. Richard Nixon, *In the Arena: A Memoir of Victory, Defeat and Renewal* (New York: Pocket Books, 1991), 191.

14. Bob Woodward, *Shadow: Five Presidents and the Legacy of Watergate* (New York: Simon and Schuster, 1999), 192, 197.

15. Quoted in Elizabeth Drew, *On the Edge: The Clinton Presidency* (New York: Simon and Schuster, 1994), 37.

16. *Myers v. U.S.* (272 U.S. 52, at 293).

17. Jacob E. Cooke, ed., *The Federalist* (Middletown, Conn.: Wesleyan University Press, 1961), no. 51, pp. 349–350.

18. Quoted in John M. Barry, *The Ambition and the Power* (New York: Viking, 1989), 304.

19. Quoted in Thomas B. Edsall, "GOP: Ideological Divide," *Washington Post,* July 14, 1990, A6.

20. Quoted in Elizabeth Drew, *Whatever It Takes: The Real Struggle for Power in America* (New York: Viking, 1997), 185.

21. Clausewitz, *On War,* 596 (see note 1 above).

22. *Congressional Record* (bound), September 8, 1980, 24683.

23. Quoted in Helen Dewar and Kenneth J. Cooper, "Jobs Bill May Strain Democratic Unity," *Washington Post,* April 27, 1993, A12.

24. Quoted in Helen Dewar, "Republicans Wage Verbal Civil War," *Washington Post,* November 19, 1984, A5.

25. John Keegan, *The Face of Battle* (New York: Penguin, 1976), 115.

26. Clausewitz, *On War,* 456 (see note 1 above).

27. David A. Stockman, *The Triumph of Politics: The Inside Story of the Reagan Revolution* (New York: Avon, 1987), 380.

28. Quoted in Phil Gailey, "Conservative Study Gives Reagan a Mixed Rating," *New York Times,* November 25, 1983, B14.

29. Quoted in Edward Walsh, "GOP Points Fingers on Tax-Bill Blunders," *Washington Post,* December 19, 1985, A6.

30. Patrick J. Buchanan, "How the Baker Boys Toppled Reagan," *Washington Post,* November 1, 1987, C1.

31. Quoted in Edsall, "GOP: Ideological Divide," A6 (see note 19 above).

32. Bill Whalen, "For Republicans, A House Divided," *Insight,* November 12, 1990, 10.

33. ABC News Nightline, May 10, 1993.

34. S. L. A. Marshall, *Men Against Fire* (New York: William Morrow, 1968 [1947]), 194.

35. Nixon, *In the Arena,* 207 (see note 13 above).

36. Newt Gingrich, *Lessons Learned the Hard Way: A Personal Report* (New York: HarperCollins, 1998), 36.

37. Charles de Gaulle, *The Edge of the Sword*, trans. Gerard Hopkins (New York: Criterion, 1960), 25.

38. Colin L. Powell, with Joseph E. Persico, *My American Journey* (New York: Random House, 1995), 207.

39. William Galston and Elaine Ciulla Kamarck, *The Politics of Evasion: Democrats and the Presidency* (Washington, D.C.: Progressive Policy Institute), 1989, 28.

40. Saul D. Alinsky, *Rules for Radicals* (New York: Random House, Vintage, 1972), 163.

41. U.S. Marine Corps, *Warfighting* (New York: Doubleday, Currency, 1995), 33.

42. Paul Kennedy, *The Rise and Fall of the Great Powers: Economic Change and Military Conflict from 1500 to 2000* (New York: Random House, 1987), xvi.

43. Quoted in William Safire, *Safire's New Political Dictionary* (New York: Random House, 1993), 745.

44. William F. Connelly, Jr. and John J. Pitney, Jr., "The House GOP's Civil War: A Political Science Perspective," *PS: Political Science and Politics* 30 (December 1997): 699–702.

45. B. H. Liddell Hart, *Strategy* (New York: Penguin/Meridian, 2nd ed., 1991 [1967]), 357.

46. Dave Grossman, *On Killing: The Psychological Cost of Learning to Kill in War and Society* (Boston: Little, Brown and Company, Back Bay Books, 1996), 216.

47. Quoted in Gingrich, *Lessons Learned the Hard Way*, 70 (see note 37 above).

48. *Congressional Record* (daily ed.), December 18, 1998, H11779. I thank Chris Wiedey for bringing this exchange to my attention.

49. Quoted in Ken Adelman, "Hat Trick: After Serving in All Three Branches of Government, Abner Mikva Likes the 'Marvelous Friction,'" *Washingtonian*, March, 1997, 31.

CHAPTER 10: Scholars and Metaphors

1. Gary J. Miller, "The Impact of Economics on Contemporary Political Science," *Journal of Economic Literature* 35 (September 1997): 1173–1204; David Lalman, Joe Oppenheimer, and Piotr Swistak, "Formal

Rational Choice Theory: A Cumulative Science of Politics," in Ada Finifter, ed., *Political Science: The State of the Discipline II* (Washington, D.C.: American Political Science Association, 1993).

2. Anthony Downs, *An Economic Theory of Democracy* (New York: Harper and Row, 1957), chap. 8.

3. Steven J. Brams, *Rational Politics: Decisions, Games, and Strategy* (Washington, D.C.: CQ Press, 1985), 10–14.

4. Steven J. Brams, *The Presidential Election Game* (New Haven, Conn.: Yale University Press, 1978), 143–145.

5. Richard M. Scammon and Ben J. Wattenberg, *The Real Majority* (New York: Berkley Books, Berkley Medallion, 1971), 337.

6. George Stephanopoulos, *All Too Human: A Political Education* (Boston: Little, Brown, 1999), 5.

7. See, among others, Kathleen Hall Jamieson, *Packaging the Presidency* (New York: Oxford University Press, 3rd ed., 1996).

8. Stephen E. Rhoads, *The Economist's View of the World: Government, Markets, and Public Policy* (Cambridge: Cambridge University Press, 1985), 203–206.

9. Martin Luther King, Jr., *Why We Can't Wait* (New York: Harper and Row, 1964), 15, 26.

10. Ibid., 27.

11. Ibid., 29–30.

12. See Michael E. Meagher, "'In an Atmosphere of National Peril': The Development of John F. Kennedy's World View," *Presidential Studies Quarterly* 27 (Summer 1997): 467–479. This article is not about courage per se but about JFK's conception of it.

13. James Q. Wilson, "The Politics of Regulation," in idem, ed., *The Politics of Regulation* (New York: Basic, 1980), 363.

14. See, among others, David L. Paletz, *The Media in American Politics: Contents and Consequences* (New York: Longman, 1999).

15. One exception is Eric M. Uslaner, *The Decline of Comity in Congress* (Ann Arbor: University of Michigan Press, 1993).

16. C. S. Lewis, *The Abolition of Man* (New York: Macmillan, 1955), 34. For a critique of rational choice theory, see Donald P. Green and Ian Shapiro, *Pathologies of Rational Choice Theory: A Critique of Applications in Political Science* (New Haven, Conn.: Yale University Press, 1994). For a recent and controversial treatment in the press, see Jonathan Cohn, "Irrational Exuberance," *The New Republic*, October 26, 1999, 25–31.

17. Dick Morris, *The New Prince* (Los Angeles: Renaissance, 1999), 123.

18. Quoted in Will Woodward, "Crime Bill Raising Status of Fetus Moves Forward," *Washington Post*, September 15, 1999, A4.

19. Eugene Bardach, "Subformal Warning Systems in the Species *Homo Politicus*," *Policy Sciences* 5 (December 1974): 422–425.

20. Some scholars and journalists have calculated general data on campaign budgets. For an excellent summary of this literature, see Paul Herrnson, *Congressional Elections: Campaigning at Home and in Washington* (Washington, D.C.: CQ Press, 1998), chap. 3. What is missing from the literature, however, are studies explaining whether certain allocations work better than others, and under what circumstances. One study does suggest that challengers get more benefit from television advertising than incumbents. See Christopher Kenny and Michael McBurnett, "Up Close and Personal: Campaign Contact and Candidate Spending in U.S. House Elections," *Political Research Quarterly* 50 (March 1997): 75–96. Over-the-air television advertisements are often impractical for House races because the boundaries of media markets do not correspond to congressional district lines. See Sara Fritz and Dwight Morris, *Gold-Plated Politics: Running for Congress in the 1990s* (Washington, D.C.: CQ Press, 1992), chap. 6.

21. Edward V. Schneier and Bertram Gross, *Legislative Strategy: Shaping Public Policy* (New York: St. Martin's, 1993), 2.

22. See for instance, Janet M. Martin, *Lessons from the Hill* (New York: St. Martin's, 1994).

23. Donald Kettl, "Clueless in the Capital," *Washington Monthly*, July/August 1999, 22–23.

24. R. Douglas Arnold, "Overtilled and Undertilled Fields in American Politics," *Political Science Quarterly* 97 (Spring 1982): 91–103.

25. Kettl, "Clueless in the Capital," 23 (see note 23 above).

26. Alexis de Tocqueville, *Democracy in America*, ed. J. P. Mayer, trans. George Lawrence (Garden City, N.Y.: Doubleday, Anchor, 1969), 218.

27. Phillip L. Gianos, *Political Behavior: Metaphors and Models of American Politics* (Pacific Palisades, Calif.: Palisades, 1982), 35.

28. Karl W. Deutsch, *The Nerves of Government* (New York: Free Press, 1966), 26.

29. Garry Wills, *Inventing America: Jefferson's Declaration of Independence* (Garden City, N.Y.: Doubleday, 1978), 93.

30. Laurence H. Tribe, "The Curvature of Constitutional Space: What Lawyers Can Learn from Modern Physics," in Theodore L. Becker,

ed., *Quantum Politics: Applying Quantum Theory to Political Phenomena* (New York: Praeger, 1991), 173.

31. Woodrow Wilson, *Constitutional Government in the United States* (New York: Columbia University Press, 1908), 56.

32. James Q. Wilson, *Bureaucracy: What Government Agencies Do and Why They Do It* (New York: Basic, 1989), 188.

33. Edward Jay Epstein, *Deception: The Invisible War Between the KGB and the CIA* (New York: Simon and Schuster, 1989), 17–18.

34. Virginia Postrel, *The Future and Its Enemies: The Growing Conflict over Creativity, Enterprise, and Progress* (New York: Free Press, 1998), 30.

35. Michael Rothschild, *Bionomics: The Inevitability of Capitalism* (New York: Henry Holt, John Macrae, 1990), 213.

36. John Vandermeer, "The Tragedy of the Commons: The Meaning of the Metaphor," *Science and Society* 60 (Fall 1997): 290–306.

37. Robert N. Bellah et al., *Habits of the Heart: Individualism and Commitment in American Life* (New York: Harper and Row, Perennial, 1986).

38. Jacob E. Cooke, *The Federalist* (Middletown, Conn.: Wesleyan University Press, 1961), no. 38, p. 243.

39. Susan Sontag, *Illness as Metaphor* (New York: Penguin, 1983), 85.

40. Michael A. Ledeen, *Machiavelli on Modern Leadership* (New York: St. Martin's Press, Truman Talley Books, 1999), 38.

41. Stephen E. Ambrose, *Nixon: The Education of a Politician 1913–1962* (New York: Simon and Schuster, 1987), 111–114.

42. Shawn J. Parry-Giles and Trevor Parry-Giles, "Meta-Imaging, the War Room, and the Hyperreality of U.S. Politics," *Journal of Communication* 49 (Winter 1999): 28–41.

43. Murray Edelman, *The Symbolic Uses of Politics* (Urbana: University of Illinois Press, 1964), 52.

44. Quoted in Al Cross, "'It's Like Doing Three Movies a Day': Clinton-Gore Caravan Often a Bumpy Ride," *Courier-Journal* (Louisville, Ky.), July 20, 1992, 1A.

45. Herbert F. Weisberg and Samuel C. Patterson, "Theater in the Round: Congress in Action," in Weisberg and Patterson, eds., *Great Theater: The American Congress in the 1990s* (New York: Cambridge University Press, 1998), 10.

46. James E. Combs and Dan Nimmo, *The Comedy of Democracy* (Westport, Conn.: Praeger, 1996), 20.

47. William K. Muir, Jr., *Legislature: California's School for Politics* (Chicago: University of Chicago Press, 1985), xii.

48. Tocqueville, *Democracy in America*, 63 (see note 26 above).

49. Ibid., 275.

50. Joseph M. Bessette, *The Mild Voice of Reason: Deliberative Democracy and American National Government* (Chicago: University of Chicago Press, 1994).

Index

Acts of War, 186
Adams, John, 192
Addison, Joseph, 45
Adler, Jonathan, 77
Advertising, 65, 107, 135–36, 147, 235n.20
Agnew, Spiro, 85
AIDS, 90
Alexander, Lamar, 131
Alexander the Great, 26, 46
Alinsky, Saul D., 39, 74, 99, 104–105, 149–50, 176, 182, 186
Ambrose, Stephen, 50
American Cancer Society, 77
American Civil Liberties Union (ACLU), 84
Ames, Aldrich, 123
Angleton, James Jesus, 195
Anti-Masonic Party, 87
Archidamus, 155
Armey, Dick, 110
Armstrong, Scott, 116
Army, U.S., 6, 63, 66, 90, 154; Army War College, 54; Center for Army Lessons Learned, 111; Training and Doctrine Command centers (TRADOC), 11–12, 65–66
Art of War, The (Machiavelli), 10
Art of War, The (Sun Tzu), 10, 12–13, 16
Assumptions, 26–30, 138–39
Attrition, 37, 63

Atwater, Lee, 37, 49, 152, 173, 182; Sun Tzu's influence on, 12–15

Baker, Howard, 47
Balaklava, Battle of, 164
Balz, Dan, 72, 105–106
Barbour, Haley, 36
Bardach, Eugene, 189
Barker, Bernard, 125
Battle cries, 96–97
Bayh, Birch, 74
Beckel, Bob, 157
Beiler, David, 108
Bekavac, Nancy, 111
Berman, Wayne, 158
Bernays, Edward L., 81
Bhopal, India, 94
Biden, Joseph, 59, 129
Bilandic, Michael, 145
Bile barrel projects, 144, 148–49
Bionomics: The Inevitability of Capitalism, 195
Birmingham, Ala., 94, 146, 187
Black, William, 48–49
Blaine, James G., 163
Blitzkrieg, 38–39, 76
Body language, 132–33, 197
Bok, Sissela, 115
Borger, Gloria, 68–69
Boycotts, 105
Bradley, Omar, 58
Brandeis, Louis, 166
Broder, John, 153
Brokaw, Tom, 14

Brownstein, Ron, 72
Brown v. Board of Education, 31
Brown, Willie, 55
Bryce, James, 61, 97
Buchanan, Patrick, 9, 171–72
Budget Enforcement Act of 1990, 191
Bullitt, Stimson, 48, 156
Bureau of Land Management, 144
Burns, Conrad, 130
Busch, Andrew, 34
Bush, George: administration, 9, 15, 124, 160, 175; character, 49–50; domestic policies, 26, 49–50, 102, 175; 1988 presidential campaign, 12, 13–15, 37, 95, 114, 138, 152; 1992 presidential campaign, 8, 34, 114, 119, 166, 173; during Persian Gulf War, 26, 102; tax policies, 15, 172–73
Bush, George W., 105–106, 157–58
Bush, Prescott, 119

Caddell, Patrick, 11, 15, 101–102
Caesar, Gaius Julius, 58
California, 9, 53, 55, 70–71, 126, 130, 145, 148, 150, 158, 164
Campaign finances. *See* Finances, campaign

Campaigns & Elections, 151
Capra, Frank, 90, 92
Carter, Jimmy, 126–27, 132
Carville, James, 8–9, 20, 36, 68, 98, 135
Casey, William, 126
Catholicism, 88, 97, 163
Cato, 45
Causes and crusades, 5, 83, 90–94, 97, 184–85
Ceaser, James, 34, 205n.63
Cedras, Raul, 40
Center for Army Lessons Learned, 111
Center for Responsive Politics, 131
Central Intelligence Agency (CIA), 123, 125, 138, 195
Challengers vs. incumbents, 25, 35, 37, 40, 65, 82, 174, 235n.20
Chancellorsville, Battle of, 163
Chang Yu, 14
Character, 44–51; theatricality in, 45–46, 193, 197–98
Checchi, Al, 129–30
Cheney, Dick, 95, 134
Chicago, 84, 105, 145
Childress, James F., 16–17
Chotiner, Murray, 29–30
Christian Coalition, 74, 84, 112, 118
Churchill, Sir Winston, 6, 26, 51, 96, 163, 164
CIA (Central Intelligence Agency), 123, 125, 138, 195
Civilian Conservation Corps, 8
Civil rights movement, 24, 31, 94, 126, 146, 187
Civil War, American, 5, 7, 8, 24, 29, 47, 74, 91, 96; Gettysburg, 29, 59, 165; Grant during, 36, 46, 49, 50, 51, 55, 90; Jackson during, 36, 101, 163; Lee during, 36, 49, 57, 95, 165; Lincoln during, 8, 50, 51, 56, 57, 75; McClellan during, 49–50; propaganda during, 89–90; Sherman during, 36, 39, 50; Shiloh, 50, 90
Clausewitz, Carl von, 10, 34, 182; on alliances, 168; on boldness, 49; on defensive warfare, 35, 36; on the enemy, 139; on enmity toward enemies, 81; on the fog of war, 162; on friction, 161; on intelligence, 133; on intuition, 55; on the key to the country, 169, 173; on moral elements, 15, 80–81, 100; on perseverance, 50; on simplicity, 161; on victory, 37, 161, 175

Cleveland, Ohio, 145
Clines, Francis X., 96
Clinton, Bill, 5, 84; administration of, 6, 9, 68–69, 76–77, 85–86, 89, 122, 166, 174; during budget showdown, 29, 32, 34; character, 9, 49, 51, 70, 111, 136, 176, 184, 188; economic policies, 168; health care policies, 26, 32, 107, 174; impeachment, 59, 86–87, 110, 113, 114–15, 128–29, 132, 179, 183–84, 186; military policies, 174; 1992 presidential campaign, 8–9, 49–50, 76, 95, 114, 119, 123, 129, 143–44, 173, 176, 198; 1996 presidential campaign, 34, 64–65, 95, 98–99, 135–36, 167–68; tax policies, 174
Clinton, Hillary Rodham, 3, 76–77, 89, 182
CNN, 129
Coalition warfare, 26
Codevilla, Angelo, 103
Coelho, Tony, 158
Cohen, Richard E., 162
Cold War, 8, 40, 79, 84, 91, 107, 126, 150, 175
The Comedy of Democracy, 198
Communication, 27, 62–63, 72–73, 75–79; as nonverbal, 132–33, 197
Competitive Enterprise Institute, 77
Compromise, 19, 193
Confidence in leaders, 50–51
Congressional Black Caucus, 159
Connor, Eugene "Bull," 94, 187
Conservative Opportunity Society, 40
Conspiracy theories, 87–90
Contact people, 122–23, 131–33

Contract with America, 32, 65–66
Coombs, James E., 198
Cooperation, 19
Coordination, 61–79, 185–86
Costikyan, Edward N., 156
Coup d'oeil, 55, 163–64
Courage, 46–49, 185
Coverdell, Paul, 178
Covert operations, 121, 123, 125–27, 131, 189
Crimean War, 163–64
Cromwell, Oliver, 90
Crowl, Philip A., 41
Crusades and causes, 5, 83, 90–94, 97, 184–85
C–SPAN, 129
Cuban Missile Crisis, 79
"The Curvature of Constitutional Space," 194

Dahl, Robert, 97
D'Amato, Alfonse, 111–12, 147
Davidson, Roger, 142
Davis, Gray, 130
Davis, Lanny, 68
Davis, Tom, 32
Dazzles, 113, 114–15
Deal, Nathan, 107
Debates, political, 101–102, 121, 126, 189
Decapitation, 102–103
Deception, 79, 119, 195; during Persian Gulf War, 38, 111; in politics, 11, 87, 101, 110–15, 130, 188; Sun Tzu on, 13, 110, 114; during World War II, 111, 113–14, 115, 117, *See also* Intelligence
Declaration of Independence, 194
Decoys, 113–14
Defectors, 107, 128
Defense Advanced Research Projects Agency, 128
Defense policies, 155
Defensive audits, 136
Defensive strategies, 4, 35–36, 184–85
De Gaulle, Charles. *See* Gaulle, Charles de
DeLay, Tom, 77, 87, 132, 158
Deliberation, 19, 193, 199
Demobilization, 107–109

Democratic Party, 33–34, 50, 85–86, 103, 125, 175–76; Democratic National Committee, 107, 161; Democratic Senatorial Campaign Committee (DSCC), 130; vs. Republican Party, 14–15, 64–65, 74, 84, 163, 183; and taxes, 170–73, 174

Demoralization, 100–103, 106–109, 188

Deniability, 116

Depression, Great, 8, 9, 57

Desert Storm. See Persian Gulf War

Deterrence, 40–41, 103–106, 158

Devine, Donald, 54

Dewey, Thomas, 28, 38, 95

Dinkins, David, 127, 131

Discipline, 61, 69, 169

Discourses, The, 10

Distraction, 113–15, 188

Dividing the opposition, 14–15, 109–10

Doctrine, 62, 63–67; in civilian organizations, 64–65, 185–86; in election campaigns, 64–65; in the military, 63–64; vs. strategy, 63

Dole, Robert, 47, 168, 171; 1988 presidential campaign, 13–14, 37, 152; 1996 presidential campaign, 34, 65, 98–99, 153

Domestic policies, 49–50, 145, 148–49, 151, 175; Great Society, 154, 178; taxes, 15, 22, 25–26, 39, 152, 169–73, 174

Douglas, Helen Gahagan, 30

Douglas, Stephen, 76, 87–88, 116, 121

Dowd, Maureen, 16

Drew, Elizabeth, 17

Drudge Report, 129

Drug war, 8

Dukakis, Michael, 13, 14–15, 114, 138, 176

Dunkirk, 26

Du Picq, Ardant, 106

Dynamism, 195

Economic Development Administration, 148

Economics. See Metaphors, market

Eddie Mahe Company, 24

Edelman, Murray, 198

Education, 55–57, 193, 198–99

Education of Cyrus, The, 10

Ehrenreich, Barbara, 91

Eisenhower, Dwight D., 160; administration, 126; character, 46, 50–51, 70, 98; on Congress, 164; 1952 presidential campaign, 22; as president, 42–43; during World War II, 46, 53, 94, 146

Eisenhower, Mamie, 70

Ellsberg, Daniel, 125

EMILY's List, 9, 69

Enemies, 81–87, 92, 98–99, 187; demonization of, 5–6, 83, 84, 93–94, 99, 186; enabling the enemy, 178–79

Engelberg, Mort, 198

Enlightenment, the, 194

Enmity, 81–87, 92, 135–36, 178, 186, 187

Evans, Rowland, 123, 172

"Fannie Mae," 40–41

Fatigue, 165–66, 174, 191

Faucheux, Ron, 21, 151

Fazio, Vic, 103

FBI (Federal Bureau of Investigation), 123, 125–26, 198

Federal Election Commission, 131

Federalist, The, 166–67, 196

Federal National Mortgage Association ("Fannie Mae"), 40–41

Federal Reserve System, 191

Feinstein, Dianne, 9

Fenno, Richard, 25, 190

Field manuals, 63–64

Finances, campaign, 18, 73–74, 117, 155–56, 157–58, 190, 197, 235n.20

Florida, 173

Foch, Ferdinand, 23

Fog of war, 162–63, 169–73, 191

Ford, Gerald, 30, 95, 131, 153, 155

Foreign policies, 145

Forest Service, U.S., 62, 68

Franco–Prussian War, 75

Frederick the Great, 45, 115, 141

Freedom of Information Act (FOIA), 116, 130

Freeman, Douglas Southall, 53–54, 57

Friction, 190–91, 194; Clausewitz on, 161; debate created by, 180; among Republicans, 169–73; among U.S. political institutions, 166–69, 179–80

Frost, Martin, 110, 179

Frost, Robert, 181, 182, 193

Fussell, Paul, 94

Future vs. past, 28–29, 139

Galston, William, 176

Games, 18, 196–97

Gaulle, Charles de, 43, 45, 46, 57, 59, 175, 184–85

Gavin, William, 60

Gay and Lesbian Victory Fund, 74

Gaylord, Joseph, 133

General Motors, 99

Genius, 55, 163–64

Geography, 27, 41, 84–85, 141–53, 169, 189–90, 192

Gettysburg, Battle of, 29, 59, 165

Gianos, Phillip, 193

Giap, Vo Nguyen, 74

Gigot, Paul, 34

Gingrich, Newt, 19, 40, 44, 84, 168, 170, 182, 185; on the Civil War, 36, 89–90; on Clinton, 174; as House speaker, 11–12, 17, 29, 32, 34, 57, 59, 65–67, 72, 86–87, 96–97, 103, 107, 159, 177, 178–79; relations with O'Neill, 102; and Training and Doctrine Command (TRADOC) centers, 11–12, 65–66

Girdler, Tom, 99

Goals, 21–26, 61–62; short-term vs. long-term, 25; survival, 23–24, 36; victory, 24, 33–34, 36

Goffman, Erving, 45

Goldwater, Barry, 53, 85, 108, 126, 155

GOPAC, 72, 185–86

Governors, state, 152, 173

Gramm, Phil, 172
Grand Strategy of the Roman Empire, 192
Grand Strategy of the Soviet Union, 192
Grant, Ulysses S., 36, 55, 90; character, 46, 49, 50, 51; as president, 19
Grapevines, 122, 189
Graves, Robert, 47
Gray, Al, 74
Great Society, 154, 178
Great Theater, 198
Green Corps, 71
Greenspan, Alan, 132–33
Gross, Bertram, 190
Grossman, David, 178
Guadalcanal, 165
Guerrilla warfare, 6, 9–10, 12, 39–40, 116, 118, 156–57, 186
Gulf War. *See* Persian Gulf War

Haiti, 40
Hamilton, Alexander, 104
Hanna, Mark, 7
Harassment, 13–14
Hargett, Edd, 151
Harrison, William Henry, 7
"Harry and Louise" ads, 107
Hart, Gary, 6, 9–10, 156–57, 182
Hatred, 81–87, 92, 135–36, 178, 186, 187
Hayden, Tom, 74
Hay, John, 7
Heads up messages, 122
Health care, 26
Heifetz, Ronald A., 42
Heraclitus, 34
Herndon, William, 116, 121
Ho Chi Minh, 99
Hofstader, Richard, 87
Holmes, Richard, 186
Honor, 187
House of Representatives, 25, 44, 117–18, 143; Democrats in, 12, 17, 36, 40, 66, 86–87, 102, 107, 110, 135, 151–52, 158–59, 167–68, 171, 174, 177, 178–79; Gingrich as speaker, 11–12, 17, 29, 32, 34, 57, 59, 65–67, 72, 86–87, 96–97, 103, 107, 159, 177, 178–79; Judiciary Committee, 129; relations with president, 167–68; Republicans in, 19, 32–33, 36, 40, 59–60, 69, 110, 129, 132,

135, 158–59, 164, 167–68, 170–73, 174, 183–84, 188; vs. Senate, 19, 40, 168, 170–71, 193, *See also* Senate
How We Won the War, 74
Human nature, 52, 161
Humphreys, Robert, 82
Hundred Years' War, 96
Hunt, E. Howard, 125
Hussein, Saddam, 5, 26, 38, 99, 102, 108, 134
Hyde, Henry, 129

Iliad, 10
Illness, 165–66
Inchon, 26, 30
Incumbents vs. challengers, 25, 35, 37, 40, 65, 82, 174, 235n.20
Indianapolis, Ind., 143
Infantry Journal, The, 44
Inflation, 86
Information technology, 75–79, 81, 121, 128–29, 137–38, 186, 189
Initiative, taking the, 14
Intelligence, 6, 16, 27, 79, 120–39, 162; clandestine intelligence, 121, 123, 125–27, 131, 189; contact people, 122–23, 131–33; definition, 120–21; evaluation of, 133–37; Internet as source of, 128–29, 131, 137–38; open-source intelligence, 127–33, 189; and party whips, 124–25; researchers, 13, 122–23, 127, 131, 137, 176, 188–89; Sun Tzu on, 13, 120, 133, 171–72; use of, 137–39, *See also* Deception
Internet, 76, 77, 78, 186, 189; as source of information, 128–29, 131, 137–38
Intimidation, 40–41, 103–106, 158
Intuition, 55, 163
Iowa, 14, 37, 144
Iran-Contra affair, 59, 116
Iraq, 129, 179, *See also* Persian Gulf War

Jackson, Jesse, 93
Jackson, Robert, 52

Jackson, Thomas J. "Stonewall", 36, 101, 163
Javits, Jacob, 154
Jefferson, Thomas, 89
Jensen, Richard, 76
Jepsen, Roger, 103
Johnson, Lyndon B., 104, 116–17; Great Society, 154, 178; 1964 presidential campaign, 108, 125–26; as Senate majority leader, 24, 52, 102, 123–24, 134; during Vietnam War, 135
Johnson, Mark, 4, 201n.2
Jones, Paula, 115
Jordan, Vernon, 122
Josephson, Matthew, 7

Kamarck, Elaine Ciulla, 176
Kamber, Victor, 33
Kashmir, 146
Kaufman, Herbert, 62
Keegan, John, 45
Kelly, Michael, 8
Kemp, Jack, 26, 170–71
Kennedy, John F., 24, 51, 79, 125, 141, 142, 165
Kennedy, Paul, 177
Kennedy, Robert F., 53, 126
Kent, Frank, 22
Kessler, David, 107
Kettl, Donald, 191–92
Khrushchev, Nikita, 165
King, Martin Luther, Jr., 39, 57, 182, 184–85
Knight, Goodwin, 164
Knowland, William, 164
Knowledge, 52–55, 118–19
Korean War, 26, 27, 30
Kosovo, 31, 128, 145
Krulak, Charles, 77, 78
Kuwait, 26, 38, 111

LaGuardia, Fiorello H., 109, 113
Lake, Celinda, 173
Lakoff, George, 4, 201n.2
Lasswell, Harold, 94, 106
Latino Academy, 72
Lauer, Matt, 89
Leaders, 25–26, 42–60, 134–35, 184–85; as actors, 45–46, 193, 197–98; boldness in, 49–50; character in, 44–51, 134; competence/knowledge in, 52–55, 59; conduct of,

55–58; as confident, 50–51; courage in, 46–49, 185; as crusaders, 90–93, 184–85; images of, 53, 111–12; as improvisers, 60; as inspiring, 43–44, 59; integrity in, 51; intuition in, 55, 163–64; perseverance in, 41, 50–51; relations with subordinates, 43–44, 53, 57–58, 68–69, 138–39, 154, 157, 186, 198; as teachers, 55–57, 193, 198–99; timidity in, 49–50

Ledeen, Michael, 197

Lee, Robert E., 36, 49, 57, 95, 165

Legal Services Corporation, 35–36

Lenin, V. I., 197

Lerner, Max, 38

Lethal Weapon 2, 84

Lewinsky, Monica, 113, 115, 128–29

Lewis, C. S., 187

Lewis, Jerry, 117, 167

Libya, 102–103

Liddell Hart, B. H., 11, 33, 34, 38, 178

Liddy, G. Gordon, 125

Lincoln, Abraham, 5, 7; during Civil War, 8, 50, 51, 56, 57, 75; Senate contest with Douglas, 76, 87–88, 116, 121

Lindauer, Charles, 142, 146

Lindsay, Bruce, 114

Lobbyists, 54, 67, 77, 122, 152

Local guides, 152–53

Locke, Gary, 23–24

Logistics, 41, 153–59, 190; definition, 141–42, 153–54

Los Angeles, 73, 144

Losing to Win, 34

Lott, Trent, 122

Loyalty, 58, 68–69, 124–25, 157, 186

Lugar, Richard, 143

Lungren, Dan, 53

Luttwak, Edward N., 192

MacArthur, Douglas, 19, 26, 27, 30, 59

McCarthy, Joseph, 88–89, 119

McClellan, George, 49–50

McCord, James, 125

McCurry, Mike, 109

McGovern, George, 6, 9–10, 74, 183

Machiavelli, Niccolò, 10, 81–82, 139, 157; *Art of War, The*, 10

McPherson, Harry, 123–24

Madison, James, 104, 166–67, 196

Maneuver, 6, 37–40, 63

Manhattan Project, 117

Mao Zedong, 11, 74, 118, 197, 203n.36

Maraniss, David, 188

Marine Corps, U.S., 54, 77, 78, 134, 149; on doctrine, 17, 63–64; on logistics, 153–54, 157; on maneuver/attrition, 37, 63; on offense/defense, 36; on overstretch, 176–77; on strategy, 21; training in, 56, 71, 73

Market metaphors. *See* Metaphors, market

Marshall, George C., 52, 53, 57, 90

Marshall, S. L. A., 45, 46, 71, 82, 153, 156, 173

Martinez, Bob, 173

Martin, Joe, 164

Masada, 23

Massachusetts, 114; furlough program in, 14–15, 95, 138

Mass/numerical superiority, 37, 140

Matalin, Mary, 9, 114

Media, mass, 78, 94–95, 147, 152, 188, 189, 235n.20

Medicare, 32

Melcher, John, 85

Metaphors, anthropological, 18

Metaphors, ecological, 194–95

Metaphors, education, 55–57, 193, 198–99

Metaphors, market, 18–19, 182, 192, 199, 204n.58; in leadership, 184–85; in strategy, 183

Metaphors, medical, 196

Metaphors, military, 3–10, 144, 182, 201n.2, 205n.63; advantages of, 183–93; battle/conflict, 4, 5, 20, 80, 82, 89, 193; blitzes, 4, 38–39, 76; Chief of Staff, 6; crusades, 5, 83, 90–94, 184–85;

good soldiers, 3, 68–69; guerrilla warfare, 6, 9–10, 12, 39–40, 116, 118, 156–57, 186; limitations of, 16–20, 19, 66–67, 69, 160–61, 181–82, 192–93, 196, 199; mobilization/demobilization, 75, 107–109; mounting attacks, 4; rallying the troops, 5–6, 24, 25–26, 80–99, 178–79, 186–87; standard-bearers, 4; warchests, 40, 117, 155, 157; war games, 73–74; war rooms, 3, 8–9, 76–77, 129, 142, 176; Young Turks vs. Old Guard, 3–4, *See also* Defensive strategies; Offensive strategies; Warfare

Metaphors, physical/mechanical, 193–94

Metaphors, sports/game, 18, 196–97

Metaphors, theatrical, 45–46, 193, 197–98

Metzenbaum, Howard, 104

Mexican War, 74

Mexico, 186

Miami, Fla., 145

Michels, Robert, 9

Mikva, Abner, 180

Mill, John Stuart, 198

Minnesota, 78

Mitchell, Billy, 66

Mondale, Walter, 11, 101–102, 137, 171, 176

Money, 40, 41, 104, 157–59; campaign finances, 18, 73–74, 117, 155–56, 157–58, 190, 197, 235n.20

Montana, 85

Morale and motivation, 27, 33, 41, 94, 136, 157; Clausewitz on, 15, 80–81, 100, *See also* Rallying the troops

Morris, Celia, 9

Morris, Dick, 29, 64–65, 85–86, 135–36, 188

Morton, Thruston, 123

Moses, Robert, 113, 115

Muir, William K., 198

NAACP (National Association for the Advancement of Colored People), 31

NAFTA (North American Free Trade Agreement), 33

Napoleon Bonaparte, 6, 8, 32, 44, 58, 80, 142, 165
Napolitan, Joseph, 21
National Association for the Advancement of Colored People (NAACP), 31
National Endowment for the Arts, 159
National Right to Life Committee, 188
National Security Agency, 128, 137
National security policies, 145, 175
National War College, 175
NATO (North Atlantic Treaty Organization), 31, 128
Naval War College, 41, 53–54
Nevada, 144
New Deal, 8, 22, 38–39, 91–92
New Hampshire, 14, 37, 152, 153
New Jersey, 98, 145–46, 152
Newman, Aubrey "Red," 53
New Mexico, 72
New York City, 85, 113, 127, 147, 156
New York State, 85, 88, 113, 115, 147, 150, 159, 193
New York Times, 174
New York Tribune, 76, 78
Nexis, 129
Nimmo, Dan, 198
Niskanen, William, 58
Nixon, Richard M., 29–30, 173–74; administration, 110, 125, 126; character, 51; 1960 presidential campaign, 156; 1972 presidential campaign, 33–34, 183; on politics, 50–51, 80, 182; and silent majority, 85, 183; and Watergate, 33–34, 96, 125, 126–27, 165–66; during World War II, 197
No Final Victories, 161
Nofziger, Lyn, 68
Nonverbal communication, 132–33, 197
Noonan, Peggy, 46
Norquist, Grover, 158–59
North American Free Trade Agreement (NAFTA), 33
North Carolina, 30
Novak, Robert, 123, 172
Nuclear waste, 149

Oakland, Calif., 148
Objectives. See Goals
O'Brien, Lawrence, 125, 161
Offensive strategies, 4, 35–36, 69, 82, 183–84
Office of Presidential Personnel, 124
Office of Strategic Services, 108
Office of Thrift Supervision, 48–49
Oklahoma City, Okla., 85–86
Oleszek, Walter, 142
O'Neill, Thomas P. "Tip," 102, 151
On Guerrilla Warfare, 74
On War, 10, 175
Overconfidence, 173–75, 176
Overstretch, 176–78

PACs (Political action committees), 72, 117, 158
Panama Canal, 30
Panetta, Leon, 6, 32
Parameters, 10
Passion vs. rationality, 187
Patronage, 150, 177
Patterson, Samuel C., 198
Patton, George, 46, 47, 58, 113–14
Paul, Saint, 26
Pearl Harbor, 161
Peloponnesian War, The, 10, 81
Perot, Ross, 173, 194
Persian Gulf War, 17–18, 134, 160; Bush during, 26, 49, 102; deception during, 38, 111; intelligence during, 137; Powell during, 55–56, 175; propaganda during, 99, 106, 108; vs. Vietnam War, 175
Philip of Macedonia, 26
Physics, 193–94
Pinkerton, Jim, 13
Plunkitt, George Washington, 52
Poindexter, John, 116
POLARIS (Political Advertising, Reporting and Intelligence System), 129
Political action committees (PACs), 72, 117, 158
Political science, 186, 192, 193–94; friction in, 190–91; rationality in, 187, 188, See

also Metaphors, market; Metaphors, medical; Metaphors, military; Politics
Politics: communication in, 62, 63, 72–73, 75–79, 132–33, 197; conspiracy theories in, 87–90; courage in, 47–49; doctrine in, 63, 64–66; enemies in, 81–87, 92, 93–94, 98–99; hatred in, 81–87, 92, 178, 186, 187; integrity in, 51; and jazz, 60; pragmatism in, 23–24; recruitment in, 63, 67–68; simplicity in, 25–26; technology in, 75–79, 81, 121, 128–29, 137–38, 186, 189; training in, 63, 70–74; women in, 9; zealots in, 23–24, See also Metaphors, market; Metaphors, military; Political science
Pork barrel projects, 135, 144, 155
Postrel, Virginia, 195
Powell, Colin, 10, 55–56, 137, 175
Pragmatism, 23–24
Press secretaries, 109, 122
Pride, 186–87
Primary Colors, 5–6, 136
Prince, The, 10
Propaganda, 78, 98–99, 106–109, 136; during Civil War, 89–90; gray propaganda, 108, 113; during Persian Gulf War, 106, 108; during World War I, 81, 84; during World War II, 87, 90, 92, 94, 95
Psychological warfare, 16, 100–119, 188
Pulaski, Art, 158
Push polling, 109
Pyrrhic victories, 33

Qaddafi, Muammar, 102–103
Quantum Politics, 194
Quayle, Dan, 93

Raglan, Fitzroy James Henry Somerset, 1st Baron, 163–64
Rallying the troops, 5–6, 24, 25–26, 80–99, 178–79,

186–87, *See also* Morale and motivation
Rationality, 187–88
Rayburn, Sam, 151–52
Reagan, Ronald, 25–26, 30, 102–103, 131; administration, 39, 58, 68, 72, 116, 162, 170; character, 46, 47, 59; competence, 59; as crusader, 97; economic policies, 178; 1980 presidential campaign, 35–36, 95, 97, 126–27, 137, 177; 1984 presidential campaign, 11, 101–102, 171; tax policies, 39, 169–72
Reason, 195
Recruitment, 62; in civilian organizations, 67–70; in the military, 67, 69–70
Reed, Ralph, 74, 118
Reform Party, 78
Reinwald, Brian R., 67
Republican Party, 32–34, 60, 72, 76, 78, 85–87, 88, 91, 109, 135–36; vs. Democratic Party, 14–15, 64–65, 74, 84, 163, 183; Republican National Committee, 7, 12, 15, 36, 127, 131, 137, 170; and taxes, 169–73, 174
Republican Study Committee, 159
Republic Steel Corporation, 99
Researchers, 13, 122–23, 127, 131, 137, 176, 188–89, 192
Richards, Ann, 9
Richie, Rob, 143
Rickover, Hyman, 128
Ridgway, Matthew, 52–53
Road to Victory, The, 21
Robertson, Pat, 74
Rockefeller, Nelson, 53
Rodota, Joe, 131
Role-playing, 73–74
Rollins, Ed, 103, 172, 173
Roman Catholic Church, 88, 97, 163
Roosevelt, Franklin D., 7–8, 22, 38–39, 109–10, 117; character, 46, 56; conduct, 57, 112; as crusader, 91–93; 1940 presidential campaign, 88, 109
Roosevelt, Theodore, 56, 91
Rothschild, Michael, 195

Rowe, James, 28
Ruckus Society, 150
Rudman, Warren, 47
Rumors, 108–109, 132
Russell, Richard, 24
Russo, Vic, 90

Safire, William, 85
Salon, 129
Savo Island, Battle of, 165
Schippers, David, 115
Schneier, Edward, 190
Schumer, Charles, 112
Schwarzkopf, H. Norman, 17–18, 119, 160, 163
SCLC (Southern Christian Leadership Conference), 31, 146
Seabury, Paul, 103
Secrecy and stealth, 87, 91, 115–18, 119, 188, 191; spies, 121, 123, 125–27, 189
Securities and Exchange Commission, 130
Senate, 24, 52, 82, 103–104; Democrats in, 168, 174; vs. House, 19, 40, 168, 170–71, 193; Johnson as majority leader, 24, 52, 102, 123–24, 134; Republicans in, 164, 170–71, 174, 177, *See also* House of Representatives
Serbia, 31, 128, 145
Shadegg, Stephen, 118
Shakespeare, William, 100
Sherman, William T., 36, 39, 50
Shiloh, Battle of, 50, 90
Sickness, 165–66
"Silent majority," 85, 183
Siljander, Mark, 92, 99
Sloan, Alfred, 99
Slogans, 7
Small Wars Manual, 149
Smith, Al, 88
Smith, Fred, 140
Smith, Robert, 82
Snowe, Olympia, 130
Socialism, 9, 195
Social Security Administration, 64, 67–68, 72
Somalia, 135
Sontag, Susan, 196
South Africa, 84
South Carolina, 28

Southern Christian Leadership Conference (SCLC), 31, 146
Southern Poverty Law Center, 137–38
Southwest Voter Registration Education project, 72
Soviet Union, 105, 192; relations with United States, 8, 40, 79, 84, 91, 107, 123, 126, 128, 150, 175
Speed, 14, 38–39, 156
Spies, 121, 123, 125–27, 189
Sports, 18, 196–97
Stahl, Leslie, 107
Starr, Kenneth, 68, 115, 129, 183
Stealth. *See* Secrecy and Stealth
Stephanopoulos, George, 3, 166, 174, 184
Stevenson, Adlai, 125
Stockdale, James B., 56
Stockman, David, 39, 162, 170
Storming the Statehouse, 9
Strategy, 6–7, 21–41, 44, 183–84; assessment of capabilities, 30–34; assumptions, 26–30; attrition as, 37, 63; defensive strategies, 4, 35–36, 184–85; definition, 21–22; deterrence, 40–41; vs. doctrine, 63; "firewall" strategy, 37; goals, 21–26, 33–34, 36, 61–62; vs. logistics, 153; maneuver as, 37–40, 63; mass/numerical superiority as, 37; offensive strategies, 4, 35–36, 69, 82, 183–84; vs. tactics, 22, 33
Success. *See* Victory
Sullivan, Gordon, 60
Summers, Harry, 101
Sun Tzu, 10, 11, 16, 34, 182; *Art of War, The,* 10, 12–13, 16; on assessment of capabilities, 32; Atwater influenced by, 12–15; on deception, 13, 110, 114; on dividing the opposition, 14; on enmity toward enemies, 81; on harassing the opposition, 13, 101; on intelligence, 13, 120, 133, 171–72; on local guides, 152; on speed, 14,

38; on taking the initiative, 14; on victory, 32, 40, 171
Sununu, John, 124, 152
Surprise, 111, 162, 183–84
Survival, 23–24, 36
Symbols and rituals, 96–98

Tactics, 6; vs. strategy, 22, 33
Taxes, 15, 22, 25–26, 39, 152, 169–73, 174
Teamsters, 36
Teamwork, 60
Technology, 75–79, 81, 121, 128–29, 137–38, 186, 189
Television, 129, 235n.20
Tet Offensive, 101
Texas, 9, 48, 105–106, 145, 151–52, 156
Theatricality, 45–46, 193, 197–98
Thirty Years' War, 81
Thompson, William Hale, 84
Threats, 40–41, 103–106, 158
Thucydides, 10, 81
Thurmond, Strom, 28
Tobacco companies, 98–99, 107, 117
Tocqueville, Alexis de, 192, 199
Today Show, 89
Training, 60, 61; in civilian organizations, 55, 63, 71–74, 185–86; in the military, 55, 56, 62, 70–71, 72–73, 82
Training for Change, 73
Training and Doctrine Command centers (TRADOC), U.S. Army, 11–12, 65–66
Tribe, Laurence, 194
Tripp, Linda, 115
Trojan Horse, 119
Truman, Harry, 5, 42–43, 86; 1948 presidential campaign, 28, 95
Tyson, Laura, 132–33
Udall, Morris, 147
Unions, labor, 28, 36, 85, 98, 99, 158, 164
United States: political geography of, 142–53, 169,

189–90; political institutions in, 161, 166–69, 179–80; relations with Soviet Union, 8, 40, 79, 84, 91, 107, 123, 126, 128, 150, 165, 175, *See also* Army, U.S.; Civil War, American; House of Representatives; Marine Corps, U.S.; Senate; Vietnam War; *and under specific states and cities*

Van Creveld, Martin, 140–41
Ventura, Jesse, 78
Vermont, 193
Vetoes, 104
Victory, 36, 94–95, 140; aftermath of, 160, 161, 173–75, 176–77; Clausewitz on, 37, 161, 175; definition, 24; as pyrrhic, 33–34; Sun Tzu on, 32, 40, 171
Vienna summit of 1961, 165
Vietnam War, 16, 17, 24, 43, 58, 82, 153, 167, 190; Johnson during, 135; vs. Persian Gulf War, 175; propaganda during, 99; Tet Offensive, 101
Vulnerability studies, 136

Wallace, George, 110
Wallace, Henry, 28
Warfare: enemies in, 80–84; guerrilla warfare, 6, 9–10, 12, 39–40, 116, 118, 156–57, 186; psychological warfare, 100–119, *See also* Metaphors, military
Warfighting, 63–64
Warren, Jennifer, 70–71
War rooms, 3, 8–9, 76–77, 129, 142, 176
Washington, George, 45
Washington Post, 69, 168, 172, 174
Washington State, 23–24
Watergate, 33–34, 96, 125, 126–27, 165–66
Waterloo, Battle of, 165
Watson, Jack, 132

Weatherford, J. McIver, 102
Weber, Vin, 102, 167, 171
Weisberg, Herbert F., 198
Wellington, Arthur Wellesley, Duke of, 154
Westmoreland, William, 16
Wheatley, Margaret, 10
Whig party, 116
Whips, party, 124–25, 132, 158
White, Theodore H., 141
Why We Fight, 90, 92
Wilhelm, David, 143–44
Willkie, Wendell, 88, 109
Wills, Garry, 194
Wilson, James Q., 185, 194–95
Wilson, Pete, 131
Wilson, Woodrow, 194
Women, 9, 73
World War I, 8, 23, 47, 179; propaganda during, 81, 84
World War II, 8, 24, 122, 160, 165, 187; Allies during, 31, 82, 135, 140, 141, 146, 147–48; *blitzkrieg* in, 38–39, 76; Churchill during, 6, 26, 51, 96, 163, 164; as crusade, 90; D-Day, 43–44, 113–14, 146; deception during, 111, 113–14, 115, 117; Eisenhower during, 46, 53, 94, 146; Germans during, 38–39, 50, 76, 86, 92, 111, 113–14, 140, 146, 147–48; Japanese during, 52, 53, 57, 90; Nixon during, 197; Patton during, 46, 47, 58, 113–14; Pearl Harbor, 138, 161; propaganda during, 87, 90, 92, 94, 95; Savo Island, 165; V-for-victory sign during, 96
Wright, Betsey, 9, 136
Wright, Jim, 48–49, 102

Xenophon, 10

Zapatistas, 186
Zinni, Anthony, 149